Intellectual Property Law
and Interactive Media

Steve Jones
General Editor

Vol. 39

PETER LANG
New York • Washington, D.C./Baltimore • Bern
Frankfurt am Main • Berlin • Brussels • Vienna • Oxford

Edward Lee Lamoureux
Steven L. Baron
Claire Stewart

Intellectual Property Law
and Interactive Media

FREE FOR A FEE

PETER LANG
New York • Washington, D.C./Baltimore • Bern
Frankfurt am Main • Berlin • Brussels • Vienna • Oxford

Library of Congress Cataloging-in-Publication Data

Intellectual property law and interactive media: free for a fee /
Edward Lee Lamoureux... [et al.].
p. cm. — (Digital formations; vol. 39)
Includes bibliographical references and index.
1. Copyright—Interactive multimedia—United States.
2. Multimedia systems—Law and legislation—United States.
3. Copyright and electronic data processing—United States.
I. Lamoureux, Edward Lee.
KF3030.1.I57 346.7304'8—dc22 2008036202
ISBN 978-0-8204-8635-2 (hardcover)
ISBN 978-0-8204-8160-9 (paperback)
ISSN 1526-3169

Bibliographic information published by **Die Deutsche Bibliothek**.
Die Deutsche Bibliothek lists this publication in the "Deutsche
Nationalbibliografie"; detailed bibliographic data is available
on the Internet at http://dnb.ddb.de/.

This book's accompanying website: *http://www.freeforafee.com/*

The paper in this book meets the guidelines for permanence and durability
of the Committee on Production Guidelines for Book Longevity
of the Council of Library Resources.

© 2009 Peter Lang Publishing, Inc., New York
29 Broadway, 18th floor, New York, NY 10006
www.peterlang.com

Printed in the United States of America

Contents

Acknowledgments

A book of this complexity requires extensive cooperation and coordination. The authors are appreciative of each other's unique perspectives. We are also deeply indebted to Marc Cooperman and Robert Resis, two Chicago-based lawyers specializing in intellectual property law. Marc and Robert authored significant portions of the case analyses presented in the book. The initials of the author for each section appear at the end of material for which they were primarily responsible.

We offer heartfelt thanks to series editor Steve Jones for his confidence in us and for his patience with the extended timeline required for a book of this nature. Editors, production, and marketing staff at Lang, especially Mary Savigar, Bernadette Shade, Sophie Appel, and Patty Mulrane, deserve praise for both professionalism and care.

Lamoureux and Baron (sometimes joined by Stewart) teach a course about intellectual property law in new media at Bradley University. They wish to thank their students for the insightful papers, projects, and class discussions that have made significant contributions to this book. Bradley colleagues Jeff Huberman, Jim Ferolo, Howard Goldbaum (now at Univ. Nevada, Reno), and

Paul Gullifor deserve special recognition for their leadership. Administrative support by Joan Wilhelm, Carrie Kroenke, Trudy Ruch, Jan Ringenberg, and Vicki Tomblin enables our collaboration.

The authors thank their families for unyielding support throughout the process; we can only do these things when you love us as you do.

Introduction

Shifting from Public to Private Interests

The following paradox captures the tone of the "new media environment" as it relates to intellectual property law: "Nothing has changed; everything has changed."

In many ways, relatively little about intellectual property law has changed in the last two hundred years or so. For example, the 1976 revision of the 1909 revision of the 1790 *Copyright Act* (amended in 1802, 1831, 1856, and 1870) kept in place, for the fruits of creative labor, a regime of protection like that afforded to real property.[1] In America, copyright laws preserve the rights of those who produce creative works or those who have acquired said rights via purchase, lease, or inheritance. The laws apply to artists and content producers by constraining them from copying the protected works of others. The laws also apply to corporate entities such as distributors to keep them from profiting by selling "illegal" copies of the protected works. The 1998 *Digital Millennium Copyright Act* (*DMCA*) clarified the application of "current" law to new media works, as well as adding a few principles specific to digital works (for example, specifying that electronic means of protecting copyrighted works should not be circumvented). The primary producers and owners of intellectual property have long been, and continue to be, large corporations. These multinational entities play a major role in the development of the legislation that affects the creation of mediated products and their distribution.

In other words, nothing has changed. Artists and writers create content that is protected by federal and state laws once the material meets the threshold requirements for protection appropriate to the form of the content. Those rights can be assigned to or be acquired by others, either freely or via economic exchange. If one violates intellectual property law by copying or otherwise using protected materials, one can be noticed, served, arrested, prosecuted, fined, and—in some cases—imprisoned.

In many other ways, virtually everything about intellectual property law has changed. Computational technologies (computers, networks, and other new media aspects) enable "every-person" to create and distribute content in ways that were heretofore the province only of professional and corporate creative producers and distributors. These technologies enable the easy copying and redistribution of content in ways that compromise the integrity of the intellectual property law system in America and, to a greater extent, globally. The sheer amount of published material has increased exponentially and crosses global jurisdictions. The in-place standards and practices of intellectual property law have not and cannot keep pace with the rate of technological change. In America, virtually every citizen who uses computational resources could probably be found to be, in one way or another, guilty of intellectual property violations, and the legal system (and the corporations attempting to leverage it) has no way to keep up with the potential case load. When everyone is a criminal, the legal system and public policy are deeply compromised.[2]

In other words, everything has changed. The laws have not kept up with the development of technology, and in many cases their enforcement is at best ineffective or at worst either non-existent or draconian. In general, citizens don't understand (or agree with or follow) the laws. The laws protect the vested interests (especially) of old media to the degradation of the development of new technologies, and the laws cannot be efficiently enforced across geographic borders such that the global interconnectivity provided by the Internet and the World Wide Web obviates most strictures. In short, the intellectual property law system is overwhelmed, overrun, and virtually helpless in the face of the new media environment. Nothing has changed. Everything has changed.

This complex situation is further exacerbated by a number of specific (and relatively recent) changes in law and technology that combine to transform the digital media landscape. Six such changes will be introduced here and will appear among the topics covered in this volume.

First, the *Copyright Act of 1976* modified the requirement for copyright holders to re-register works for which protection had expired and for which the rights owner wanted continued protection; ratification of the *Berne Convention* in 1988 ended the registration requirement. As a result of this revocation of the traditional requirement to renew, there is no longer a material difference, with regard to rights protection, between works in which rights holders retain an interest and those in which that interest has waned. As a result, when the term of copyright protection is extended, orphaned works (those in which no living person has an identifiable economic interest in the protections afforded by intellectual property law) receive the same protections as do works that are still generating return for owners. Under this practice, even works in which owners are uninterested do not enter the public domain.[3]

Second, the *Copyright Extension Act of 1998* (the so-called "*Sonny Bono Act*") added, in general, twenty years to the terms of all copyrights. In itself, this extension was not remarkable; Congress had previously extended copyright terms a number of times.[4] However, this extension came at the historical moment at which the early works of modern mass media were scheduled to come into the public domain. As the era in which radio, television, and other electronically recorded materials were beginning to come into the public domain approached, large media interests pressed for political action that led to the extension and raised concerns that in the new media environment a series of extensions are sure to follow. Roughly speaking, then, anything made after 1923 for which protections were about to expire (read: virtually all of the work in the modern media era) had its protection extended another twenty years. When combined with the 1976 and 1988 removal of the registration requirement, the *Extension Act* virtually locked the public domain for twenty years. While this situation might be reasonable for some works (for example, the early Disney drawings and animations), the result also applies to all printed works, whether or not they are orphaned, leading to an enormous amount of material being blocked from entry into the public domain. The degree to which large corporations like Disney (which took much material out of the public domain and transformed it in order to build their empires but do not want any of their materials to enter the public domain) deserve for their works to be forever protected is highly contestable.

Third, the *Digital Millennium Copyright Act of 1998* (*DMCA*) contains anti-circumvention requirements that trump many traditional fair-use provisions. An activity that has been traditionally protected by fair use may now be illegal due to the *DMCA*. Take, for example, the case of backing up a legally purchased movie for private use: Owners can't "crack" DVDs in their collections to make back-up copies. While making back-ups taken from videotape (an analog source) is legally protected by fair use, making the same back-ups from a DVD (a digital source) is illegal, as doing so constitutes a *DMCA* anti-circumvention violation. Just as the public domain promotes the public's interest in developing and furthering research and creative production, so fair use produces the same palliative effect on the ability of citizens to use otherwise protected intellectual property under certain conditions and following specific protection principles. The dual losses of the public domain and of fair use at the hands of the legislative and legal systems in the current era cause many to wonder if corporate entities have gained too much of an upper hand to the detriment of the public interest.

Fourth, a number of court cases have validated "click through/shrink wrap agreements." These implied contracts and the court actions supporting them allow contract law to trump intellectual property law protections (including those in the otherwise draconian *DMCA*). So, for example, while the *DMCA* and the *Copyright Act of 1976* both protect reverse engineering, the courts have said that if the usage agreement (the click/shrink wrap) says that opening the software package engages the user in a contract with the provider/producer and the contract says you can't reverse engineer, then one can't reverse engineer after agreeing to the contract by opening the product (even in cases in which that agreement is not displayed on the outside of the container). The outcome stifles technological innovation and competition based on reverse engineering, a protection that is supposed to be built into the affirmative protections of intellectual property law.

Fifth, the specter of increased control over property rights management through digital rights management (DRM) regimes appears to threaten that every sort of digital material will be watermarked as proprietary so that the controls suggested in points one through four, above, will be strictly enforced, perhaps at the code level (in the background, within machines and networks), rather than at the content level (where users encounter the material). Software makers and entertainment media providers are collaborating in pushing digital rights management protocols, ostensibly as a way to combat piracy and illegal downloading. However, the implications of the technologies threaten a sort of prior restraint that might very well have been illegal in the analog/offline world.

Sixth, and finally, our elected officials generally want little part in efforts to alleviate these matters on behalf of the general public, though many politicians are more than enthusiastic about further protecting the rights of corporate interests. There are obvious reasons why politicians don't like advocating in favor of the public in these matters. The media provide both campaign support (through corporate donations and by providing access to celebrities who are under contract and who are willing to fundraise on behalf of politicians) and access to media in a direct way through news coverage (or the lack of it). Politicians do not want to "mess with" big entertainment or big information (news). Additionally, the details of intellectual property law in the new media environment are highly technical. Historically our so-called representatives have turned over the task of drafting legislation to working groups of industry representatives (usually via their stables of intellectual property lawyers). As a result, players who are the current holders of intellectual property advocate the crafting of laws that favor their positions, and the laws are written in ways that protect their interests and appeal more to high-level legal wrangling than to everyday common sense about right and wrong.[5]

Taken together, these practices disturb the traditional balance between promoting creativity via distribution to the public domain and protecting the economic interests of creative producers and their sponsors and distributors as a way to support further research and/or creativity. The balance is now strongly in favor of corporate producers and the regime of control. Laws that are written by and for elite corporate interests apply to every person, every day. The system is strained almost to the breaking point. [ELL]

Property Law Governing Products of the Mind

Rapid advances in technology have challenged the legal system to apply traditional legal constructs to new problems of ownership of intellectual property. More to the point, the digitizing of property and the ease and speed with which that digitized property can be copied, transmitted, and shared across the globe has posed pressing legal problems for both traditional owners and those who desire to share information freely. This tension is played out nearly daily in the court system and, increasingly, in the media. As reflected in *The Wall Street Journal*, *The New York Times*, *The Washington Post*, or virtually any major news source, the amount of coverage generated by disputes about intellectual property has multiplied in recent years. Some of the cases arise when competitors in highly specialized industries battle over technologies. But as the recent Supreme Court decision in *Metro-Goldwyn-Mayer Studios, Inc. v. Grokster* demonstrates, some cases involve the rights, directly or indirectly, of the citizenry at large to share information (e.g., peer-to-peer sharing of digitized information).

> Tony Long, copy chief at *Wired News*, writes about the degree to which the pursuit of IP rights enforcement by big media is both frustrating to consumers and, perhaps, counter-productive to the long-term business interests of rights holders. In his article "RIAA Hits a Sour Note with Its File-Sharing Witch Hunt," Long recounts the case of Jammie Thomas, a single American Indian mother of two making $36,000 a year, who lost the first court decision based on filings by the Recording Industry Association of America (RIAA). Thomas was convicted of violating copyright law and was ordered to pay the recording industry $222,000 in damages. Long makes a number of points, including that Thomas was found to have downloaded a small number of songs, that the recording industry is overly inefficient and therefore their products are overly expensive, and that most of the profit goes to RIAA member companies instead of artists. Long notes the bad public relations for the recording industry in this and other RIAA actions and predicts that such action will produce only hollow victories for the industry.
>
> The reference citation URL, for each of these "inset" notes is provided in the Works Cited section at the end of the book. Readers are encouraged to enter the link in a browser and read the entire article.

For each landmark case that winds its way through the legal system, there are thousands more that are fought out and resolved every day in lower courts, corporate boardrooms, and backroom settlements (sometimes between corporate giants and beleaguered and overmatched private citizens). The battles will only escalate and spread to an international stage as technological development continues at a rapid, global pace. Emerging economic powerhouses like China and India, which have vast populations to employ and an increasingly sophisticated work force, are challenging the developed nations' approaches to remaining economically competitive in the twenty-first century. While the contours of American intellectual property law change on a daily basis, it is safe to say that many emerging economies are less concerned with abiding by the principles of ownership found in American intellectual property law than they are with capitalizing on the strength of their vast labor forces. The result is an increasing tension between the creators of intellectual property, who wish to reap the economic rewards of their creativity, and the exploiters of intellectual property, who—with the aid of technology and cheap labor—desire to capitalize the same intellectual property. Simply put, when Universal Studios invests $100 million in a film, it does not want a bootlegger in China to distribute 25,000 unauthorized pre-release copies of the film on the streets of Beijing for one dollar each. But the digital age makes it possible for a single "pirate" to copy and transmit the data to an outlet overseas that can then burn the DVDs for literally pennies apiece and have them to market in the span of a day or two. Whether the law (or international diplomacy) can stop such conduct is a pressing concern for the American economy.

Against this contemporary backdrop, it is necessary to take a step back and understand how the American legal system has come to classify the products of the mind as property (intellectual property). What did the framers of the Constitution mean when they specified, in Article I, Section 8, that "The Congress shall have Power ... To promote the Progress of Science and useful Arts, by securing for limited Times to Authors and Inventors the exclusive Right to their respective Writings and Discoveries"?

One wonders if the American legal system has remained true to the intent of the framers concerning intellectual property. On the most basic level, given America's position as a global leader in many fields of science, technology, literature, and other arts, it is easy to conclude that American intellectual property law has amply achieved the Constitution's goal of promoting the progress of science and art. But as the American economy has become increasingly reliant upon and, indeed, fueled by its ability to leverage science and art for commercial gain, so too have American economic interests become increasingly determined to expand intellectual property law in a way that focuses more on corporate rights and less on the good of the public domain.

In general, American law classifies and protects intellectual property in a variety of ways with a suite of protections across a number of jurisdictions. For example, copyrights and patents are largely the product of federal law (with Constitutional foundations, as noted above). Both federal and state laws govern trademarks; trade secrets are, at least for now, largely the domain of state law. One also finds that the active lifespan of each form of intellectual property varies. For example, a drug company's patent on a particular drug expires in twenty years, but Coca-Cola's trade secret formula for its famous beverage will live on in perpetuity, provided that it remains a secret. The methods of securing ownership in each form of intellectual property vary as well. Under copyright law, the author owns a work the moment it is "fixed in a tangible medium of expression." Under trademark law, a trademark owner must use a mark (in a specified geographic territory) in commerce (in a particular business segment) in order to acquire rights. Under patent law, an inventor must convince the US government, via a detailed application procedure, that the invention is "new, useful, and non-obvious" to someone who is skilled in the same art or area of study.

American law also features a number of ways to enforce the rights of intellectual property owners. Intellectual property disputes are largely resolved through litigation or—if the parties have otherwise agreed—arbitration. We will study these processes and come to know them largely through reading excerpts of judicially made case law. The most potent traditional remedy available to the owner of intellectual property is a court-ordered injunction that prohibits an infringer from distributing infringing material and may even require the infringer, at its own cost, to destroy the stock of infringing material. In the digital age, the destruction of infringing material may be akin to blowing on the dried petals of a dandelion. The seeds float to the ground, and from there we can hardly count the next generation's weed patch. Of course, no legal remedy is complete unless money changes hands, and American intellectual property law has developed elaborate mechanisms to compensate victims of intellectual property misappropriation and punish so-called pirates. Through all of the legal processes, there are transaction costs—lawyer's fees and court costs—that tip the scales of justice largely in favor of those who can most afford pursuing relief and against those who can least afford legal representation. Although certain intellectual property laws have attempted to build in mechanisms to shift fees to the losers, in the American justice system the general rule is that each party generally bears its own legal expenses, irrespective of the outcome.

The American legal system copes with the rapidly evolving technology rather poorly. It must run to catch up, and the moment it catches up, it falls behind again. The simple truth is that law evolves through a slow, incremental, and deliberative process, both at the legislative and the judicial level. In contrast, technology evolves as quickly as the human mind allows. The result is an increasingly wider "guidance gap"—the space between the new technology and the old law. There is no better exemplar of this gap than the *Grokster* defendants' efforts to rely on the Supreme Court's decision from the 1980s in the *Sony/Betamax* case (*Sony Corp. of America v. Universal City Studios, Inc.*) to bolster their argument that peer-to-peer file sharing is no different, legally, than Sony's manufacture and distribution of Betamax machines that allowed users to record and time-shift shows from their televisions. While a twenty-year span between Supreme Court decisions on related topics may be marginal in the law, it is literally light years in the development of technology. Ultimately, the Supreme Court did not accept the Betamax analogy, but the larger question remains as to whether we have reached a point at which the guidance gap between law and technology has become so large as to be unworkable.

Additionally, a student of the media (new or old) might ponder why it is necessary to poke around in the law at all. Isn't that the domain of lawyers? When it comes to the law, isn't a little knowledge a dangerous thing? The answers, of course, are "yes" and "yes." However, in today's environment, where we have fingertip access to more intellectual property than ever in the history of humankind, it is safe to say that those who venture out into the world with a blindfold and hope for the best may one day wonder why a legal summons has arrived at their doorstep. A sage philosopher might say that it is better to study lawsuits (difficult though they may be) than to be a party to them. [SB]

Information Stewards' Rights and Responsibilities

Recent advances in technology and resulting changes in intellectual property laws present particular challenges for librarians, archivists, and museum professionals. These and other information stewards have been entrusted with the responsibility to collect, preserve, and provide access to information and cultural objects for the long-term benefit of society as a whole. They have long acknowledged that this role requires a close understanding of the law and an obligation to balance the interests of all stakeholders. As technology changes the fundamental nature of information, both the forms and the rules of stewardship are changing.

Traditionally, libraries, archives, and museums house legally obtained copies of books, recorded sound, three-dimensional objects, films, manuscripts, maps, data sets, and other content forms. When the private papers of a famous person are deposited in an archive, the archivist must act with awareness of the ethical and legal rights of privacy and publicity. Academic libraries that receive copies of dissertations might temporarily restrict access to a dissertation if the researcher intends to apply for a patent for any part of the research. By and large, however, the most important legal issue for an information steward is copyright. While it might be a stretch to say that before the digital revolution copyright law was simple to understand and apply, it is certainly true that clear guidelines had been established to interpret the law and govern everyday practices. Many of these guidelines fail to translate to a digital environment.

Libraries have historically acquired the bulk of their collections through purchase. Section 109 of the *United States Copyright Law* specifies that the copyright holder may control only the first sale of a copy of a work; the purchaser then has the right to re-sell or lend the copy. This so-called "first-sale doctrine" is essential to the operation of libraries (and also, incidentally, to video and video game rental stores). Increasingly, however, libraries do not purchase materials outright but rather pay to electronically subscribe to titles in their collections. These subscriptions are governed by a contractual license between the library and the copyright holder. In this situation (like other instances we'll examine involving digital materials), contract law trumps copyright law, and exemptions such as section 109 no longer apply. The best illustration of the consternation this causes may be seen in the explosion of full-text electronic journals in the 1990s and the resulting crisis in library budgets. Among American research libraries, the unit cost of serials increased by 188% and overall serial expenditures by 273%, well above the unit cost increase for books (64%) and the overall increase in the Consumer Price Index for the same period (63%).[6] Many believe that since these monies are paid to access, and not to own, libraries are now paying more and getting less. Even those who believe they are paying more to get more, since the electronic text is infinitely easier to search and to use than paper copies, are concerned for the long-term implications of such a shift. If libraries no longer own copies of these works, how will they preserve and maintain access to them far into the future, when the copyright expires, or when it is no longer financially profitable for the rights holder to license access? With the rapid growth in popularity of electronic books and music subscription services, it cannot be long before the "subscribe vs. own" phenomenon shifts even further toward the subscription model.

Preservation is a vital activity for all information stewards. The complexity of new media technologies and changes in copyright law make it more difficult than was the case with analog media to retain and preserve access to materials over the long term. Old forms, such as books and sculpture, were somewhat simpler in configuration than, say, an animated Web-based work of art that might require specific, and possibly proprietary, software for viewing. How is a museum curator to maintain such an object? While storage may be relatively easy, future access (the end-goal of curation and storage) may be problematic. Further, if the artist has applied digital rights management (DRM) technology to prevent use on more than one computer workstation, how will the museum ensure that it can be viewed by future generations of museum visitors? Thanks to the 1998 *Digital Millennium Copyright Act*, it is now illegal, in many circumstances, to defeat rights-protection measures. This creates a true dilemma for the curator.[7]

At an even more fundamental level, changes in law and technology may dramatically test the image of society's information stewards as members of not-for-profit organizations. The emergence of services such as eBay and the

Google Books project challenge our concept of a repository, which traditionally has encompassed not just the housing but also the arrangement and description of objects. Although eBay exists to make money, it is one of the most unique research tools available in the world today. Likewise, Google's existing Web search product and its proposed Google Books project, will create one of the largest information repositories ever known. Access to such repositories will unquestionably benefit society at large, but how will they be seen in legal terms? US copyright law mentions not-for-profit use and not-for-profit institutions repeatedly in its exemption sections, and courts have traditionally cast a more favorable eye on fair use and other such claims by these institutions. How will the question of profit in a technological environment change the interpretation of the law?

Information stewards who select, purchase, and care for materials support and promote the interests of creators and other copyright holders. They represent a significant revenue stream, particularly for materials that are further along the "long tail" than materials with mass-market appeal, and by preserving the expression of an idea, ensure that the idea itself will be accessible far into the future.[8] At the same time, the social contract obligates them to make access as unfettered as possible for scholars, researchers, and the general public, who seek to use the material to advance the interests of society. Balancing these interests when both the law and technology are in a period of rapid change is likely to be more expensive and less clear, a potentially dangerous combination. [CS]

Types and Categories of Intellectual Property Law

Intellectual property law establishes relationships among and between the concretized ideas produced through research, creativity, and innovation by applying principles about ownership drawn from property law. The system is supposed to encourage creativity and innovation by using the legal protections of property to provide economic incentives and rewards to creators for introducing culturally enriching new creations into citizens' lives.

As is the case with all things constitutional, the correct interpretation of Article I, Section 8 is problematic. What is meant by "for limited Times"? Numerous congressional extensions of copyright terms, for example, have locked up intellectual property across lifetimes and generations with little expectation that further extensions won't follow. Since the majority of intellectual property rights are held by corporate entities, one wonders if the constitutional rights that might encourage "Authors and Inventors" to "promote the Progress of Science and useful Arts" are actually being used, instead, to suppress innovation in favor of those who hold the rights to the old media that innovation would replace. These and other issues are central to the intersection of intellectual property and new media. Wide ranges of legal principles are at play in these matters, and a brief review will introduce and orient the in-depth analysis of developments to follow in later chapters.

This book will discuss the legal ramifications of *copyright* (including questions of fair use, the public domain, file sharing, and digital rights management); *patents*; *trademarks* and *trade dress*; *trade secrets*; and various *content torts*, including the *rights of publicity and privacy* as well as laws related to *defamation*. Additionally, we will consider some of the ramifications of international/global contexts and virtual environments on these legal aspects. All intellectual property issues depend on the relationships among the creative forces and contractually specified employment arrangements under which the works were created. For example, the status of "works made for hire" modifies rights and categories (as do other contractual arrangements). Further, the copyright categories often overlap and interact with each other. For instance, the rebroadcast of a photo opportunity-style event featuring Hollywood stars may well involve negotiations over copyrights, rights of publicity, and trademarks. Let us begin by introducing the categories; details will follow in dedicated chapters.

Copyright protects original works of authorship, be they literary, dramatic, musical, or artistic. Copyright gives the rights holder legal preference for the reproduction, performance, distribution, display/performance, and reworking (derivative works) of the creative production. Copyright protection is in place whenever material is fixed into a tangible medium of expression (pen is put to paper, bits are set by typing and saving a file, musical notes are written on a score or generated into a sound file). For citizen/human authors, rights are secured for their lifetime plus seventy years. For a corporate author, the rights are secured for 95 years from publication or 120 years from creation—whichever is shorter. One's standing in legal cases adjudicating copyright issues can be improved/augmented by displaying the copyright symbol © with the work. One can further extend protections by registering the work with the US Copyright Office. Derivative works present new combinations of rights and protected owners; these relationships sometimes make it difficult to determine whom to ask for permission or whom to pay a royalty for using materials. Although there are a variety of clearinghouses and professional organizations involved in copyright, there is no single path for ascertaining copyright ownership and/or rights acquisition, especially in the interdisciplinary spaces in which multimedia operate. There is, however, heated interest (and there are dominant players) in each industry, as rights management is a key issue in the digital era.

The Internet adds a number of complexities to traditional copyright considerations. For example, publishing companies often assign rights to other companies when doing business across international borders, so the use of works on the net may require permissions from a number of rights holders to the same work. Additionally, authors of Web sites may be required to acquire a range of rights for the use of a single item; for example, the public display and/or public performance rights may be needed for the use of third-party materials.

Virtually all mass-mediated materials feature multiple considerations in addition to those initially presented by authorship (regardless of the analog or digital nature of the media and delivery methods). The media production environment raises issues of joint or collaborative authorship. In professional production, authorship relationships are often managed through contracts and/or employment agreements. In some ways, these agreements simplify the copyright situation by assigning the rights to a single entity. However, the arrangements could empower a range of people with a variety of rights across the project, thereby making rights management difficult. Careful legal research and analysis is needed to determine the rightful owner of protections. Assignment of rights to others, as is often the case with photographs/photographers and in the case of "works made for hire," can also complicate rights ownership and management questions. In many professional contexts, some parent organizations are able to pay blanket fees that enable employees to freely use a wide range of materials in production, while smaller enterprises find themselves having to clear permissions and pay fees one item at a time.

Distribution of materials in the media is often controlled by industry or legal standards and practices that work in concert with copyright laws. For instance, various permission, licensing, and royalty arrangements attend to the use of materials at television or radio stations (including Internet-based radio). These practices are regulated by laws that mandate regulatory agencies to work with and/or to exert various amounts of control over industries. Large and experienced Web-based firms or game designers may be in step with these procedures; smaller firms may be unaware of standard industry practices.

Copyright protection of music adds complexities because of the multiple layers of rights involved and the use of a compulsory licensing system. First, there are rights associated with the basic musical composition. These rights are often held by the original composer or are assigned (sold or given) to a music publishing company. Second, there are rights associated with sound recordings of the music, as the work of players, singers, and technicians join to create unique artistic artifacts. In addition to the five copyright categories (reproduction, performance, distribution, display/performance, and reworking/derivatives), music protection and use also includes considerations of the "mechanical right" (the right to use songs through a license and royalty rather than permission system—more about this in the section concerning the compulsory license in Chapter 1), various synchronization rights (allowing protected music to be used in concert with images), and rights to use particular recordings or excerpts of a recording in other works.

Trademarks ™ can be words, graphic images, designs, sounds, distinctive colors or color combinations, or smells (and combinations of those elements) that identify and distinguish the source of the goods of one party from those of others. A service mark ™ is the same as a trademark, except that it identifies and distinguishes the source of a service rather than a product. In order to establish a trademark, one should be the first to publicly use the mark in commerce in a specific category of business activity in a specified geographic location. Trademarks can be registered ® within each state or nationally with the US Trademark Office for a renewable term of ten years (for federal protections). The mark must be deemed to be distinctive, ranging on a continuum from "fanciful" (the strongest type of mark) to "generic" (generic marks are sometimes so "usual" that protection for them is denied). As is the case with copyrights being established when authors/creators fix a work in tangible form, basic trademark protections accrue immediately upon the use of the mark in commerce. However, additional protections/rights are added through the registration process.

Trade dress is the form, shape, and look of a product or service's distinctive packaging and presentation. In intellectual property law, elements of trade dress are treated in ways similar to trademarks and service marks.

Patents are the grant of a property right to the inventor(s), issued by the US Patent and Trademark Office. Patents provide the right to exclude others from making, using, offering for sale, or selling the invention in the United States or importing the invention into the United States. Applications must be filed in the US Patent and Trademark Office. Any person who "invents or discovers any new and useful process, machine, manufacture, or composition of matter, or any new and useful improvement thereof, may obtain a patent," including practically everything that is made by humans and the processes for making the products. There are also "business process" patents that protect certain "ways of doing" that produce material and/or services, and there are "plant patents" that apply to seed varieties, certain hybridization procedures, and the like. In recent times, certain aspects of software became patentable.

Patent law specifies that the subject matter of the application (the invention) must be useful, that is, the subject matter has a useful purpose, and it works as described in the application. The subject matter wanting patent must be sufficiently different from what has been used or described before, such that it may be said to be non-obvious to a person having ordinary skill in the area of technology related to the invention. For example, the substitution of one color for another or changes in size are ordinarily not patentable.

Generally, patents protect the inventor for twenty years from the date on which the application for the patent was filed in the United States. In special cases, the protection extends from the date on which an earlier, related application was filed, subject to the payment of maintenance fees. US patent grants are effective only within the United States, US territories, and US possessions, although a variety of international trade agreements carry implications for respecting patents across borders. In general, the laws of nature, physical phenomena, mere ideas or suggestions, and abstract ideas are not patentable subject matter.

Trade secrets consist of information with economic value. The information is not generally known, and the holder of the intellectual property has made reasonable efforts to maintain secrecy surrounding the information. For example, the formula for Coca-Cola is a closely guarded trade secret. Protection afforded trade secrets is not engendered through application or registration. Protection of trade secrets is provided by the information holder, via the steps taken to keep the secret closely held. However, the intellectual property legal system recognizes the validity of trade secrets and will enforce limitations, constraints, and sanctions when petitioned by the holder of intellectual property who faces damage by the release of closely held trade secrets.

There are a number of additional aspects of intellectual property law sometimes referred to as *content torts*, as they hinge on the status of the informational content contained in acts of communication that have purportedly led to material damage to one of the parties. These activities fall within the purview of intellectual property in that they seldom have any relationship to actual damage to or loss of property. Instead, they involve perceived damage to one's image.

Defamation is defined as a false statement of fact that causes damage to the reputation of another person. Defamation may exist where one party makes claims that the second party committed a crime, has a disease, or suffers from unfitness or lack of integrity in office or employment, or has an inability in trade or profession. One may defame both private citizens and public figures.

However, the threshold standard for proving defamation in the case of a public figure is much more restrictive/challenging than for a private citizen. Public figures may only be defamed through "actual malice," meaning that the source entertained serious doubts that the information was true but published it anyway (with the intent to do malice to the public figure). In the case of private citizens, the defamation case hinges on the degree to which the proposed defamatory communication is not true and is actually damaging.

One's privacy rights are violated (*invasion of privacy*) when others take actions that invade the party's seclusion or put their image into false light. In a related tort, citizens have rights to control their image via the *right of publicity* that specifies, in general, the need to get permission to use a person's image in commercial contexts. The use of pre-existing material (for example, from films or television) may also involve payments for re-use that are associated with rights accorded by actors' union membership. [ELL]

Finding, Reading, and Analyzing the Sources of Intellectual Property Law

Intellectual property law in the United States derives from two principal sources, legislation and common law. Legislation governing intellectual property is largely—though not exclusively—the domain of Congress. Copyrights, patents, and trademarks, three significant forms of intellectual property, have been shaped and guided by acts of Congress.[9] Indeed, in the areas of copyrights and patents, federal law largely preempts state law from impinging upon this subject matter. Trade secrets are the one form of intellectual property that remains predominantly controlled by state law. Presently, forty-two states have enacted legislation based on model legislation known as the *Uniform Trade Secrets Act*.[10] In 1996, however, Congress passed the *Economic Espionage Act of 1996*, which, among other things, gave sweeping authority to the Justice Department to prosecute theft of trade secrets both inside and outside the United States.[11]

Although legislation may give initial definition and guidance to any area of intellectual property, the common law or case law adds a significant contribution (and complexity) to the interpretation of the law. The common law consists of the body of law derived from judicial opinions issued by judges on a case-by-case basis.[12] When judges—particularly those who sit on courts of appeal—render written opinions, those opinions become binding law not only upon the parties who are involved in the case before the court, but also upon other parties who, in the future, may be similarly situated. The fundamental concept that underlies the common law system is known in Latin as *stare deci-*

sis, which, in effect, means that a judge's decision becomes precedent for future cases.[13]

Naturally, there is great interplay between legislatively created law and judicially created law. Congress may introduce new legislation precisely as a result of a judicial interpretation of existing legislation. An example of this emerged when the US House of Representatives passed the *Trademark Dilution Revision Act of 2005*.[14] The proposed legislation followed the Supreme Court's 2003 decision in *Moseley v. V Secret Catalogue, Inc.*, 537 U.S. 418. In that decision, the high court ruled that the current trademark dilution law requires a showing of *actual* harm, as opposed to a lower threshold of *likelihood* of harm. The proposed bill clarifies Congress's intent that dilution must be actionable at the outset (before actual harm occurs) to ensure that the goodwill associated with famous marks is not eroded over time.

Organization of the US Court System

In this textbook you will be introduced to many examples of the common law, largely in the form of appellate judicial opinions. In order to understand the value of any such opinion as precedent, it is important to have some familiarity with the organization of the court system of the United States. The nature of the court issuing the opinion will directly govern the scope and effect that the opinion will have on the law at large.

In general, courts may be divided between those that handle trials and those that handle appeals. Trial courts are the ports of entry for parties who have legal disputes that they cannot otherwise resolve without resorting to the legal system. Initially, the parties present their disputes to the trial court through submission of legal papers and evidence. Trial courts are typically staffed by a single judge who may hear and rule upon legal issues in the case and, unless there is a jury, make ultimate factual determinations and legal conclusions. If trial courts are the ports of entry, then appeals courts are the final destination for litigants. The courts of appeal are established to review the application of the law to the facts in the case and to determine if there was an error of law in the trial court that would mandate a reversal of the result or a return of the case for further proceedings in the trial court.

In the federal court system, there are three tiers of courts. The Federal District Courts are the trial courts—the ports of entry into the federal court system. There are presently ninety-four districts across the country with more than 450 judges occupying courts in those districts. Although the decisions of a trial judge will control the outcome of the questions before the court, those decisions do not serve as controlling legal authority in other cases.

The second tier of courts consists of the Circuit Courts of Appeal. The country is divided into eleven judicial circuits with approximately 170 Circuit Court judges. Each Circuit Court hears appeals that arise from the District Courts located within the circuit. The Circuit Courts typically operate in panels of three judges, but there may be times when a matter of significance will be heard *en banc*, which means the entire collection of Circuit Court judges hears arguments, deliberates, and participates in the decision-making process.

The third and highest tier in the federal court system is the US Supreme Court, which is comprised of nine justices. The Supreme Court is the final arbiter of case law in the United States. The Supreme Court's decisions on issues of law become the law of the land. In recent years, the number of cases that arrive in the Supreme Court on an annual basis has skyrocketed to over seven thousand; however, the court typically hears and issues full opinions on only about eighty to ninety cases each year. Of those eighty to ninety cases, only a handful (at most) involve intellectual property disputes.[15] Every judge in the federal system is appointed by the president of the United States and confirmed by the Senate.

Table 1. Federal Court System

Tier	Court	Number of Judges (2004)
First	US District Courts	94 districts, 680 judges
Second	US Circuit Courts of Appeal	11 judicial circuits, 167 judges
Third	US Supreme Court	9 justices

In state courts, there is a similar, though not necessarily identical, framework of trial and appellate courts. All states have an entry-level trial court system and typically at least two levels of review by appellate courts. The executive branch in some states appoints judges; in other states, judges are elected.

Specialized Tribunals for Certain Intellectual Property Disputes

In addition to federal and state courts, there are other tribunals that hear and decide intellectual property disputes. The Trademark Trial and Appeal Board (TTAB) is affiliated with the US Patent and Trademark Office. The administrative law judges of TTAB hear proceedings relating to disputes over trademark applications. Although the TTAB may issue written rulings relating to these disputes, the rulings do not serve as binding precedent, but they may be looked upon for guidance.

As the Internet has grown rapidly in recent years, so has the number of disputes over Internet domain names, which may be considered a form of intellectual property. Although the process of obtaining and registering a domain name is relatively easy and inexpensive, certain domain names may have very high intrinsic value. Early in the evolution of the Internet, there were many examples of prescient cybersquatters who had the foresight to obtain registrations of domain names that were likely to be in strong demand—for example, the names of Fortune 500 companies, followed by ".com."[16] Once these cybersquatters had valid registrations in their possession, they were in a position to leverage their ownership and sell them to the companies who were themselves rapidly coming to understand the importance of owning and controlling the right uniform resource locator. In the wake of this phenomenon, Congress passed the *Anticybersquatting Consumer Protection Act* (1999), which, among other things, makes illegal the intentional, bad-faith registration, trafficking, or use of a domain name that is identical or confusingly similar to a famous name or mark.[17]

Disputes involving ownership and use of domain names often wind up in the federal courts. However, in the last several years, various administrative hearing panels have emerged that specialize in and are authorized to hear disputes involving domain names. The World Intellectual Property Organization, or WIPO, is one such body that hears and decides matters involving domain names.[18] Like federal appellate courts, WIPO cases are heard and decided by a panel of three arbitrators. However, the arbitrators are limited to determining whether a domain name should be transferred or retained by the registrant. WIPO panels do not award monetary damages or other legal relief but rule solely on issues of ownership of domain names. There are several other bodies that have been authorized to hear and resolve domain name disputes, including the National Arbitration Forum,[19] the CPR Institute,[20] and the Asian Domain Name Dispute Resolution Centre.[21]

How to Locate Intellectual Property Law

We assume that the reader of this textbook has access to Internet-based resource material, which affords the public unparalleled access to legal resources that until recently were only available in law libraries or to those with online, for-pay subscription services such as Westlaw or Lexis. Today, much is available free of charge to those with a computer and Internet service.

Beginning with federal legislation, all relevant acts of Congress are easily accessible online. The *United States Code* (U.S.C.), which contains all acts of Congress, including those involving intellectual property, can be accessed at the US government site.[22] Before engaging in a search, it helps to know the title and the section number of any given act, although keyword searching is available. For ease of reference, we include in Table 2 below a shorthand reference for easy access to the major acts of Congress pertaining to intellectual property.

Table 2: Significant Federal Acts Related to Intellectual Property

Act	Title and Section Number
Copyright Act	17 U.S.C. § 101 et seq.
Trademark Act	15 U.S.C. § 1051 et seq.
Patent Act	35 U.S.C. § 1 et seq.
Economic Espionage Act of 1996	18 U.S.C. § 1031 et seq.

The federal judiciary also maintains a general Web site that serves as an easy portal into the various courts that make up the federal system (<http://www.uscourts.gov/>), and the courts that make up the federal judiciary also maintain their own independent sites, including District Courts (e.g., <http://www.ilnd.uscourts.gov/>), Circuit Courts of Appeal (e.g., <http://www.ca7.uscourts.gov/>), and the US Supreme Court (<http://www.supremecourtus.gov/>). In recent years, these courts have begun to post every reported decision that is published by the court. Obtaining judicial opinions that were issued before the era of online posting may pose a challenge to the Internet-only researcher. There are university-based research sites that have augmented their collections to include historical Supreme Court decisions, some of which are organized topically (e.g., <http://www.law.cornell.edu/supct/index.html>).

Beyond federal law, most states also provide online access to their legislative and common law. Fifty-state entry portals are also available and offer efficient starting points for state law research (e.g., <http://www.law.cornell.edu/states/listing.html>).

Reading the Law

Of course, finding applicable law is only the first step in a larger analytical process. In the course of this book, we will explore various texts, both legislative and common law, in order to gain an understanding and appreciation of how to read and understand these primary source materials. We will also explore how the law develops incrementally through the common law, with occasional sea changes that emerge from legislation or groundbreaking Supreme Court precedent.

We assume the reader has had little or no experience reading common law judicial opinions. This is usually the provenance of law students, who must spend three years mastering the process of deconstructing case law and arguing it back to their law professors. For the uninitiated, delving into an appellate court's opinion—which may range in length from a page or two to over one hundred pages and is fraught with legal terminology and analysis of precedent—will certainly be a daunting task. To make this journey slightly more accessible, we provide here a synopsis of a sample legal analysis similar to those that the student is likely to encounter.

Let us start with the following recent example from the US Supreme Court:

(Slip Opinion) OCTOBER TERM, 2004 1
Syllabus

SUPREME COURT OF THE UNITED STATES
Syllabus
METRO-GOLDWYN-MAYER STUDIOS INC. ET AL. v.
GROKSTER, LTD., ET AL.
CERTIORARI TO THE UNITED STATES COURT OF APPEALS
FOR
THE NINTH CIRCUIT

No. 04.480. Argued March 29, 2005. Decided June 27, 2005.

Here one finds the caption of the Supreme Court's opinion in a case that pitted various entertainment companies that made and distributed films and music against various computer software companies that made and distributed peer-to-peer file sharing software. End-users who acquired the peer-to-peer file sharing software were able to share their own music and film entertainment with other end-users without paying a fee to the entertainment companies. The entertainment companies believed that the peer-to-peer file sharing software companies should be held legally responsible for contributory copyright infringement. The case began in Federal District Court in California and made its way to the Supreme Court.

But let us return to the caption and see what information we can glean solely from the title of the case itself. First, we know that the case was decided during the Supreme Court's 2004 session, which actually ran from October 2004 through June 2005. Officially, the Supreme Court is not in session during the summer. Second, we know that *Metro-Goldwyn-Mayer Studios Inc., et al.* (meaning "and others") has a legal dispute with *Grokster, Ltd. et al.* Third, we see that the case was issued on a *writ of certiorari* to the 9th Circuit Court of Appeals. In other words, the case arrived at the Supreme Court from the 9th Circuit (the federal appellate circuit that covers a sizeable part of the western United States). When a case arrives at the Supreme Court, it comes on a petition for a *writ of certiorari*. When the Supreme Court decides to take the case, it grants the writ. Finally, we know that the case was "argued" on March 29, 2005, which is the day that the lawyers assembled in Washington, D.C., and appeared in the courtroom of the Supreme Court to present their respective cases to the justices. Most certainly, for many months leading up to the oral argument, the parties submitted lengthy written "briefs" for the justices to consider. About three months after the oral argument, on June 27, 2005, the Supreme Court issued its opinion.

The next part of the opinion is the "syllabus," which is not really part of the official opinion but rather is a short summary of the case. The syllabus may be a useful tool to gain entry into a much lengthier opinion, but the reader should not rest on the syllabus alone.

After the syllabus comes the opinion itself. Here is how the Court's opinion in *Metro-Goldwyn-Mayer* begins:

> SOUTER, J., delivered the opinion for a unanimous Court. GINSBURG,   J.,   filed a concurring opinion, in which REHNQUIST, C. J., and KENNEDY, J., joined. BREYER, J., filed a concurring opinion, in which STEVENS and O'CONNOR, JJ., joined.
>
> The question is under what circumstances the distributor of a product capable of both lawful and unlawful use is liable for acts of copyright infringement by third parties using the product. We hold that one who distributes a device with the object of promoting its use to infringe copyright, as shown by clear expression or other affirmative steps taken to foster infringement, is liable for the resulting acts of infringement by third parties.

Here we see the identity of the author of the opinion, Justice Souter, one of the associate justices of the US Supreme Court. Justice Souter provides a succinct summary of the question (as he sees it) that is presented to the Court, together with the Court's "holding" or legal answer to the question. In any case, the holding is the controlling part of the legal opinion—that part of the judicial decision that binds the conduct of the parties and serves as a signpost for future cases. It is important to distinguish the holding of the case from *dicta*, which is the extraneous commentary in the opinion. *Dicta* in a judicial opinion is not binding on the parties or future litigants but is added to an opinion to help explain the Court's reasoning or to distinguish one proposition from another.

After an introduction to the case, the author of the opinion presents a recitation of the material facts of the case, including a description of the parties and the nature of the dispute that brought them to the Court. For example, here is how Justice Souter describes the peer-to-peer parties and the dispute:

> Respondents, Grokster, Ltd., and StreamCast Networks, Inc. defendants in the trial court, distribute free software products that allow computer users to share electronic files through peer-to-peer networks, so called because users' computers communicate directly with each other, not through central servers. The advantage of peer-to-peer networks over information networks of other types shows up in their substantial and growing popularity.
>
> Because they need no central computer server to mediate the exchange of information or files among users, the high bandwidth communications capacity for a server may be dispensed with, and the need for costly server storage space is eliminated. Since copies of a file (particularly a popular one) are available on many users' computers, file requests and retrievals may be faster than on other types of networks, and since file exchanges do not travel through a server, communications can take place between any computers that remain connected to the network without risk that a glitch in the server will disable the network in its entirety. Given these benefits in security, cost, and efficiency, peer-to-peer networks are employed to store and distribute electronic files by universities, government agencies, corporations, and libraries, among others.
>
> * * *
>
> A group of copyright holders (MGM for short, but including motion picture studios, recording companies, songwriters, and music publishers) sued Grokster and StreamCast for their users' copyright infringements, alleging that they knowingly and intentionally distributed their software to enable users to reproduce and distribute the copyrighted works in violation of the Copyright Act, 17 U.S.C. §101 *et seq.* (2000 ed. and Supp. II).

Judicial opinions usually also trace the procedural history of the case in the lower courts. So, in the case of the Supreme Court, the opinion will tell the reader what happened in the District Court and the Circuit Court of Appeals. Here is Justice Souter again:

> After discovery, the parties on each side of the case cross-moved for summary judgment. The District Court limited its consideration to the asserted liability of Grokster and StreamCast for distributing the current versions of their software, leaving aside whether either was liable "for damages arising from past versions of their software, or from other past activities." (259 F. Supp. 2d 1029, 1033 (CD Cal. 2003).

The District Court held that those who used the Grokster and Morpheus software to download copyrighted media files directly infringed MGM's copyrights, a conclusion not contested on appeal, but the court nonetheless granted summary judgment in favor of Grokster and StreamCast as to any liability arising from distribution of the then current versions of their software.

Distributing that software gave rise to no liability in the Court's view, because its use did not provide the distributors with actual knowledge of specific acts of infringement. Case No. CV 01 08541 SVW (PJWx) (CD Cal., June 18, 2003), App. 1213.

The Court of Appeals affirmed. 380 F. 3d 1154 (CA9 2004). In the Court's analysis, a defendant was liable as a contributory infringer when it had knowledge of direct infringement and materially contributed to the infringement. But the Court read *Sony Corp. of America v. Universal City Studios, Inc.*, 464 U.S. 417 (1984), as holding that distribution of a commercial product capable of substantial noninfringing uses could not give rise to contributory liability for infringement unless the distributor had actual knowledge of specific instances of infringement and failed to act on that knowledge. The fact that the software was capable of substantial noninfringing uses in the Ninth Circuit's view meant that Grokster and StreamCast were not liable, because they had no such actual knowledge, owing to the decentralized architecture of their software.

The court also held that Grokster and StreamCast did not materially contribute to their users' infringement because it was the users themselves who searched for, retrieved, and stored the infringing files, with no involvement by the defendants beyond providing the software in the first place.

The Ninth Circuit also considered whether Grokster and StreamCast could be liable under a theory of vicarious infringement. The court held against liability because the defendants did not monitor or control the use of the software, had no agreed-upon right or current ability to supervise its use, and had no independent duty to police infringement. We granted certiorari. 543 U.S. (2004).

After tracing the procedural history of the case in the District Court and the Ninth Circuit Court of Appeals, Justice Souter then launches into the heart of the opinion, which is the Court's analysis of the law and how the law should be applied to the facts. His analysis begins, as do many Supreme Court opinions, with a very broad perspective:

> MGM and many of the *amici* fault the Court of Appeal's holding for upsetting a sound balance between the respective values of supporting creative pursuits through copyright protection and promoting innovation in new communication technologies by limiting the incidence of liability for copyright infringement. The more artistic protection is favored, the more technological innovation may be discouraged; the administration of copyright law is an exercise in managing the trade-off. See *Sony Corp. v. Universal City Studios, supra*, at 442.

* * *

The tension between the two values is the subject of this case, with its claim that digital distribution of copyrighted material threatens copyright holders as never before, because every copy is identical to the original, copying is easy, and many people (especially the young) use file-sharing software to download copyrighted works. This very breadth of the software's use may well draw the public directly into the debate over copyright policy, Peters, Brace Memorial Lecture: Copyright Enters the Public Domain, 51 J. Copyright Soc. 701, 705.717 (2004) (address by Register of Copyrights), and the indications are that the ease of copying songs or movies using software like Grokster's and Napster's is fostering disdain for copyright protection, (Wu, When Code Isn't Law, 89 *Va. L. Rev.* 679, 724.726) (2003). As the case has been presented to us, these fears are said to be offset by the different concern that imposing liability, not only on infringers but on distributors of software based on its potential for unlawful use, could limit further development of beneficial technologies. See, *e.g.*, Lemley & Reese, Reducing Digital Copyright Infringement Without Restricting Innovation, 56 *Stan. L. Rev.* 1345, 1386.1390 (2004); Brief for Innovation Scholars and Economists as *Amici Curiae* 15.20; Brief for Emerging Technology Companies as *Amici Curiae* 19.25; Brief for Intel Corporation as *Amicus Curiae* 20.22.

Note that Justice Souter cites an earlier Supreme Court decision, the case of *Sony Corp. v. Universal City Studios,* that the Court decided twenty years earlier and that involved a different (but at the time groundbreaking) technology—the Betamax machine. It is this very process of looking back to earlier precedent (binding law) and attempting to analogize to the current set of facts before the Court that is at the heart of how the common law evolves. The entertainment industry that fought the Betamax machine twenty years earlier and lost (because the Court found that the Betamax had substantial non-infringing uses) had to convince the current Court that its decision in *Sony* was distinguishable from the current technology of peer-to-peer file sharing.

Justice Souter signals the ultimate outcome of the case early on when he states the following:

The argument for imposing indirect liability in this case is, however, a powerful one, given the number of infringing downloads that occur every day using StreamCast's and Grokster's software. When a widely shared service or product is used to commit infringement, it may be impossible to enforce rights in the protected work effectively against all direct infringers, the only practical alternative being to go against the distributor of the copying device for secondary liability on a theory of contributory or vicarious infringement. See *In re Aimster Copyright Litigation*, 334 F. 3d 643, 645.646 (CA7 2003).

Ultimately, Justice Souter, writing for the majority of the Court, concludes that the *Sony* decision is distinguishable:

In sum, this case is significantly different from *Sony* and reliance on that case to rule in favor of StreamCast and Grokster was error. *Sony* dealt with a claim of liability based solely on distributing a product with alternative lawful and unlawful uses, with knowledge that some users would follow the unlawful course. The case struck a balance between the interests of protection and innovation by holding that the product's capability of substantial lawful employment should bar the imputation of fault and consequent secondary liability for the unlawful acts of others. MGM's evidence in this case most obviously addresses a different basis of liability for distributing a product open to alternative uses. Here, evidence of the distributors, words and deeds going beyond distribution as such shows a purpose to cause and profit from third-party acts of copyright infringement. If liability for inducing infringement is ultimately found, it will not be on the basis of presuming or imputing fault, but from inferring a patently illegal objective from statements and actions showing what that objective was. There is substantial evidence in MGM's favor on all elements of inducement, and summary judgment in favor of Grokster and StreamCast was error. On remand, reconsideration of MGM's motion for summary judgment will be in order.

The judgment of the Court of Appeals is vacated, and the case is remanded for further proceedings consistent with this opinion.

[SB]

Preview

This introduction, then, has presented important cultural, legal, and information science perspectives on intellectual property law in new media. In the chapters that follow, we will discuss these intellectual property topics in some detail. Each will begin with a legislative history: How did US law evolve to address questions of intellectual property? What changes in technology and society motivated lawmakers? Who were the stakeholders and how was the law drafted? The legislative history will be followed by an overview of key court cases and decisions, first from classic cases dealing with traditional/analog media and then moving to more recent cases dealing with digital materials. Each chapter will conclude with a brief discussion of the intellectual property issues raised as they relate to crucial questions in new media practices. [ELL]

Discussion Questions

1. To what extent do citizens, especially young adults, seem to want to "take it out on big business" by pirating media with a "steal from the rich and give to the poor" mentality? Does this mindset create an environment in which legitimate businesses develop a "bunker mentality" for self-preservation of their industries?
2. Intellectual property laws appear to be developed in favor of large

content holders. (a) Why is this generally the case? (b) What are the implications for common citizens? (c) What are the implications for artists and content producers?

3. What are the political motivations of elected officials regarding active legislation on intellectual property issues? Domestically? Internationally?

4. Assuming that the laws and the courts cannot, generally, keep up with developing technologies, what are alternatives for ordering the system and avoiding massive lawlessness?

5. A commonplace of the digital era is that "information wants to be free." What are the pros and cons of doing without a system of intellectual property protections?

CHAPTER ONE

Copyright

Let's consider three copyright conundrums before taking up a historical review of the legislation through which US copyright law has emerged.

First:

- The film *Titanic* is being shown on a broadcast television network; you receive it over your digital cable service Sunday night at 7. The film will be presented with limited amounts of advertising. You set your TiVo to record it so you can watch it later that evening. When you watch it, starting at 10 PM, you fast-forward through all the ads.

This is *probably legal*.

- You are working on a criticism project for a film appreciation class you are taking at the university. You go to Blockbuster to rent a copy of the film *Titanic*. However, your DVD player is on the fritz, so you borrow a video cassette copy to play in your VCR. Using your computer and a video deck, you "pull out" a short segment of the movie,

digitize it, and include it in the PowerPoint presentation you'll do when you present your project to the class.
This is *probably legal*.

- Later, your DVD player comes back from the shop. You go to Blockbuster and return the videotape and rent a DVD copy of the film *Titanic*. Returning to your computer and DVD deck, you use a piece of software you bought that "rips" DVDs, and you extract the short portion of the film to use on your iPod.
This is *probably not legal*.

Second:
- You were fortunate to receive a new Apple iPod for Christmas. You immediately use your computer to "visit" the iTunes Store where you download a skit from *Saturday Night Live*. Some skits are priced; others are free. You select a free skit. You then sync your iPod to your computer so that you can watch the episode while you are on the bus headed back to school for evening classes.
This is *probably legal*.

- You were fortunate to receive a new Apple iPod for Christmas. You use your computer to access the same skit from *Saturday Night Live* that you recorded on your TiVo. After moving the segment from the TiVo to your computer, you use a piece of software to compress the episode for transfer to your iPod. You sync your iPod to your computer so that you can watch the episode while you are on the bus headed back to school for evening classes.
This is *probably not legal*.

Third:
- In the process of completing a project for a class at school, you need some background music to enhance a presentation you are going to do. You digitize a copy of the latest single release by Coldplay from a CD you've purchased. The work is presented in class; you turn in a copy of the files to your teacher for grading. After grading, the teacher returns the work to you and you throw it away.
This is *probably legal*.

- In the process of completing a project for a class at school, you need some background music to enhance a presentation you are going to do. You digitize a copy of the latest single release by Coldplay from a CD you've purchased. The work is presented in class; you turn in a copy of the files to your teacher for grading. After grading, the teacher returns the work to you. You put a copy of the file on your Web site so that family, friends, and future employers can see your work.

This is *probably not* legal.

By way of example, then, the situations illustrate some of the complexities found in the paradoxical nature of copyright law. In the first instance, while it is legal to use a digital device to record and time-shift the television broadcast of a movie so that you may watch it whenever you want without commercial interruption, and it is legal to digitize segments of that film from a rented videotape copy to use in a fair-use-protected academic environment, it is probably not legal to copy segments (or the whole) of the DVD of that movie for convenient privateviewing on another device. The anti-copy protection circumvention clauses of the *DMCA* make the process of "ripping" a DVD illegal in most instances, although there are some exceptions for libraries, archives, and the like.

In the second instance, it is legal for you to use digital content across a number of players/viewers/platforms if and when the content provider supports that flexibility. Materials you obtain from, for example, the iTunes store, can be displayed on your computer, copied across a number of machines, played (shared) across multiple machines via "internal" networks, or downloaded to your iPod at your discretion; one is also able to burn a limited number of legal copies to CDs. It may not be legal, however, for you to convert the very same material for the purpose of cross-platform flexibility. In the case of Apple computer products, the digital rights management (DRM) technology "FairPlay" is used to control/limit the amount and type of copying and transfers that can take place within the bounds of Apple's use agreements with consumers. Court rulings against software firm 321 Studios combined with *DMCA* anti-circumvention aspects show that platform conversion in the face of digital rights management prohibitions is not legal.

The third instance further illustrates the changed nature of the fair-use environment in that activities that are protected offline are not encouraged online, though both sets of activities are similar and usual in the everyday lives of students. One can, then, freely borrow and use copyright-protected material in the context of academic work under the protection of fair use. The amount and type of material borrowed constrain the scope of the use, but, in general, as long as the work is turned in to the teacher and then thrown away after return to the student, fair use protects the learning enterprise. However, many of the activities of learning take place online today. The *Teach Act* specifies a number of provisions under which academic folks may array materials online. The open posting of copyright-protected materials, even if only a very small portion of either the protected work or a segment of the student work containing the protected work, is not allowed under, or protected by, the *Teach Act*, *DMCA*, or the *Copyright Act*.

Copyright law and its application develop along three tracks. The first can be thought of as normal technological development. The pace at which technology changes, historically speaking, varies wildly. One gets the sense that the end of the last century and the start of the new one were times of profound and rapid change. In such an environment, the pace of legislative and legal developments appears glacially slow as compared to the rate of technological advances. In short, the law just can't keep up with changes in an environment such as this.[1] The result of this track finds citizens empowered with technologies and uses for them prior to the requisite development of legal parameters that effectively and equitably control the uses of the technology.

The second track is played out in the courts via litigation (and pre-trial settlements). Even lay observers of the American justice system can't help but sense that the wheels of justice grind very slowly in the United States. Legal wrangling over ownership, infringement, and remuneration can take years, sometimes decades (i.e., Apple Computing and Apple Records argued over their intellectual property-related differences from 1978 to 2006).[2] Later in this chapter we will review some of the most important court cases in the development of US copyright law and will thereby illustrate the difficulties inherent in trying to settle intellectual property differences in court. The result of this track finds citizens faced with enormously complex legal circumstances such that applying the law to everyday needs in this area has become overly problematic, almost to the point of anarchy.[3]

The third track, the legislative process, provides the basis for litigation activities, so will be taken up first. Without oversimplifying the matter, the following two ideas will be exemplified through the historical review that follows. First, copyright law has developed as the handmaiden and tool of corporate interests. The laws were designed for corporate entities. These legislative activities paid little attention to the interests and/or needs of common citizens. Second, not only has copyright law been most appropriately used by corporate interests, it has also been largely authored via corporate influence such that the governmental representation afforded citizens through the political process has been negated. In effect, large, corporate IP content holders (variously labeled Big Entertainment/Big Media/Big Content) have made their own laws, and "we the people" have been relatively unrepresented in the process. The result of this track produces the largest challenge for intellectual property law today. Because technological progress has recently placed the means for production and distribution of content into the hands of common citizens, legislative controls must take citizen concerns into consideration and must be developed by those who represent them in the governmental process. And neither of these aspects is the case. The law doesn't work for common people, and legislative representatives don't get much involved; often, when they do, they advocate on behalf of large, corporate, IP content holders for more controls and stronger penalties rather than for citizens' rights and interests. When the law fails to keep pace with technological change and in the process fails to protect citizens' rights, the need to litigate burgeons, and the entire process grinds toward an unsatisfactory state.

Copyright infringement cases in the digital realm now often involve everyday citizens who lack both the resources and legal background to participate on equal footing with corporate interests. As discussed in the Introduction, the RIAA won its first case at trial in 2007; previous "victories" were from out-of-court settlements. Here we examine a landmark case in which a citizen fought back against industry legal tactics.

In "Mother Fights Record Companies' Lawsuit on Her Own," Kathy Mclaughlin of the Associated Press recounts a 2005 case in which a New York woman, Patricia Santangelo, was sued by the RIAA after insisting on a settlement of $7,500 for illegal downloading. Santangelo claimed that she had not downloaded any illegal music. Racking up large legal bills, Santangelo fought the RIAA, sometimes using lawyers and other times defending herself. She claimed that while her children might have used her computer to download music, she was not aware of it. After protracted arguments, the RIAA withdrew its suit against the mother; however, it later sued the children.

Legislative Development of US Copyright Law

Copyright Legislation: 1780–1910

Early English Influences

American copyright (and patent) law originated as an outgrowth of legal considerations inherited from the British. England's intellectual property history dates roughly from the period 1518–1542.[4] For a time after the introduction of the printing press in England in 1476, the primary issue with regard to the control of intellectual property was royal censorship of various books. With the rise of the Stationers' Company, a closely held, guild-based co-op started in 1403 but royally chartered in 1557, the Stationers' copyright became a controlling legal consideration. This principle was developed as a private consideration of the Company, but subsequent law failed to challenge the Stationers' rights for approximately 150 years. The copyright granted the stationer—as publisher of a work—the exclusive right to forbid any unauthorized printing of the same work. This right enabled the Stationers' Company to control the availability of most written works.

The English government controlled the second important aspect of intellectual property law in this period. The printing patent provided press owners with exclusive rights over the fruits of their labor in the printing of certain types of government-authorized works (e.g., bibles, reading primers, textbooks, and medical books). The government usually granted its printing patents to favored printers aligned with the Stationers' Company, giving that group even tighter control of information dissemination.

These two systems of protection, the copyright and the printing patent, intermingled with royal censorship decrees as the principles that controlled the distribution of books and other printed materials, and the resulting profits, through the early 1600s. During the mid-to-late seventeenth century, Parliament enacted a number of laws that manipulated the licensing results inherent in the situation; some of this legislation compromised the position of the Stationers' Company such that after its exclusive rights expired in 1694, it petitioned Parliament for relief. The resultant legislation was the *Statute of Anne*—a work that significantly changed the copyright situation in England (to the detriment of the interests of the Stationers' Company) and set the tone for later American laws.

The *Statute of Anne* was introduced just prior to 1709 in order to clarify the legal chaos that resulted from the revisions to the copyright laws in the late

1600s and to address the monopolies over publication and printing that were the result of the combination of the Stationers' copyright and the royal printing patents. The statute also aided a lessening of the negative effects of government censorship. It did, however, continue various practices that enabled the government to exert controls over the situation by enacting a large number of required registrations and procedures for those who sought to exercise their copyrights.

After the *Statute of Anne*, authors (rather than publishers or printers) were seen as the rightful owners of copyright. However, the British Parliament took almost sixty years to fully enact the various changes inherent in the statute. American copyright law is modeled after the *Statute of Anne*.

Early American Scene

The American colonies followed English law with regard to copyright. However, soon after the Revolution, the need for copyright laws became apparent as American trade in books and other printed materials flourished. The Continental Congress of 1783 mandated that the states should draft copyright legislation.[5] In response to economic/trade needs, early American colonial governments had adapted the *Statute of Anne* and other principles, but in a somewhat uneven fashion from state to state.

Early laws underscored a number of important principles: that copyright protects the rights of authors; that copyright should promote learning; that copyright helps bring order to the book trade; and that copyright helps prevent monopoly.[6] Of course the proper balance and emphasis of these features are at the very center of historic copyright arguments and legal developments and were reflected in the uneven application of the principles across various colonies' laws. Further, the Americans also adapted copyright principles drawn from continental influences other than the British. These approaches characterize the author's right of control over the fruits of his or her labor as a fundamental natural right (rather than one merely granted by the state through legal protocol).[7]

The importance of protecting creativity was further illustrated by the inclusion of America's guiding (national) copyright principle in Article 1, Section 8 of the *Constitution*: "To promote the Progress of Science and useful Arts, by securing for limited Times to Authors and Inventors the exclusive Right to their respective Writings and Discoveries."

This constitutional mandate has been interpreted in a variety of ways that fuel controversy over the proper implementation and application of the law.

The "protection" aspect specifies that the government will encourage (relative) monopolies (for a fixed time) in order to enable authors to reap benefits from their industry. This aspect is thought to encourage creativity via economic incentive. The "progress" aspect promotes the general welfare by promoting creativity (through the protection clause) and then mandating an end to that protection (by limiting its duration) such that the fruits of creativity come into the public domain for the mutual benefit and free use of others in their creative efforts.

Article 1, Section 8 created both national patent rights and copyrights. While many colonies had not passed significant patent legislation, all but one had enacted copyright laws. Later, this promoted controversy as the government and courts tried to balance pre-existent state statutes (a strong form of common law when cross-applied in national contexts) with the national mandate for Congress to make policy in the copyright domain.

In response to the constitutional initiative, the Congress, in its first session in 1790, passed "an act for the encouragement of learning, by securing the copies of maps, charts, and books, to the authors and proprietors of such copies, during the times therein mentioned."[8] The rights were granted for fourteen years (with a fourteen-year renewal possible) and, essentially, provided a mechanism for US citizens to protect their maps, charts, and books from piracy. The statute established the author's rights, encouraged the promotion of learning, established the governmental power to grant the rights, and promoted monopoly on the part of creative forces. However, section 5 of the *Copyright Act of 1790* permitted the pirating of foreign works.

Generally, the *Copyright Act of 1790* shifted the emphasis away from the thrust of a number of state statutes that leaned toward the general form of the *Statute of Anne*. The *Act* vested the right primarily through the regulatory procedures rather than, for example, in the natural rights of the author.

Having established the principles underlying American copyright law,[9] the *Copyright Act of 1790* stood for more than one hundred years (with revisions). Jessica Litman describes the processes through which these revisions were enacted:

> The legislative process accompanying copyright enactments differed little from the process yielding most statutes: interested parties sent petitions to Congress.
> The majority of bills were drafted by representatives of affected interests, who then requested members of Congress to introduce the bills, wrote petitions to Congress in their support, and testified in their favor during Patent Committee hearings. ("Copyright Legislation" 282–83)

Unfortunately, the revisions, noted below, left the body of copyright law with numerous and confusing amendments that conflated copyright, patent, and trademark law and that were met with the inability of the Patents Committee to amend the difficulties. By 1900, the leadership of the governmental administrative offices called for Congress to revise copyright laws. Major amendments to the *Act* during the 1800s included revisions in 1802, 1831, 1834, 1846, 1856, 1870, 1891, and 1897.

In 1802, the statutes were revised to include prints and to require the inclusion (at the start of each printed work) of the copyright notice designed by the government. In 1831, the revision extended the statutes to musical compositions as well as mandating provisions enabling widows and children of deceased copyright holders to apply for continued protection (for twenty-eight years, renewable for fourteen). The 1831 revisions also made it illegal to falsely claim a copyright when none had been registered. The 1834 revision provided for the assignment of rights to others, while the changes in 1846 clarified the "deposit" requirements (specifying a copy for both the Library of Congress and the Smithsonian Institution). Revisions in 1856 added the right of public performance for dramatic works to the list of protected activities. In 1870, categories and provisions were added for fine arts, translations, and dramatizations, and the registration requirement was moved from the Federal District Courts to the Library of Congress.[10]

Crucial events occurred in 1886 as nations worldwide joined the agreements made in the *Berne Convention*, provisions that moved toward standardization of copyrights across international boundaries. The United States did not participate in drafting the agreement and refused to sign the treaty for a variety of reasons. Tenets of the *Berne Convention* would have overturned US copyright law in ways that were unacceptable to the United States at the time. The philosophy underlying the *Berne Convention* tended more in the direction of natural rights than the US outlook assumed. For example, the *Berne Convention* did away with most of the administrative procedures of registration by assigning copyrights to authors at the point of authorship. US procedures did not fully drop registration requirements until 1988. Another philosophical issue that delayed America's agreement to *Berne* reflected the in-place administrative prejudice against "foreign" works, since at the time of *Berne*, the *Copyright Act of 1790* still protected works by US citizens but specifically did not protect foreign works. Adoption of *Berne* would have overturned that preference, and American legislators/negotiators were not yet ready for that change. Five years later, in 1891, the United States adopted the *International Copyright Act* and extended copyright protection to foreign works, but did so without assenting to the full range of policies specified by *Berne*.

The year 1897 brought passage of revisions that recognized the right of public exercise of musical performances. By this time, however, a number of factors indicated both the general breakdown of the effectiveness of the in-place system and the need for a thorough revision of the *Copyright Act of 1790*. First, the law itself had been sufficiently vague (with regard to important issues such as the nature of publication, etc.) that one hundred years of court interpretations still left the boundaries of the bill in some question. Second, technological advances challenged the intent and application of the procedures. Third, the numerous revisions forced patchwork accommodations on the *Act* when, perhaps, a thoroughgoing revision would have produced a more uniform approach.

The first major rewrite of the *Copyright Act of 1790* was passed in 1909 after roughly eight years of negotiations. After the Register of Copyrights and the Librarian of Congress repeatedly asked Congress in 1901 to appoint a special commission to revise the law, the Senate Patent Committee first declined, then suggested that the Librarian of Congress should call an unauthorized conference on his own.[11] And so begins the history of the ill-fated process that corrupts and hinders copyright legislation by making it the handmaiden of professional industries, drafted behind the backs of elected officials.

The resultant conference (in 1906) included representatives of authors, dramatists, painters, sculptors, architects, and composers; photographers, publishers, libraries, and printers' unions (representatives of old/existing media); but it did not include representatives from new media that had not previously been granted legal status. The fledgling motion picture, piano roll, and phonograph ("talking machine") industries were absent, as were elected representatives of "we the people."

After two years of meetings, the resultant bill would have revoked extant case law that held the piano roll did not infringe (by giving all rights to make or sell mechanical devices for reproducing sounds to copyright owners). The bill would also have made unlicensed phonograph records illegal. After another year of discussion, representatives of songwriters sat down with those of the piano roll and phonograph companies and produced an acceptable compromise bill, establishing a compulsory license for mechanical reproduction of music and exempting the performance of music on coin-operated devices. The bill contained some additional "side agreements" made by other parties (for example, between authors and typographers' unions concerning printing books in foreign languages). The resultant bill was enacted in 1909. Note carefully that the bill that was passed into law as the new US copyright law was drafted, negotiated, revised, and presented via discussions among representatives of professional trade organizations, not elected officials. Congress approved the bill without substantial on-the-record discussion once the presentations to Congress indicated that the "warring" parties were satisfied with the compromises that led to the final draft of the bill. The fact that this process required almost ten years to draft a workable document should have given elected officials and the public pause for thought. Within two years, events showed the folly of having followed these procedures.

In 1911, the Supreme Court found that showing motion pictures (*Ben Hur*) specifically infringed the copyright of the novel (*Kalem Co. v. Harper Brothers*). The crux of the difficulties in the new procedures used for drafting copyright law quickly became apparent. A new media technology, moving pictures, was not represented in the previous set of professionalized talks through which law was written. Without adequate representation, the interests of new media were ignored or—even worse—specifically (and somewhat underhandedly) legislated against. Representatives of in-place industries (old media) used the law-drafting conferences as a venue for solidifying their position against future encroachment, effectively using the law to slow the course of technological development. The rights of citizens to utilize the newest and best technologies, unrepresented in the so-called legislative process, were infringed by the very laws that were supposed to promote science and the arts among "the people."

The solution to the issue for the motion picture industry completes this preview of the process and subsequent difficulties. Frustrated with the complaints of representatives on all sides, members of Congress called on industry representatives to sit down among themselves and work out a compromise they could live with. By 1912, the movie people joined with the others, and a bill was brought forward and approved by Congress. Technological and sociological changes would soon again challenge the process: radio, talking pictures, the exportation of media abroad, the rise of the music authors' and publishers' unions, and licensing cooperatives (ASCAP). These and other advances would call for yet more side deals, inter-industry negotiations, and revisions to the law that were accomplished without the careful consideration and involvement of elected officials. In short, by the very early 1900s, the process of legislating copyright law had been turned over by Congress to large, corporate, IP content holders, and the results were neither good for our representative form of government nor for emergent new media industries.

Twentieth-Century US Copyright Legislation: 1913–1950

The fractured process through which the initial major revisions of copyright law took place did not provide an adequate platform for orderly change in the first half of the twentieth century. Time after time, new media, or calls for modified practices within the old, came forward with challenges to the *Copyright Act of 1909* (and its revision in 1912), only to suffer the same fate. In some cases initial proposals for change came from elected legislators, in others from new industries. Numerous committees and negotiation teams were called, charged, and dismissed. National trade organizations and public interest groups alike joined congressional efforts, all in vain. The next major revision of copyright law would not take place until 1976.

After noting that the talks previous to the *Act of 1909* left out the piano roll and talking machine interests and that the motion picture industry did not attend sessions that led to the *Act*, Litman further writes:

> The 1912 negotiations between motion picture and theatre industries to frame the Townsend Amendment [extending copyright to movies] yielded a compromise that handicapped authors and publishers of nondramatic works, who did not participate. The conferences in the 1920s that led to the Dallinger bill [seeking to address the authors' issues] included no representatives of the [new and burgeoning] broadcasting industry; the Dallinger bill [which never passed] gave publishers and composers rights at the broadcasters' expense. The broadcasters walked out of the conferences that produced the Vestal bill [which tried to mediate disagreements among trade groups]; the Vestal bill addressed none of the broadcasters' concerns [and was not passed]. ("Copyright Legislation" 299)

Additional unsuccessful revision efforts, variously sponsored by Congress, trade groups, and private interests, were made through the end of World War II.

Twentieth-Century US Copyright Legislation: 1950–1976

Copyright law drafted in the early part of the twentieth century faced enormous challenges in the latter half. Since numerous revision efforts had failed, by the mid-to-late 1950s the law contained no provisions specific to radio, jukeboxes, sound motion pictures, Muzak®, or television (among other media). The businesses controlled by copyright law had to try to accommodate changing needs through industry practices, collective bargaining agreements, and a host of "practical contortions" (Litman, "Copyright Legislation" 305). Since the law did not specify arrangements for media industries developed after 1909, it had to be applied "by analogy." This worked in some cases but not in others. For example, "motion pictures and television programs recorded on film could be copyrighted as unpublished motion picture photoplays. . . . [but] Live or taped television programs, radio programs, and phonograph records were deemed uncopyrightable" (Litman, "Copyright Legislation" 307). Further, the *Act of 1909* specified only one right under copyright law: mass media always implicate multiple rights (authorship, performance, derivative works, etc.). Questions concerning these and similar issues were worked out, often with great rancor and long court battles, by the professional parties. By 1956, complaints about the situation encouraged Congress to appropriate funds targeted toward a revision of copyright law.

The revision process began with a panel of copyright lawyers invited by the Copyright Office to work toward recommendations. This effort might have negated somewhat the problems with the processes used earlier. However, leadership change in the Copyright Office soon led to resumption of the industry-based conference process. The resultant *Copyright Act of 1976* took nearly fifteen years to produce and almost totally ignored private use (the ways that common citizens would use intellectual property) and was negotiated by industry operatives as opposed to legislated by elected representatives (Litman, "Copyright Legislation" 313–15). As had been the case in negotiations at the start of the century, soon-to-emerge new media (or any other group marginal to large, corporate, IP content holders) were not represented. Among others left out were painters, sculptors, choreographers, and theatrical directors. Further, a wide range of interests that would develop in the years following passage of the act were unrepresented because they did not yet fully exist as a factor in the marketplace. Computer programmers, video cassette manufacturers, cable and direct satellite broadcasters, digital audio technicians, motion picture colorizers, and online database distributors, just to name a few, were not of issue in the years leading up to 1976 but would soon present enormous challenges to the efficacy of the law.

The *Copyright Act of 1976* did establish a number of very important legal changes. The law expanded the scope of protection to all written works once they were put into tangible form, even if they were unpublished. This loosened the requirements for formal notice and registration. The *Act* extended the copyright term to the life of the author plus fifty years (seventy-five for corporate authors). The *Act* explicitly preempted most state and common law practices in the copyright area, and it established for the first time in the law the concept of "fair use" (the idea that otherwise protected materials might be put to non-infringing uses). The *Act* codified treatments that had developed both informally (via inter-industry agreements) and formally (via the courts) as to the bundle of rights inherent within the copyright (copying, distribution, performance, derivative works).[12] In short, the *Copyright Act of 1976* provides the basic configuration for modern US copyright law.

In addition to encouraging revisions of the general copyright law, digital media challenged the status quo by presenting an entirely new type of intellectual property for the law to consider. The law did not speak to the status of software or its underlying code structures. As we'll see later, some aspects of software eventually came to fall under the rubric of patents. However, initial protection efforts focused on implications for copyright.

In 1974, in response to the challenges, Congress empowered the National Commission on New Technological Uses of Copyrighted Works (CONTU) to make recommendations concerning which aspect of intellectual property protection best suited software. After four years of deliberation, CONTU recommended that software be extended copyright protection, and—with amendments to the law enacted beginning in 1980—Congress adopted most of CONTU's recommendations. This protection presents a conundrum: the underlying processes implemented by software are seen as non-protectable via copyright; however, their expression via computer programs apparently can be protected. This dichotomy produces a fine line that comes to stand at the heart of much copyright litigation dealing with software.

Twentieth-Century US Copyright Legislation: 1976–1998

The major copyright revision of 1976 faced almost immediate challenges requiring negotiation and revision. In fact, initial challenges came to the fore during the writing of the *Copyright Act of 1976*. Since the procedures used to develop the law followed the usual pattern of excluding new technologies, it became evident as early as 1974 that the *Act* might not adequately account for new media (as we conceive them in the contemporary digital age). The CONTU recommendations concerned the interests and needs brought about by a variety of new or emerging technologies, particularly computers, software, databases, and photocopying. Some of the early recommendations of the committee were considered and became part of the 1976 *Act*; other aspects would wait until 1980 for implementation. Not everything recommended by the committee became law.

Between 1976 and 1988, then, there were three revisions that had major implications for new (digital) media. First, the majority of the CONTU-influenced refinements of copyright law went into the 1980 *Computer Software Copyright Act*, which mandated for the first time that software could be legally copyright-protected. This modification adjusted the treatment of software, computers, and databases. Note that the industry-specific nature of this modification continued trends established through the first part of the century, as adjustments accommodated technologies that were not included in earlier negotiations and rule making. In this fashion, the law evolves and improves but also becomes more complex and more in need of thorough revision. The year 1984 brought the *Record Rental Amendment of 1984*, a revision that was motivated by the development of technological means to copy recorded material. The revision stands as the first major abridgment of the "first-sale doctrine," the principle that purchasers of intellectual property (say, an audio record or tape) have the right to resell, rent, or otherwise use the material as they see fit. The *Record Rental Amendment (RRA)* made it illegal to rent audio recordings as an industry protection against piracy-based copying. The revision does not comport easily with the legal bifurcation that developed after the "*Sony/Betamax*" case (to be discussed in the case section below) that allows users to videotape television signals and that (in essence) also permits Blockbuster-style videotape rentals while the *RRA* outlaws the same services in audio recordings. The *RRA* later became the model for treatment of software in the *Computer Software Rental Agreement (CSRA) of 1990*, discussed below.[13]

Another revision with implications for new media occurred in 1988 through the *Satellite Home Viewer Act (SHVA)*. The cable television industry had been able to operate under the terms of the 1976 act by using the limited statutory license to pay royalties into a fund to compensate copyright holders. However, the language that enabled and allowed this was too narrow to apply to satellite carriers, who demanded a license of their own.[14] The *SHVA* granted satellite carriers a new and more restrictive license. The arrangement allowed them to transmit television signals to home dishes for private viewing but only in cases in which viewers could not otherwise receive those signals. Many homeowners are now aware of the implications that this arrangement had for everyday citizens. While the side deal negotiated between cable companies, satellite operators, and broadcasting firms worked for the industries, the result often puts consumers in difficult straits. In television markets receiving free local stations' over-the-air broadcasts, consumers who want to receive satellite programming and local programming have to pay extra to add the local service to the feeds going to televisions connected to satellites, as satellite providers are not allowed to offer the local material at no cost.

Perhaps the most significant adjustment to the *Copyright Act of 1976* during the 1980s took effect in 1988 when the United States finally signed on to the (by then over-one-hundred-year-old) *Berne Convention*. Through this action, the United States agreed to bring some of its procedures in line with international standards. For example, all remaining protocols for registration, notice, and renewal were dropped from the basic coverage afforded authors at the point of fixed authorship. Signing on to the *Berne Convention* was an interesting example of give and take in political wrangling. On the one hand, the United States was required to recognize and cooperate with a wide range of international law that it had previously treated with modest disrespect. It was also required to make small modifications to US law and practices. In return, the United States gained leverage in its ability to require that other countries conform to, and to some degree adopt, US-style intellectual property laws. Negotiations over ratification of the *Berne Convention* were carried out in cooperation with international trade negotiations at the World Trade Organization. In the current global economy, intellectual property arrangements have international implications. Further attention will be paid to international IP law in Chapter 7.[15]

In 1990, the older *Copyright Act* was revised to protect fine artists in cases in which their work has been modified and they wish to remove themselves from association with the work. The *Visual Artists Rights Act* (*VARA*) *of 1990* allows artists to remove their names from modifications of their work and sets forth provisions for agreements between building owners and artists when architectural changes involve modifications of the works of art built into the architecture.

Again in 1990, the *Copyright Act of 1976* was further revised, this time to accommodate digital audio recorders. Digital audio technologies (referred to variously as DAT—digital audio tape—and DCC—digital cassette tape) had been available, especially through imports from Japan, for nearly a decade prior to the revision. However, US recorded music IP holders had negotiated with Congress various trade constraints out of fear that the recorders would damage the US music industry. By the early 1990s, however, US media corporations (beginning with Phillips) wanted both to import and to manufacture such units and sought legislation that would control the technology while advancing its market. The *Audio Home Recording Act* (*AHRA*) permitted home digital audio recordings and devices but added royalty fees (maximum $8 for a single unit; $12 if the unit has multiple digital recorders) to the production costs of the unit as a way to contribute to funds for composers and artists. The *AHRA* also prohibits manufacturers from adding copyright information to the resultant copies and forbids serial copying by requiring all units to include a Serial Copy Management System.

Between 1994 and 1997, spurred by invitations from various Clinton Administration officials, a number of working groups of copyright stakeholders met to discuss issues in copyright law of particular importance to libraries, archives, and distance education. Recommendations of the *Conference on Fair Use* (CONFU) did not lead directly to specific legislation; however, the information they generated helped inform the process that led to the eventual passage of the *Teach Act* (below). Additional conferences on matters of particular interest to libraries and archives were taken up from 2005 through 2008 under the auspices of the Library of Congress.[16]

Twentieth-Century US Copyright Legislation: 1998

1998 saw the passage of two extremely important pieces of legislation: the [*Sonny Bono*] *Copyright Term Extension Act* (*CTEA*), became law in January 1998; and the *Digital Millennium Copyright Act* (*DMCA*), became law in December of that year. Each had a significant impact on the US copyright landscape.

In some respects, *CTEA* was unremarkable in that Congress had extended the term for copyright protection a number of times since the passage of the original *Copyright Act*. The 1998 extension, however, featured distinctive elements. Although a small number of the oldest products of modern mass media had, by the 1990s, begun to enter the public domain, the principal works of modern mass media were set to lose copyright protection in the early 1990s. Powerful copyright holders sought to protect their economic interests by keeping their work out of the public domain longer. As an example, protections afforded the Disney Company for their image of Mickey Mouse were set to expire in 1993. Disney was not the only company with mass media content at risk, but its particular history provides a fortuitous example of many of the issues.

Much of Disney's success can be attributed to its appropriation and repurposing of material taken from the public domain. From *Snow White and the Seven Dwarfs* to *Pinocchio*, *The Little Mermaid*, *Beauty and the Beast*, and so on, Disney took material out of the public domain and transformed it into widely successful, economically enriching content. However, when pieces of its creativity were supposed to begin entering the public domain such that others in the public could take those images and repurpose them for advancement and profit, Disney was no longer interested in the riches of the public domain (at least not in adding further value to it). Instead, it moved strongly, with expensive and powerful lobbying, to block the material from the public domain, seeking an extension of copyright protection.

On the one hand, it seems almost natural that Disney would want to protect its interest in the image of "the mouse" (as well as other properties). After all, Disney created both the images and their cultural legacy. But the constitutional framers specified that the protection of such content would be for a limited period (a time frame already legislatively extended many times over), and they specified the other side of the equation: that intellectual property must eventually enter the public domain for the furtherance of creativity among the citizenry.

Former rock-and-roll star (and movie/television personality) Sonny Bono was, at the time, serving in the US Congress as Representative from California (Palm Springs district) and was more than willing to sponsor the extension for his colleagues in the entertainment industry. The legislation passed with very little discussion. Its influence, however, was far-ranging. Not only did *CETA* protect the content representing the works of the entertainment and mass media industries, it also kept all other content (whose protections were due to expire) from coming into the public domain for an additional twenty years. This included an overwhelming amount of content that held little if any interest to big entertainment, including printed literature and the like. Currently complicating the situation even further are new media/Internet-related efforts to make content available to wider populations through networked technologies.

The implications of the extension were exemplified in the subsequent court cases involving Eric Eldred. In his efforts to digitize and Web-post literature collections, Eldred had eagerly anticipated the flow of new material that would enter the public domain in the 1990s—the first decade in which the Internet fully empowered the possibility of global library collections. *CTEA*, essentially, put that collection work on hold for twenty years. Eldred sued, questioning the legality of the extension (generally on the grounds that Congress did not have the authority to limit free speech in this way) and lost both at trial and on appeal. However, due to the questions raised by the action, the Supreme Court took up the case. In ruling against Eldred, the Court upheld *CTEA* and re-iterated the Congressional right to extend copyright. An important implication of this decision is this: Not only does the public domain remain closed for an additional twenty years, but there is a worry that Congress will continue to extend the copyright term (which is already the rough equivalent of two human lifetimes), thereby effectively closing the public domain forever. It's hard to believe that, for example, Disney will be any more willing to give up the protection of its content—and thereby allow the public to make use of, and profit from, images of Mickey, Donald, and the like—in twenty years than they were in 1987. Analysis of *Eldred v. Ashcroft* will appear in the section on cases later in this chapter.

The other legislation that took effect in 1998 may well stand as one of the most important and far-reaching revisions of US copyright law in history. The *DMCA*, though somewhat limited in terms of size and scope (that is, it was not a complete re-write of the law), made fundamental changes that threaten both the public domain and the first-sale doctrines, two of the most important legal principles at the heart of copyright law.

Following the 1993 deployment of Mosaic, the first widely used Web browser, and spurred by rapid growth of the World Wide Web/Internet, content owners began articulating concerns that an unregulated Internet could lead to either the loss of US intellectual property via piracy from abroad or the lack of US-generated content on the Web due to owners' fears about piracy. Vice President Al Gore and others in the first Clinton Administration "re-visioned" the "information superhighway" as the "National Information Infrastructure" and appointed a task force, led by Patent Commissioner Bruce Lehman (an official with ties to the content industries prior to his government appointment) to examine the effects of digital communication media on copyright law.[17]

After holding a public meeting and deliberations, the Lehman Working Group issued its initial report, sometimes referred to as the *Green Paper*. This report generally reflected the concerns of leaders in the content industries as it proposed numerous protectionist measures, many of which, had they been accepted, might have derailed the very technological innovations they were intended to protect. The *Green Paper* threatened to define every copy made by a computer system as a protected copy, such that all computing would be subject to systems of permissions and/or royalties (due to RAM/cache copies). The group also proposed principles that conflated transmission of data with performances (following the copyright protection of performance) by suggesting that data transmissions should *not* be afforded the general protection of the first-sale doctrine. Hence users who shipped files of copyright-protected material around the Internet without the explicit permission of the rights holder could be said to be in violation. In general, the group called for stringent new levels of copyright protection. In its earliest form, most of the report virtually ignored the Internet and its implications. A working draft of the *Green Paper* was released in September 1995.

The *Green Paper* set off an enormous amount of discussion and negative feedback from a wide range of user groups. Representatives of libraries, universities, Internet service providers, and many others raised numerous concerns about the breadth and potential harm that could ensue if the approaches taken by the *Green Paper* were enacted. The Lehman group continued its work in an effort to reshape the *Green Paper* into a form that would continue to protect media industries but that would meet the approval of at least some of the user groups/critics.

Further work on the issues produced the *White Paper*, which proposed that in-place copyright law was adequate for dealing with digital materials *if* the law were properly iterated. This move was meant to mollify opponents by making the changes seem as though they were less thorough than they appeared in the *Green Paper*. The report then went on to propose a number of refinements for how the copyright law should be applied in the digital arena. The *White Paper* maintained the "RAM copy" position such that using computers would require a license/royalty each time one viewed online material. The paper proposed that both individuals and ISPs/providers would be held liable for copyright violations taking place in networks, and the group added the soon-to-become standard and crucial (in the *DMCA)* anti-circumvention language that makes it illegal to circumvent an anti-circumvention scheme on a digital product. The *White Paper* urged harsh criminal penalties for copyright infringement, a major change in the way that copyright infringement was handled. The report also sought to undermine the principle of fair use, claiming that fair use would no longer be necessary, because licensing would be so easy and cheap that consumers would be willing to "pay per view." The report also undermined the first-sale doctrine, noting that what "was then first sale . . . is now copying and distributing" [read: piracy].

Two bills that would have enacted the *White Paper* proposals, H.R. 2441 and S. 1284, were appended to the report. These legislative proposals died in committee in 1996 as numerous interested parties responded strongly and neg-atively to the changes proposed in the report. For example, the Digital Future Coalition (DFC) consisted largely of law professors and librarians who op-posed most of the proposals. The Home Recording Rights Coalition (HRRC) carried forward arguments that had been made since the *Sony/Betamax* case concerning citizens' rights to record and the first-sale doctrine.

Various telephone companies, ISPs, libraries, and schools wanted "safe ha-ven" from responsibility for illegal use of their network facilities, and they were not offered protection under the terms of the *White Paper*. Though defeated in the short term, the *White Paper* laid the groundwork for action that would, in time, become the framework for the *DMCA*.

In absence of enactment of the recommended statutes, forces who wanted tight copyright controls were given another venue for action by the December 1996 World Intellectual Property Organization (WIPO) Conference. At WIPO, US representatives introduced into international trade negotiations a number of the new copyright principles that had been proposed by the *White Paper*. When the WIPO conference passed a watered-down version, the US Congress was virtually mandated to re-open the copyright revision process and direct it along the lines of the *White Paper* as the US delegation had proposed, advocated, and then signed on to the principles as part of international treaty negotiations.

As a result of the pressure exerted by the WIPO agreement, both the House and Senate produced multiple versions of copyright revision legislation. The final version of the *DMCA* retained many of the principles articulated in the *White Paper* (though others were modified). The *DMCA* was signed into law on October 28, 1998. It enacted neither the "RAM/cache" copying principle nor the idea that ISPs are responsible or liable for the content that travels their networks.

The *DMCA* prohibits the manufacture, sale, and distribution of circumvention technology. Technologies must neither be primarily designed to circumvent nor have few uses other than circumvention. This principle, for example, was the issue on which the *Grokster* case (to be discussed later) turned when the Supreme Court upheld an earlier ruling that the peer-to-peer technology was primarily for the purpose of illegal file sharing (though there are conceivably some uses that are not illegal). The *DMCA* enumerates two sets of control mechanisms: access control mechanisms, through which anti-circumvention controls manage users' abilities to open and operate software and devices, and copy control mechanisms, through which content owners fight against piracy/illegal copying.

The *DMCA* added impetus to content industry plans to develop and implement code and machine-level copyright management information systems (to be addressed more fully in Chapter 8, "Digital Rights Management"). The *DMCA* makes it illegal to remove any copyright identification information in files and systems and also makes it illegal to falsify copyright management information with the intent to induce, enable, facilitate, or conceal infringement. The *Act* followed the recommendations of both the *Green* and *White Papers* by introducing new criminal penalties of up to five years in prison for first offense and up to ten years in prison for the second.

The *DMCA* did vary from the form of the *Green* and *White Papers* with regard to holding networking institutions/utilities liable for infringement/violations. The *DMCA* offers ISP protections, sometimes referred to as "safe harbor," that limit the liability of service providers to injunctive, rather than monetary, relief. The statute also sets forth circumstances that must apply in order for the service provider to be exempt from liability, including that ISPs must register with the US Copyright Office and that they have particular behavioral responsibilities when they are notified of potential violations running through their systems (through a variety of notice and takedown rules).

The *DMCA* also took into account some special circumstances in which copying is necessary and should be protected (even if—from a strict constructionist viewpoint—it is illegal). For example, in the area of digital performances of sound recordings, the *DMCA* permits the making of temporary copies for transmission purposes. The law further details some notable but limited exceptions, including those allowing some library purchases to be "cracked" so that libraries can determine their materials and software purchase plans, as well as a number of small exceptions that protect personal privacy and enable encryption research. The *DMCA* also put periodic rulemaking by the Library of Congress into the fabric of the law.

Implications of the *DMCA* have already been discussed often in this book; suffice it to say that the *DMCA* changed the very nature of copyright law for the digital age. In particular, the law destabilized the positions of fair use and first sale, since in both instances activities that are protected (as a citizen right) by copyright law are trumped by the *DMCA* such that many acts that appear to be legal under the *Copyright Act of 1976* are illegal under the *DMCA*. For example, under the *Copyright Act of 1976* one can make a legal copy of a movie purchased on videotape. One cannot make a similar copy from a DVD, as doing so requires circumvention of anti-circumvention technology and is thus a *DMCA* violation. Under protections afforded by the first-sale doctrine, the *Copyright Act of 1976* would allow someone who has purchased a DVD to watch the movie on any computer (anywhere in the world). However, region-specific controls on DVDs set the region of the world where the film can be watched to match the region in which it was purchased (as an anti-piracy measure) such that use by the original purchaser across machines (if they are region-coded in different regions) is generally not possible. Other activities illustrate both fair-use and first-sale doctrine implications of the *DMCA*. For example, at the time of this writing, there is debate over the now relatively common practice of moving music from legally purchased CD-ROMs to mobile music players (like the iPod) via computers. Most users would probably maintain that practice to be fully legal, as they paid for the music and are just varying the players and locations for playing it. Recording industry executives take a different view and would prefer that consumers purchase each format separately. Such arguments label shifting files across platforms as piracy and a violation of the *DMCA*.[18]

Twentieth-Century US Copyright Legislation: 1999–2005

There have been a number of additional revisions to the *Copyright Act of 1976* in recent years, and there are continuing legislative discussions toward further action. The *Digital Theft Deterrence and Copyright Damages Improvement Act of 1999* increased the statutory damages for various types of piracy.

The *Teach Act*, enacted in 2002, mandates procedures for the use of digital media in distance education. The *Teach Act* specifies (among other things) that accredited, nonprofit, educational institutions or governmental bodies can make fair use of small amounts of otherwise copyright-protected digital materials if the institution is in compliance with a number of aspects of the *Act*. For example, the *Act* mandates that the institution must educate its population about copyright law (and how to follow it) and must have institutional policies and practices that limit piracy; must control the exposure of the material to students enrolled in particular courses; and must seek (in most cases and whenever possible) permissions rather than falling back on fair use as an easier alternative. Procedures for management of the digital materials are specified, including constraints on amount (small), numbers of copies (few), and archival issues (most materials must be destroyed after use). In general, the *Teach Act* has allowed, for example, institutions of higher education to maintain the use of digital materials in distance education programs. However, it does so at the cost of engaging the school as a full-fledged member of the "copyright police," essentially giving the school the right to use materials in exchange for re-energized participation in a copyright control regime.

The 2004 *Family Entertainment and Copyright Act* clarified and strengthened criminal penalties for copyright infringement, especially for in-theater piracy and for piracy of media works in progress (doubling the previous sentencing guidelines). This revision also allows a "family friendly" circumvention so that consumers who have paid for copies of motion pictures can produce edited copies that exclude certain portions of the program. For example, a parent could engage a digital technician to re-record a popular film for family viewing after removing violence and sex from the work.

The *Copyright Royalty and Distribution Reform Act* of 2004 replaced copyright arbitration panels with copyright royalty judges. It empowered a panel of judges to determine and adjust terms and rates of royalty payments under

statutory licenses, to adjust royalty rates for secondary transmissions, to authorize and make determinations on royalty fees collected, and to accept or reject
royalty claims based on timeliness or failure to establish a foundation for the
claim.

The *Intellectual Property Protection and Courts Amendments Act of 2004* seeks
to prevent and punish trafficking in counterfeit copyright-protected material.
The act significantly raises the levels of penalties and damages accrued from
convictions of those found to be trafficking in counterfeit copies. [ELL]

Compulsory Licensing

As we have seen thus far, a copyright holder possesses exclusive rights to maintain control over the work that is the subject of copyright protection. Those
rights include the right to reproduce, prepare derivative works, distribute copies, perform, and display the work.[19] Under current law in the United States,
however, there are circumstances under which, by law, a copyright holder must
cede some control to others. One such example is the compulsory license.

In the most basic sense, a compulsory license requires (i.e., "compels") a
copyright holder to share with others certain limited rights in the copyrighted
work, provided the others pay a set fee. It is the government's way of balancing
private intellectual property rights against a public right of access. In theory, if
there were not a mechanism in place to force copyright holders to offer up certain types of works for use by others, creative development would be stifled.

Congress initially enacted a form of compulsory license in the *1909 Copyright Act* when there was concern about the potential for music publishing
companies to form "a great music monopoly."[20] The 1909 provisions of the
Copyright Act provided the first compulsory license for the act of mechanically
recording music on phonographs or piano rolls. To this day, a compulsory license is still sometimes referred to as a "mechanical" license.[21]

With the advent of new technologies, Congress has revisited the compulsory license from time to time. Most recently, Congress passed the *Digital
Performance Right in Sound Recording Act of 1995* to contemplate "digital phonorecord delivery" or the delivery of a phonorecord by digital transmission.[22]
In other words, where the original compulsory license covered the "mechanical" reproduction of previously published composition, the law has not had
to contemplate that music is delivered through digital transmission where no
tangible object is created.[23]

US copyright law provides compulsory licenses for non-dramatic musical
compositions, public broadcasting, re-transmission by cable systems, subscrip-

tion digital audio transmission, and non-subscription digital audio transmission such as Internet radio.[24]

Let us illustrate how the system works for musical compositions. Under current copyright law, once a composer authorizes a recording of his song, others are free to record the same song, as long as they pay the original composer a fee set by law.[25] In other words, provided that a requesting party meets all of the statutory requirements, a copyright holder may be compelled to grant permission to allow others to record the song. By way of example, if Bob Dylan writes a song called "Mr. Tambourine Man," he can sell the song to the highest-paying recording artist, say, The Byrds. Once The Byrds distribute their recording of the song to the public, however, the compulsory license is activated. Any other performers who wish to sing the song can now also record it, if they pay the compulsory license, which, by law, is approximately one half of one cent per minute, per record distributed. In other words, the compulsory license compels the composer to allow additional users to record his song at the regulated price. In this example, the performer is free to negotiate directly with Bob Dylan; however, if Mr. Dylan cannot be located or otherwise refuses to deal, the performer can invoke the compulsory license provisions of US law.

The compulsory license only covers "nondramatic musical works."[26] Thus, it does not apply to literary or dramatic works and does not allow for reproduction of the soundtrack of a motion picture, which is considered an audiovisual work, not a nondramatic musical work.[27] It also does not cover the sound recording.[28]

With a major paradigm shift in the traditional music industry underway, there have been thoughtful calls for an expansion of compulsory licensing to the world of peer-to-peer file-sharing. In a white paper published by the Electronic Frontier Foundation (EFF), a proposal has been set forth to collect a monthly fee (approximately $5–$10) from end-users.[29] According to the EFF, in the United States alone, if sixty million file-sharing computer users paid such a fee, the record industry could collect $3 billion in net profit, the recording artist could be fairly compensated, and the end-users could continue to enjoy an exhaustive catalogue of music for a reasonable price without excessive government intervention.[30] [SB]

Pending Legislative Action

As part of the *DMCA* mandate for continued study, the Copyright Office in 2005 completed the first round of comments about the operation of the *DMCA*, began the second round, set in motion discussions about library/

archive-related amendments, and solicited comments about orphaned works. The orphaned works issue gave rise to a proposal (H.R. 24) referred to as *PRO-USE* (*Preservation and Restoration of Orphan Works for Use in Scholarship and Education Act*).[31] The *PRO-USE* act contains provisions that would exclude authorized federal entities from copyright limitations so that films, television, and other electronic media could be copied and preserved, especially in cases in which all of the rights holders cannot be located (so rightful permissions cannot be garnered). H.R. 1201, *Digital Media Consumers' Rights Act of 2005*, would amend the *Federal Trade Commission Act* to provide that the advertising or sale of a mislabeled copy-protected music disc is an unfair method of competition and an unfair and deceptive act or practice.[32] The passage of this act would force labels for digital media to correctly identify the digital rights management schemes included in the software.

Even more radically (with regard to orphaned works), H.R. 2408, the *Public Domain Enhancement Act*, would allow orphaned works to enter the public domain after fifty years by reinstating the registration (and fee) requirement for renewing copyright protections (thereby placing any materials not re-registered into the public domain.)[33] As noted in the evidence presented to the Supreme Court in the *Eldred* case, perhaps as little as 2% of the body of copyright-protected works since 1923 have ongoing commercial value, yet the *Bono Extension Act* places all materials under the terms of the extension. H.R. 2408 would seek to rebalance that situation.

H.R. 4536, the so-called *BALANCE Act* ("Benefit Authors without Limiting Advancement or Net Consumer Expectations"), is a significant proposal seeking to restore some of consumers' fair-use rights lost to the *DMCA*.[34] The act seeks "to safeguard the rights and expectations of consumers who lawfully obtain digital entertainment" by enabling them to make archive copies or cross-media copies for personal, non-commercial use (much as the *Sony/Betamax* ruling enabled the use of the VCR for analog copying). H.R. 2408 and 4536 were proposed by Rep. Zoe Lofgren (CA).

Three proposals would significantly extend restrictive protection practices. H.R. 4569, the *Digital Transition Content Security Act*, would restrict application of the *Sony/Betamax* ruling to analog-to-digital recordings that bypassed DRM protection codes on the analog source.[35] H.R. 4861, the *Audio Broadcast Flag Licensing Act*, would authorize the Federal Communications Commission to impose licensing conditions on digital audio radio to protect against the unauthorized distribution of transmitted content.[36] In April 2006, Rep. Lamar Smith (TX) began promoting the *Intellectual Property Protection Act of 2006*. The act would strengthen the DMCA's anti-circumvention and grant federal police more wiretapping and enforcement powers.[37]

In 2008, bills proposed by Sen. Patrick Leahy (VT) and Rep. Howard Berman (CA) addressed the suggestion by the Copyright Office that changes should be made to the ways that orphaned works are treated under the *Copyright Act* and *DMCA*.[38] Those bills faced immediate opposition from a variety of rights-holder groups. [ELL]

Everyday citizens are not the only ones caught up in the complexities of copyright law as it applies to new media. Major corporations still battle over rights issues. Ted Bridis of the Associated Press reports in "XM Faces Lawsuit about Handheld 'Inno'" on a suit seeking $150,000 in damages in which the RIAA sued XM Satellite Radio over its new handheld device that can store up to fifty hours of music.

Traditional Media Copyright Cases with New Media Implications

Baker v. Selden, 101 U.S. 99 (1879)

The Supreme Court in *Baker v. Selden* considered what aspects of Selden's book relating to an improved bookkeeping system could be protected by copyright. Selden's book contained mostly bookkeeping forms and some description of how to use the new bookkeeping system. The case involved an attempt to keep Baker from selling a book describing a similar system. The Court held that, although copyright law granted Selden the right to prevent others from printing or publishing any material part or his entire book, "copyright of a book on bookkeeping cannot secure the exclusive right to make, sell and use account books prepared upon the plan set forth in such a book."

This is an early case dealing with the idea versus expression dichotomy in copyright law. The system that Selden devised was merely an idea and therefore not subject to copyright protection. The Court went on extensively to distinguish copyright and patent laws, clarifying that the particular description of the system itself could be protected by copyright, but not the abstract idea of the method or system—ideas must be protected by patent; it is the expression of ideas that is governed by copyrights. In contrast, the specific layout and presentation of Selden's book was subject to copyright protection, but Baker was not copying the text or presentation from Selden.

Feist Publications, Inc. v. Rural Telephone Service Co., 499 U.S. 340 (1991)

In *Feist*, the Supreme Court addressed what satisfies the minimum original-ity requirement as specified by the Constitution to be eligible for copyright protection. Rural provided telephone service in Kansas and was statutorily re-quired to provide a phone directory to customers free of charge. Feist compiled telephone directories from larger areas than Rural. When Rural refused to license its local directory to Feist, Feist copied Rural's listings. Rural was able to detect the copy because it had placed some phony numbers in its listings for just that purpose.

Rural sued Feist for copyright infringement, alleging that its "compilation" of the phone numbers copied from its listings warranted copyright protection. The Court held that effort and the expenditure of resources are not protected by copyright and rejected the "sweat of the brow" doctrine that had previously existed in copyright law. Prior to *Feist*, the "sweat of the brow" doctrine pro-vided copyright protection to those who invested a significant amount of time and energy into a work.

Feist clarified that the point of copyright protection as laid out by the Constitution is to encourage creative expression, thereby "promot[ing] the Progress of Science and useful Arts." Prior to *Feist*, it had long been settled that information itself could not be protected by copyright, but that collections of information could be. The Court in *Feist* then indicated that in order to be copyrightable, a work need not be novel, but it must possess "a minimal degree of creativity" and that the copyright only applies to those creative aspects of the work. The Court held that an author's selection and arrangement of a compila-tion of facts can warrant copyright protection. However, the Court concluded that Rural's arrangement of names and phone numbers in alphabetical order was not remotely creative and did not warrant copyright protection.

Sony Corp. of America v. Universal City Studios, Inc., 464 U.S. 417 (1984)

In *Sony*, various movie studio companies elected to sue Sony for copyright in-fringement based on its production of home video recorders. Sony argued that: (1) recording copyrighted broadcasts to be watched at a later time for noncom-mercial use was simply "time-shifting," which—even if unauthorized—is a fair use; and (2) there were substantial non-infringing uses, including the copy-ing of non-copyrighted material or copyrighted programming whose owners consent to such copying. The studios countered that, even if there are non-infringing uses, the primary purpose of the home video recorders was to make unauthorized copies of copyrighted material.

The Supreme Court established a test for determining whether recording devices violate copyright law. This test has presented some problems for the courts when attempting to apply it to file sharing commonly used for music. In a narrow majority, the Court stated that "the sale of copying equipment, like the sale of other articles of commerce, does not constitute contributory infringement if the product is widely used for legitimate, unobjectionable purposes." The Court then set forth the test as being whether the allegedly infringing device "is capable of commercially significant non-infringing uses."

The Court then agreed with Sony that there were substantial non-infringing uses and that recording programming for a noncommercial home use is a fair use of the copyrighted material. The Court emphasized that the public was invited to view the broadcast free of charge, and the home video recorder allows them to do just that, but at a later time.

Mazer v. Stein, 347 U.S. 201 (1954)

In *Mazer*, Stein designed statuettes of male and female dancing figures intended for use as bases for table lamps. The statuettes, without any of the components used for lamps, were registered with the Copyright Office as works of art. Stein then sold the statuettes as lamp bases of fully equipped lamps. Mazer copied the designs of the lamp bases and sold them as fully equipped lamps as well. Stein sued Mazer for copyright infringement. The Supreme Court evaluated whether a work of art, intended for use as an element in a useful manufactured article, is copyrightable. The Court affirmed the appellate court and held that such a use of a copyrighted work of art does not affect the ability to protect against copyright infringement of the work of art. The Court held that the statuettes in *Mazer* were an original, tangible expression of the author's ideas and that the reproduction of the statuettes as lamps did not bar or invalidate the statuettes' copyright registration.

The Court found that the statuettes were subject to copyright protection and that "the dichotomy of protection for the aesthetic is not beauty and utility but art for the copyright and the invention of original and ornamental design for design patents." The Court went on to hold that just because an item is used or intended for use in industry does not mean that the registration of such an item for copyright should be barred or invalidated. Furthermore, the Court stated that it is not a misuse of copyright to register a work of art after it has been used as an element in a manufactured article.

Harper & Row v. Nation Enterprises Case Media, 471 U.S. 539 (1985)

Former President Gerald Ford licensed his publication rights to Harper & Row for his memoirs relating to his decision to pardon Richard Nixon. Harper & Row had in turn contracted with *Time* magazine to print Ford's memoirs. *The Nation* magazine obtained and published significant portions without permission of any of the involved parties—Ford, Harper & Row, or *Time* Magazine. Once *The Nation* published those excerpts, the value of the publication rights were minimal, so *Time* chose to withdraw from its contract with Harper & Row, as allowed by a clause in the contract. Harper & Row then sued *The Nation* for copyright infringement.

The Nation attempted to claim that the public interest in learning of Ford's reasons for pardoning Nixon was vital, and that its appropriation and publication should therefore constitute a fair use. The Court found that there was no exception to copyright protection merely because the memoirs were those of a public figure. The Court applied the traditional fair-use test and found that the factors weighed in favor of no fair use because it was a commercial use of the significant portion of the copyrighted material that caused an actual harm (the cancellation of the contract) despite the fact that the nature of the work was informative.

New Media Cases and Copyright Law

Kelly v. Arriba Soft

- *Leslie A. Kelly, et al. v. Arriba Soft Corp., et al.,*USDC (C.D. Cal.), Southern Division Case No. SA CV 99–560 GLT[JW] (1999)
- *Leslie A. Kelly, et al. v. Arriba Soft Corp., et al.*, Appeal from USDC (C.D. Cal. Feb. 6, 2002), *Gary L. Taylor, District Judge, Presiding*
- *Leslie A. Kelly, et al. v. Arriba Soft Corp., et al.* (9th Cir. 10; July 7, 2003). *Withdrawn July 7, 2003, Re-filed July 7, 2003*

In 1999, Leslie A. Kelly, a professional photographer, brought a suit for copyright infringement against the Arriba Soft Corporation. Arriba operated an Internet search engine that functioned by presenting image search results in the form of thumbnails: reduced-size versions of entire images. Kelly requested summary judgment against Arriba's use of thumbnail images, arguing both that Arriba infringed his copyright and, in removing copyright management information, violated the *DMCA*. Judge Gary Taylor, central district of California, disagreed with Kelly, finding that Arriba's use was fair and that no *DMCA* violation had occurred.

At the time the suit was filed, most search engines operated by presenting search results in textual form. Arriba's was among the first to operate by displaying a downsized version of the content itself, an approach now ubiquitous in Web searching. The case was an important test of the application of copyright law and traditional infringement defenses in an Internet environment.

Arriba conceded that it had both copied and displayed Mr. Kelly's images at reduced size on its site but denied removing or altering any copyright management information. One of the major additions introduced by the *DMCA* requires that copyright management information, including the title of the work and the identification of the copyright owner, not be falsified, removed, or altered. Judge Taylor found that, since the copyright identification information was in the text surrounding—but not included within—the images on Mr. Kelly's Web site, no removal had occurred in the act of copying images to Arriba's database. Although the thumbnails were displayed in the Arriba search engine without the text accompanying them on Kelly's site, "Defendant's users could obtain a full-sized version of a thumbnailed image by clicking on the thumbnail. A user who did this was given the name of the Web site from which Defendant obtained the image, where any associated copyright management information would be available, and an opportunity to link there" (*Kelly v. Arriba*).

Arriba argued that its use of Kelly's images was permissible under section 107 of the copyright law, the so-called fair-use exemption. In his analysis of the four fair-use factors, the judge found that two of the factors weighed in favor of a fair-use finding, and two against. The first factor, the character and purpose of the use, focuses on the way the work is used. Although Arriba used the images in the context of a commercial enterprise, the judge found the use less exploitative in relation to other types of commercial use, where the image might be offered for sale or directly used to promote sales of a product. In addition, he found that the use of Kelly's work was transformative, that is, the work was used in a substantially new way in the process of creating a new and useful service. The transformative evaluation, introduced in a 1990 *Harvard Law Review* article by Pierre Leval and famously applied by the US Supreme Court in the *2Live Crew/Pretty Woman* parody case (*Campbell v. Acuff-Rose Music, Inc.*) is increasingly seen as an important part of a fair-use evaluation.

Evaluation of the second factor, nature of the copyrighted work, weighed against a fair-use finding. The works were of a highly creative nature, which typically receives more copyright protection than factual works. The third factor determines whether the amount of the work copied was reasonable in light of the intended purpose. Here, the judge evaluated both the thumbnail-sized display and an intermediate linking page that displayed the image full-size alongside a link to the originating site. Although the thumbnail display prevented users from reprinting or otherwise reproducing the image at full size, the judge also felt that the intermediate page created a problem and was not necessary to fulfill the purpose of the search engine: "The Court finds the third factor weighs slightly against fair use."

The final factor evaluates the use against its likely effect on the market for the work. Kelly argued that the Arriba search service made it more likely that users could copy and reuse his work in violation of his copyright, while Arriba argued that the service would increase Kelly's market. Since Kelly did not present any evidence of actual harm, the judge found Arriba's argument more compelling and ruled in favor of fair use for the fourth factor.

Although two factors favored fair use and two did not, the use was found to be fair overall, with the first factor playing a key role in tipping the scales: "Defendant's purposes were and are inherently transformative, even if its realization of those purposes was at times imperfect. Where, as here, a new use and new technology are evolving, the broad transformative purpose of the use weighs more heavily than the inevitable flaws in its early stages of development."

The case took a strange turn when Kelly appealed the District Court ruling. Because Judge Taylor had mentioned the in-line display of full-sized images in his fair-use finding, the 9th Circuit appeals court judges also evaluated the use of full-size images, this time separating the two uses and finding that, while the use of thumbnails was fair, the use of full-size images was not. It remanded the case but, upon rehearing arguments, withdrew its opinion on the basis that Judge Taylor had improperly ruled on the full-size image question. Since Arriba had never conceded that it infringed the copyright in displaying full-size images, it was improper for the judge to rule on that question in a summary judgment phase, and it therefore could not be evaluated in the appeals phase. The case was remanded but was never fully tried; Mr. Kelly was able to obtain a default judgment against Arriba in 2004 after it failed to appear in court to answer his charges on the issue of full-size images. Despite the lack of a direct ruling on the full-size images question, the ruling on use of thumbnail images was an important interpretation of the application of a fair-use defense in an Internet environment.

DeCSS and DVD-Related *DMCA* Cases

The *DMCA*, which was almost a footnote in the Arriba case, took center stage in a series of cases involving the distribution of a computer program designed to circumvent the Contents Scrambling System (CSS) used in many commercial DVDs to prevent unauthorized access. In 1999, Jon Johansen, a teenager living in Norway, reverse-engineered the CSS encryption. The version of the Linux operating system that Johansen was using did not have a DVD software player licensed by the DVD Copy Control Association (DVD-CCA), so he wrote a software program to defeat CSS and copy unencrypted movie contents to a computer. This code, which he released as a Windows program called DeCSS, was later redistributed and linked to from hundreds of sites around the world, including the online "hacker" magazine *2600*. The publishers of *2600* and others who had linked to or posted the code were sued in New York and Connecticut by eight movie studios for violation of the *DMCA*, and in California, several individuals were sued by the DVD-CCA for violation of trade secrets. [See Chapter 5, pages 143-144, for a DeCSS and trade secret case]

Universal City Studios, Inc. v. Reimerdes, No. 00 Civ. 0277 (LAK), USDC (S.D.N.Y. Aug. 17, 2000, amended Sept. 6, 2000) [Defendants' Reply Brief in]

In defending themselves against the accusation that they violated section 1201 of the *United States Copyright Act* (the anti-circumvention portion of the law enacted by passage of the *DMCA*), Eric Corley (publisher of *2600*), Shawn Reimerdes, and Roman Kazan argued that they had been improperly targeted as parties in the suit, cited the encryption research anti-circumvention exemption, and argued that the *DMCA* was unconstitutional because it violates both the fair-use exemption in the copyright law and the right to free speech guaranteed by the First Amendment (Defendants' Reply Brief in *Universal City Studios, Inc. v. Reimerdes*). District Court Judge Lewis Kaplan disagreed with these arguments and enjoined the sites from posting or linking to DeCSS; in late 2001, the Court of Appeals upheld his ruling. Kaplan found the fair-use argument irrelevant, since the suit had been brought for violation of anti-circumvention provisions, not for infringing the plaintiff's copyrights. In other words, only the circumvention actions were challenged, not the copying of any video content. The free-speech argument consumed most of the Court's attention in both the district and appellate stages, but ultimately the judges felt that, while it could plausibly be argued that computer code is speech, the functional aspects of the computer program could not be so protected (Merges et al. 514).

DVD-CCA v. Bunner, Court of Appeals of the State of California, 6th Appellate District, HO21153 Santa Clara County Super. CT. No. CV786804, (Feb. 27, 2004)

While the Universal case was unfolding in New York, the DVD Copyright Control Association (DVD-CCA) was pursuing a trade secrets case against a number of individuals, including Andrew Bunner, in California State Court. A preliminary injunction was initially denied, then granted, then reversed on appeal; eventually the Court found that the DVD-CCA had not met the standard for demonstrating that Mr. Bunner's activities were instrumental in disclosing a trade secret. By the time he posted a link, DeCSS had already been widely published and circulated. In 2003, the California Supreme Court further ruled that posting the DeCSS code qualified as protected speech. Shortly after, the DVD-CCA requested that the case be dismissed.

321 Studios v. MGM Studios, No. C 02–1955 SI, USDC (N.D. Cal. 2004)

Despite the ruling in *Universal*, 321 Studios, a small San Francisco software company, attempted to market software to copy the contents of DVDs, including a package called "DVD X Copy," which allowed DVDs encrypted with CSS to be duplicated to a blank DVD disc. In 2002, 321 Studios, fearing a suit from the film industry, proactively asked a California District Court to find that, because its software had substantial non-infringing uses and allowed consumers to use content as allowed under the fair-use clause, its manufacture and distribution were not in violation of the *DMCA*. The non-infringing uses argument refers to the standard established in the *Sony/Betamax* case, when the US Supreme Court found that, because the commercial videocassette recorder could be used for a variety of purposes (including many that did not infringe copyrights), its manufacture could not be prohibited. In ruling on the *321 Studios* case, however, US District Court Judge Susan Illston instead relied heavily on the rulings in the *Universal* DeCSS case. She declined to rule specifically on the claim that DVD X Copy supports fair use, focusing instead on the circumvention and trafficking bans and finding 321 Studios in violation of both. Not long after, 321 Studios went out of business.

Copyright Term Extension and Eldred

Eldred v. Reno, 74 F. Supp. 2d 1 (1999)

Eldred v. Reno, 239 F.3d 372 (2001)

Eldred v. Ashcroft, U.S. Court of Appeals, D.C. Cir. (Jan. 15, 2003)

Eric Eldred, a former computer systems administrator, had been publishing online editions of public domain texts for several years. He had been looking forward to expanding his project when he learned that Congress had passed the *Copyright Term Exension Act*, lengthening the term of copyright protection from life of the author plus fifty years to life of the author plus seventy years. "Dozens of library groups and other public organizations opposed the bill, but there were no public hearings or debates, and not a peep between the bill's passage and its signing by the president" (Eldred). Eldred joined forces with several groups that were also using public domain works, and with the support of noted copyright scholars including Lawrence Lessig and Jonathan Zittrain, he filed suit in Washington, D.C., District Court in 1999 to challenge the constitutionality of the *Copyright Term Extension Act*.

The plaintiffs argued that Congress exceeded its authority in extending the term, by violating both the constitutional mandate that copyrights be secured for only "a limited time" and the First Amendment right to free speech. The District Court (*Eldred v. Reno*, 1999) and the appeals court (*Eldred v. Reno*, 2001) both disagreed with these arguments. The US Supreme Court agreed to hear the case. On October 9, 2002, Lawrence Lessig argued the case before the Court; on January 15, 2003, in a 7–2 opinion, the Supreme Court agreed with the lower courts that the *Act* was constitutional and must be allowed to stand.

Key factors in the Eldred case were the true meaning of the phrase "limited times," specifically as it pertains to existing copyrights, and the question of whether the right to free speech in any way applies to the use of copyrighted works. The justices did not agree that repeated extensions of the copyright term were, in effect, creating a perpetual and unlimited right, even when the extensions applied both to new and existing works. Although a life-plus-seventy-years term is considerably longer than the fourteen-year term granted when the copyright law was enacted for the first time, " . . . a timespan appropriately 'limited' as applied to future copyrights does not automatically cease to be 'limited' when applied to existing copyrights. And as we observe . . . there is no cause to suspect that a purpose to evade the 'limited Times' prescription prompted Congress to adopt the *CTEA*" (*Eldred v. Ashcroft*, 2003). The Court likewise rejected the First Amendment argument, finding that a limited monopoly on expression is not incompatible with the right to free speech, further noting that the *United States Copyright Act* already contains limitations, such as the 107 fair-use exemption, which act as safeguards in cases where the protected speech must involve the use of a copyrighted expression.

Peer-to-Peer File Sharing

In the mid-1990s, a compressed audio file format known as MP3 (officially: MPEG-1, layer 3) began to make serious waves as a popular format for sharing recorded music online. The bulletin boards and newsgroups that were once popular for swapping pictures and other media had been replaced by Web sites and so-called "peer-to-peer" file sharing systems.

A&M Records, Inc. v. Napster, Inc., 239 F. 3d 1004 (9th Cir. 2001)

Shawn Fanning, then a freshman at Northeastern University, wrote a simple program he called Napster, which allowed users to share lists of the music stored on their computers and to directly connect to and swap the actual music files. Record companies and the Recording Industry Association of America (RIAA) began to take notice of Napster and the other peer-to-peer, or P2P, services that were springing up. In 1999, they filed suit against Napster in California District Court, alleging both contributory and vicarious infringement on their copyrights.

Napster attempted to have the case dismissed, arguing that it qualified for protection under the *DMCA*'s safe harbor provision limiting liability for the Internet service providers (ISPs) who merely provide bandwidth and base services for users to transact their network activities. The record companies countered that Napster had both the right and the ability to monitor and prevent the illegal activity of its users, and, since it had attracted more than $13 million in venture capital, had a strong financial incentive to support the infringing behavior of its users. The District Court agreed that Napster had failed to qualify for any ISP protections, agreed with the record companies' argument, and ordered Napster to halt trading copyrighted files. Although an appeals court gave Napster a brief reprieve, the injunction was eventually allowed to stand. Napster's assets were purchased by Bertelsmann, which closed down the P2P service before an appeal could be considered.

Metro-Goldwyn-Mayer Studios Inc. v. Grokster, Ltd. (04–480) 545 U.S. 913 (2005)

The Napster suit was only one of the first against a P2P service. Dozens of other such services had sprung up, and in late 2001, a coalition of film and recording studios filed suit against another group of P2P services, including Grokster. These services operated on a slightly different basis than had Napster in that they were completely decentralized, without a central catalog of music residing on a specific computer or (set of) server(s). The *Grokster* case was eventually argued before the US Supreme Court, and, as with the *321 Studios* case, the defense raised the *Sony* standard, arguing that technology with substantial noninfringing uses cannot be prohibited under US copyright law. In a unanimous but narrow ruling, the justices declined to respond to the noninfringing uses argument, finding instead that Grokster was liable for inducing the infringing behavior of its users. After the ruling, both sides claimed victory—the content industries for successfully making an inducement argument, and Grokster for successfully preserving the *Sony* standard. The decision did not definitively resolve the P2P issue one way or the other, but as with *321 Studios* and *Napster*, although the case was remanded to the lower court for further action, Grokster ceased operations shortly after the Supreme Court decision was handed down.

Recording Industry Association of America, Inc., v. Verizon, Inc., 359 U.S. App. D.C. 85 (2004)

Responding to what they perceived as serious threats to their members' businesses and profitability, the RIAA began, in 2001, to take direct action against users sharing music online through P2P systems. As part of their copyright infringement suits against users (or "pirates," as they called them), the RIAA sought to compel Internet service providers (ISPs) including Verizon, Inc., to disclose the identity of users who were engaging in large-scale music sharing. Several providers did identify their users, but when presented with a subpoena, Verizon refused to do so. The RIAA then took Verizon to court. Verizon argued that limitations on Internet service provider liability in section 512 of the *United States Copyright Law* (another addition of the *DMCA*) exempted them from responsibility for activities that involve content that travels across Verizon-administrated network connections but is not directly stored on servers or other devices operated by them. Verizon further argued, based on this exemption, that section 512 is not constitutional, both because a subpoena issued without a substantive copyright infringement claim would lack jurisdiction, and because the statute violates the First Amendment right to assemble anonymously. The D.C. District Court disagreed with all three of Verizon's arguments, but the Court of Appeals agreed: "We conclude from both the terms of § 512(h) and the overall structure of § 512 that, as Verizon contends, a subpoena may be issued only to an ISP engaged in storing on its servers material that is infringing or the subject of infringing activity." However, the Court declined to consider the constitutional arguments that Verizon had raised. [MC]

Summarizing Copyright and New Media

Although the authors of this book think otherwise and therefore examine a wide panoply of intellectual property rights and law, copyright for many is virtually synonymous with—and covers the most interesting range of—intellectual property rights. Press coverage of circumstances surrounding P2P file sharing, illegal downloading, and lawsuits by (and settlements with) the RIAA draws attention to the importance of copyright in the digital era.

To some, the US copyright system is irreparably broken, because it only advantages the rich and powerful. From this perspective, the US regime is totally bound to the interests of large, corporate content holders, who wield rights almost as a club against consumers.[39] Further, the government coerces our international partners into accepting the terms of our copyright regime. From this point of view, the system does not deter infringement but rather makes criminals out of most consumers. Politicians do not advocate for pro-consumer changes but instead choose to further the advantages of the wealthy and greedy corporate content (and rights) holders to the detriment of both consumers and artist/creators. From this point of view, the copyright system has tilted too far toward corporate profit in ways that degrade the public domain, diminish incentives and raw material for creative artists, and virtually ignore the realities of the everyday lives of common citizens who now regularly engage in digital enterprises.

To others, the US copyright system is broken because it is no longer strong enough to effectively deter illegal downloading and piracy. From this perspective, too much economic value is lost to pirates, and everyone along the content pipeline—from artist/creators to the industries that support them—is threatened with extinction as a result. Far too many international partners do not cooperate with thorough enforcement, with the result that the global marketplace seems more a black market than a promising zone for economic expansion. To this contingent, corporate profits in the content industries provide the strongest platforms and assurances available for the continuation of artistic excellence. Replacing these with user-created content, much of which is formed from illegally sampled or pirated primary materials, leads to cultural deterioration (see Keen). From this point of view, the system is broken, and the "fix" features stronger laws, enforcement, and penalties.

Regardless of one's stance regarding whether the system needs repair, the status quo features in-place laws and enforcement. The courts use current copyright laws to adjudicate conflicts among and between rights holders (industries, artists, creators) as well as disagreements between rights holders and consumers. At least to some degree, the system continues to work/operate to constrain and punish illegal infringement, to protect the rights of artists and those to whom they grant rights, and to promote further creativity. Feeling that the system should change has the same status as ignorance of the law: neither gives valid excuse in a court of law for illegalities.

The nature of digital media has changed the copyright landscape exponentially and in perpetuity. Never again will copyright law apply primarily (or only) to large corporations and their business with each other (although the laws do continue to apply in those venues). In the digital age, copyright law must be relevant to everyman, as citizens are the principal users of digital content. American capitalist democracy does not function well when anarchy rules. One worries that ineffective copyright law, and the negative responses to it from almost every corner—consumers, corporate entities, the courts alike—may be one of the few factors that has the weight to slow the digital revolution. At this point in history, it seems silly to claim that any single force could turn back the clock from digital to analog. However, copyright is a crucial element of intellectual property law and plays a central role in encouraging or discouraging creativity. Antiquated and ineffective copyright laws that work well for neither consumers nor corporate interests cannot long serve American interests.

Yet, the current system is in place and requires understanding and adherence. Chapter 2 of this volume extends treatment of copyright by examining three important issues: fair use, the public domain, and orphaned works. Although, technically speaking, the public domain and fair use involve materials and issues of relevance to a variety of rights, they are in the main treated with regard to copyright. [ELL]

Discussion Questions

1. Discuss making copies of digital materials for the purpose of private use across playback devices. Should copyright law permit this, or are industry forces that insist that new copies be purchased for each device correct? Would this kind of copying further encourage piracy?
2. Discuss making backup copies of digital materials for private use. Should copyright law permit this, or are industry forces that insist that this kind of copying further encourages piracy correct?
3. Should elected officials be more actively involved in copyright legislation? What are the pros and cons of their higher involvement: to them, to the process, to "the people"? Perhaps the "expert system" that is in

place is actually best?

4. Discuss the subtle and philosophical differences between the US system, in which copyright is granted on fixing the form and is furthered by registration, with the European perspective of copyright as a "natural right." Are the differences significant enough to warrant defending one approach over the other?

5. Regarding extending copyright terms: If you represented large, corporate, mass media rights holders, would you ever be in favor of allowing your materials into the public domain? For example, should others ever freely use Disney or Warner Brothers' classic cartoon characters?

CHAPTER TWO

Three Copyright Issues

Although it is certainly the case that copyright law is principally applied in order to protect the rights of content creators (and those to whom they assign rights), the law is also designed to promote progress through use—by "the people"—of creative works. In most instances, creative progress can be made when citizens either pay for the use of works or when they receive the copyright holder's permission to use the works without cost.

However, there are numerous circumstances under which neither monetary exchange nor the negotiation of permissions functions as a way to encourage further creativity via the circulation of the material among the people. For example, certain uses might be opposed by the rights holder in such a way that one can neither purchase rights nor obtain permission for use ("You may want to use our work to criticize or parody us in artistic or editorial ways"). In other instances, materials might be wanted for educational purposes in classroom situations during which neither payment nor permission seems to be a valid demand. Studying excerpts or samples may simply not justify the purchase of complete works, and the technical procedures of rights clearance may be onerous for large amounts of curricular material. Some works have been out of cir-on for so long that it is either difficult or impossible to find rights holders with whom to negotiate. In such cases, "current" users may be willing to pay or to seek permission for use but are unable to determine whom to contact. Most important, contrary to the outcomes of the numerous extensions of copyright terms, having creative work enter into free and common usage "greases the creative wheel" for all citizens who might want to model, iterate, build on, or otherwise re-purpose creative content for fun, learning, or profit.

This chapter examines three important copyright issues: (1) Fair Use: the various ways in which parts of otherwise protected works can be utilized without payment or permission; (2) the Public Domain: the conceptual and practical notion that, at some point, after the creative work has been protected long enough for its creator(s) to recover development costs and make enough profit to encourage them toward further creativity, the works' protection expires, and the citizenry at large may utilize it without fee or permission; and (3) Orphaned Works: items that are so far removed from usage, commerce, and in some cases history itself, that reasonable efforts cannot locate a rights holder with interests needing protection.

Fair Use

One of the first sections of the 1976 *United States Copyright Law*, section 106, enumerates the exclusive rights of the copyright holder. It is short and direct, particularly when viewed in comparison to the rest of the law. The section immediately following, 107, is even shorter. It defines the "fair-use" exemption and the four factors that must be weighed in order to determine whether or not a use without remuneration, permission, or license is fair. Fair use is one of the most fundamental and important characteristics of American copyright law and the one arguably most closely tied to the constitutional underpinnings of copyright, "to advance the progress of science and the useful arts." To make a fair use means to exercise the rights of the copyright holder without their permission but for a purpose that society feels is beneficial, one that it wishes to promote and protect. Education is a beneficial use that the fair-use clause specifically mentions. Teachers who use newspaper articles in political science classes, clips from television news for journalism, and sample audio recordings in music class should not be required to seek explicit permission from copyright holders. News reporting, criticism, and parody are other socially valuable uses that have traditionally enjoyed protection from findings of copyright infringement thanks to the fair-use doctrine. In this section we will look at the scope and origins of the rule, as well as a number of specific cases in which a fair-use defense has succeeded or failed.

The full text of section 107 is as follows:

> Notwithstanding the provisions of sections 106 and 106A, the fair use of a copyrighted work, including such use by reproduction in copies or phonorecords or by any other means specified by that section, for purposes such as criticism, comment, news reporting, teaching (including multiple copies for classroom use), scholarship, or research, is not an infringement of copyright. In determining whether the use made of a work in any particular case is a fair use the factors to be considered shall include—
>
> (1) the purpose and character of the use, including whether such use is of a commercial nature or is for nonprofit educational purposes;
>
> (2) the nature of the copyrighted work;
>
> (3) the amount and substantiality of the portion used in relation to the copyrighted work as a whole; and
>
> (4) the effect of the use upon the potential market for or value of the copyrighted work.
>
> The fact that a work is unpublished shall not itself bar a finding of fair use if such finding is made upon consideration of all the above factors.
>
> (17 U.S.C. § 107)

This section is so short as to seem almost simplistic, a common-sense doctrine, something easily understood by any normal person. Congress refers to fair use as an "equitable rule of reason." In reality, however, each one of the four factors has been carefully studied, interpreted and reinterpreted, and passionately debated. The lack of specificity in the fair-use clause is both its greatest strength and its greatest weakness, inviting, as it does, both overly broad and overly restrictive interpretations. The *DMCA* further raises the stakes in the fair-use debate, and it remains to be seen whether its anti-circumvention provisions effectively trump fair use.

It was something of an understatement for the Supreme Court to say, in its opinion in *Williams & Wilkins* (1975), an important library fair-use case, "The development of 'fair use' has been influenced by *some tension* between the direct aim of the copyright privilege to grant the owner a right from which he can reap financial benefit and the more fundamental purpose of the protection 'To promote the Progress of Science and the Useful Arts'" (emphasis added). In *Williams & Wilkins*, a publisher of four medical journals brought a suit for copyright infringement against the National Library of Medicine, operators of a photocopying and interlibrary loan service to provide copies of recent medical articles to researchers. The Supreme Court, reversing the decision of the lower court, found the library's use was not an infringement, and in its opinion summed up the tests courts had developed in the fifty years since the law was last revised—the four factors that would formally become the section 107 fair-use exemption when the major 1976 revisions became law the following year. The Court captured succinctly the balance that fair use was intended to protect. The monopoly of copyright is limited, both in duration and in scope, in order that authors will have the incentive to create works, but also so that other authors can use those works to create new works. Fair use is an additional weight in the balance pan.

Even though fair use was not formally incorporated into the law until 1976, it had been employed in US courts as early as 1841, when Massachusetts Circuit Court Justice William Story ruled that the Rev. Charles W. Upham had certainly violated the copyright of the publishers of a seven-thousand-page, twelve-volume work, *The Writings of President Washington*, by reprinting 353 pages of its letters in his much shorter *Life of Washington*. Story regretfully summarizes the facts of the case, concluding that although his preference is to promote production of condensed works for the educational market, there had undoubtedly been excessive taking: "We must often, in deciding questions of this sort, look to the nature and objects of the selections made, the quantity and value of the materials used, and the degree in which the use may prejudice the sale, or diminish the profits, or supersede the objects, of the original work" (*Folsom v. Marsh*). We see here the beginnings of a multipart test, where quantity, nature, and—perhaps most important—financial effect, are evaluated to determine whether the benefit to society is greater than the known or anticipated injury to the author.

The so-called Gentlemen's Agreement of 1935 between the National Association of Book Publishers and a group of academic researchers led by professor Robert Binkley is one of the first known examples of a formal set of rules or guidelines, albeit quite limited in scope, exempting certain kinds of copying along the lines of what we now recognize either as fair use or as the exemptions granted to libraries and archives in section 108 (Hirtle, "Research, Libraries and Fair Use"). Binkley sought to promote scholarly use of the most exciting new technology of his day, reprographic photography. An interesting historical document for this reason, the Gentlemen's Agreement also epitomizes a fundamental problem both with fair use and the many sets of guidelines that have been developed to interpret it. Creating rules like these, as nebulous as they are, subtly shifts from the stance that some behaviors and uses are simply outside of the scope of copyright law toward the view that any use is a potential copyright infringement. Indeed, this concern was raised by some of the experts Binkley consulted as he was simultaneously working on the Gentlemen's Agreement and advocating for copyright law revisions in order to codify a fair-use provision (Hirtle, "Research, Libraries and Fair Use" 31). Private copying by researchers, with no intent to reproduce for the purpose of selling or otherwise distributing copies of a work, was now formally presumed to be an acceptable unauthorized exercise of the author's rights.

Understanding the four-factor test will be furthered by a closer examination of its use in specific instances. Following this brief review, we will look at some broad fair-use theories and discuss their evolution and recent application in light of the new technological uses of copyrighted works.

Purpose and Character of the Use: Parody and 2Live Crew

Parody, which involves taking a specific work and reworking it in some way to poke fun or ridicule, is an activity that society often wishes to promote and protect in defense of free speech. We exercise our creativity as we amuse and entertain. Sometimes the purpose of parody is just to be silly or attract attention, but some parodists use humor to poke fun at or criticize powerful people and interests by turning their own words and creations against them as a means of maintaining a balance of societal power. One of the most well-known parody fair-use cases is *Campbell v. Acuff-Rose Music*. The rap group 2Live Crew wrote and recorded a song, "Pretty Woman," which they claimed was a parody of Roy Orbison's 1964 song, "Oh, Pretty Woman," substituting unflattering comments about a woman (hairy woman, two-timin' woman, etc.) to make fun of the original's obsequiously fawning lyrics. The 2Live Crew song followed the same basic song structure and incorporated looping sections from Orbison's musical recording, including the very distinctive bass riff. The 2Live Crew song, therefore, is obviously a derivative work. The copyright holders of the Orbison song, Acuff-Rose Music, brought a suit for copyright infringement against 2Live Crew, naming the song's author, Luther Campbell, and the other members of the group, alleging both that too much of the original work was used and that it failed to qualify as a fair use at all, since the work was developed for commercial purposes.

The Tennessee District Court granted Campbell's reply request for summary judgment, finding that the fact that the work was commercial was not in itself a reason for not finding it to be a fair use, and that the amount of the original work taken was necessary to create the link between the new work and the old and therefore establish it as a parody. On appeal, however, the 6th Circuit Court reversed. In the decision, Judge Charles W. Joiner grudgingly agreed that the 2Live Crew song was a parody, although he inserted the observation that "because the text of section 107 lists specific fair uses, we find that the term parody must be either subsumed within the statutory terms 'criticism' or 'comment,' or be an entirely separate category of exception." Arguing that the work is a parody addresses the purpose of the use, but the Court then proceeded to separately consider the character of the use, also mentioned in section 107 as an element of the first factor. In this evaluation, the Court uses language from the decision in the *Sony v. Universal Studios* case, otherwise known as the *Sony/Betamax* case, where the discussion about the nature of the use contains this passage: "If the Betamax were used to make copies for a commercial or profit-making purpose, such use would presumptively be unfair. The contrary presumption is appropriate here, however, because the District Court's findings plainly establish that time-shifting for private home use must be characterized as a noncommercial, nonprofit activity." Joiner bases his conclusion about factor one on this "presumptively unfair" statement and, furthermore, uses it to evaluate the fourth factor as well.

In the *Campbell v. Acuff-Rose Music* opinion reversing the Circuit Court's decision, the US Supreme Court briefly discusses the nature of a parody, refraining from commenting on the quality of the parody in this case, but nevertheless affirming its presence: "The threshold question when fair use is raised in defense of parody is whether a parodic character may reasonably be perceived. Whether, going beyond that, parody is in good taste or bad does not and should not matter to fair use." Moving on from this interesting discussion of the nature of parody, the Supreme Court addresses the crux of the problem: the fact that the use was for a commercial purpose does not presume that it cannot be fair. In explaining its reasoning, the Court quotes from the opening sentences of section 107, noting that the list of fair uses (criticism, reporting, etc.) is only meant to be illustrative, and is not, as the lower court seems to suggest, to be taken as a comprehensive list of all known fair uses. Furthermore, the standard applied by the lower court in this case was not subtle enough for the Supreme Court, and it takes issue with the application of the "presumptively unfair" comment from the *Sony/Betamax* case. The fact that the work is commercial is a separate factor that must be weighed and, while it might tend to tip things away from fairness, is not by itself enough to make a factor-one decision.

Even though in this case the Court performed a complete four-factor analysis, it is the nature of the use that was the key to crafting an evaluation. This does not merely mean that the Court felt factor one was the most compelling, but rather that factors two through four (nature of work, amount, market effect) were evaluated entirely through the lens of factor one (nature of use). In remanding the case back to the lower court, the Supreme Court found that all of the other factors turned on whether or not the amount was appropriate for a parody, and whether the nature of the work should be taken much into account for parodies, since they are almost always employed in conjunction with highly creative works. Can we conclude from this, therefore, that not all of the four fair-use factors are equivalent, but some are more important than others? Do the courts evaluate each factor completely independently, or do they, as they did in this case, use one of the factors as the prism for looking at the others? The case leaves no clear and definitive answers to these questions.

Nature of the Work: J. D. Salinger's Unpublished Letters

In October 1986, famously reclusive author J. D. Salinger sued biographer Ian Hamilton for copyright infringement, seeking an injunction to prevent Hamilton and his publisher, Random House, from releasing a biography containing paraphrased excerpts and short quotations from forty-four of Salinger's unpublished letters. The original recipients deposited the letters in the libraries of Harvard, Princeton, and the University of Texas, where Hamilton was granted permission to view the letters but was required to sign agreements stating that he would not copy or publish them without the permission of the copyright holder. Even though Salinger had refused to cooperate with the biography, Hamilton sent him a copy of the galleys in May 1986 and revised the manuscript at Salinger's request to remove a number of direct letter quotations, reducing them down to some two hundred words and substituting close paraphrasings. The changes failed to placate Salinger, who brought his suit alleging copyright infringement, unfair competition, and breach of contract, the last charge relating to the agreement forms Hamilton signed with the libraries.

Hamilton mounted a fair-use defense to the copyright charges, arguing that because his purpose was commentary and criticism, and because he limited the amount of direct quoting, he was entitled to make use of the letters in his biography. The New York District Court denied Salinger's request for a preliminary injunction, but the Circuit Court of Appeals overturned and remanded the case along with an order to issue the injunction. As with the "Pretty Woman" parody case, both courts completed a four-part, fair-use analysis, but the entire evaluation was colored by one of the factors, in this case the second, the nature of the work. Indeed, before he begins to look at the factors in turn, Judge Newman writes, "The Court begins its discussion of fair use by considering the application of the doctrine to unpublished works.... Following the Supreme Court's approach in *Harper & Row*, we place special emphasis on the unpublished nature of Salinger's letters and proceed to consider each of the four statutory fair-use factors. Application of these four factors points in Salinger's favor." On the first factor, the purpose and nature of the use, the Circuit Court judge agreed that a fair-use argument could be made on the grounds that the biography was a work of scholarship and literary criticism. Newman agrees with the District Court judge that the second factor, nature of the work, weighs heavily in Salinger's favor, because previously unpublished works ought to receive more protection under the law, and therefore the ability to argue fair use in publishing them—even in small portion—ought to be constrained. On the third factor, the amount of the work copied, the District and Circuit Court judges do not agree. The higher court very strongly weighs in Salinger's favor, finding that the paraphrased passages so faithfully represent not only the factual essence of the letters, but their expressive contents as well, and that, in aggregate, a larger portion of Salinger's work has been taken than would be apparent from a strict counting of the number of verbatim passages. On the final factor, the market effect, Judge Newman also disagrees with District Court Judge Pierre Leval finding that, although Hamilton's excerpting wouldn't directly compete with published copies of the full letters (were Salinger ever to agree to their publication), they are substantial enough to give readers the sense that "they have read Salinger's words, perhaps not quoted verbatim, but paraphrased so closely as to diminish interest in purchasing the originals."

Finding three of the four factors in Salinger's favor, the Circuit Court rejected the fair-use defense and granted the injunction. The Salinger case is believed to be one of a small handful that led to a 1992 modification of section 107 to include the phrase "The fact that a work is unpublished shall not itself bar a finding of fair use if such finding is made upon consideration of all the above factors" (Madison 401).

Amount and Substantiality: Cake-Decorating Instruction Booklets

In 1982 the 9th Circuit Court heard an appeal from Elise Marcus, whose request for summary judgment and complaint of copyright infringement against Shirley Rowley had been denied by the Southern California District Court. Marcus and Rowley were both teachers of home economics, and Rowley copied twelve pages from a cake-decorating booklet that Marcus had developed and copyrighted for her own course-teaching materials. In a fairly straightforward, four-factor analysis, Circuit Court Judge Mariana Pfaelzer found in Marcus's favor on two of the four, and found the fair-use defense without merit.

Even though education is mentioned as one of the favored purposes in the evaluation of the first factor, nature and purpose of the use, the judge took the analysis further in order to determine whether the use for both works was substantially similar. This case was argued at least a decade before Pierre Leval's introduction of the transformative use standard, discussed later in this chapter. In finding that Rowley's use was effectively identical to the use for which the work was originally developed, the judge in this case anticipates the evolution of this transformative use test as a refinement of the first factor. Because the work has both informational and creative aspects, the second factor is not conclusive. The key in this case is really the analysis of the third factor, the amount and substantiality of the copying. Large portions of the booklet were copied verbatim, and so the Court had no difficulty finding that the use was not fair according to the third factor. Although Marcus sold her booklets to her students for $2 while Rowley distributed hers for free, the Court was not able to find that a market for the work was significantly damaged by the second work, so there could be no solid conclusions on the market-effect factor. Nevertheless, the strong finding on the third factor, amount used, was sufficient for a finding against application of fair use in this case.

Market Effect: *Hustler* v. Moral Majority

The November 1983 issue of adult magazine *Hustler* printed an advertisement parodying an ad for Campari liquor, in which the Rev. Jerry Falwell, an evangelical Christian pastor and founder of the political organization the Moral Majority, is depicted having a drunken sexual encounter with his mother in an outhouse. The Moral Majority copied and distributed the fake ad in several mass mailings appealing for financial support, and Falwell filed suit against *Hustler* and its publisher, Larry Flynt, for libel, invasion of privacy, and intentional infliction of emotional distress. The libel and invasion of privacy charges were decided in favor of *Hustler* by a judge and a jury, respectively, but the emotional distress charge went all the way to the Supreme Court before also being decided in the magazine's favor. In the meantime, *Hustler* had countersued the Moral Majority for copyright infringement for copying and distributing the fake advertisement without permission. Falwell mounted a fair-use defense, and in 1985 the D.C. District Court agreed that his copying was fair.

In analyzing the first factor, purpose of the use, the Court found that Falwell's use was arguably commercial in nature, since it was used to solicit donations, but that the use was significantly different from the purpose the creator originally intended, and therefore met in some way the test for being a new and productive, or transformative, use. Furthermore, the Court agreed that it would be appropriate to characterize the copying and distribution as a form of criticism, since Falwell used it as an example of what he considered to be Flynt's outrageous assault on decency. In his opinion, Judge Gadbois observes that the use was part of a productive ongoing public debate between the two groups. Flynt wrote in part:

> The First Amendment and the Bill of Rights belong to me and the people who read HUSTLER as much as they belong to Reaganites and the Falwellians of the world and their Moral Majority. The court believes that, in view of the context in which the parody appeared, the public interest in free expression would be served by facilitating an effective response by Falwell. (*Hustler v. Moral Majority*, 1536)

The judge found no compelling argument for either side on the second factor. While the ad was certainly a creative work, Falwell's use did not exploit it as such but rather used it to make commentary and criticize it. In the analysis of the third factor, the amount and substantiality used, the Court took into account not just the ad itself, but the entire corpus of *Hustler* publications. Since Falwell's use was intended to criticize Flynt's enterprise and publication as a whole, copying a single ad does not amount to substantial taking. The final factor, the market effect, seems to have been the most straightforward and definitive in this case, as the magazine issues in which the ads appeared were no longer available for purchase. As for Flynt's assertion that there was some enduring value (in terms of a financial market) in the ad that would be damaged by the copying, the Court said: "This argument is disingenuous at best. For one thing the membership of the Moral Majority would probably not be counted among the regular readers of *Hustler*. But even those who are would not logically have been deterred from buying the March, 1984, issue because of Falwell's actions."

Fair Use in Practice

As interesting as these individual cases are, even close examination fails to determine whether a consistent approach is taken by the courts in doing a four-factor analysis. We may have a sense that the overall evaluation of the use is probably colored most strongly by the first and fourth factors, but cases such as Salinger's also show that some quite important cases depend more heavily on the second or third. Sometimes the entire case is evaluated through the lens of one factor, as with *Campbell* and *Salinger*, but at other times the evaluation seems to take each factor as a truly independent test, as it seems to do with *Marcus v. Rowley*. Does the Court get a general sense for a case first, and then write the factor analysis to fit the conclusions it has already drawn, or does it approach each with an open mind and draw a conclusion more or less mathematically? At this point, one cannot be sure.

Theories suggesting general approaches to the fair-use question have circulated over time. These are worth brief discussion here, particularly in light of the massive technological change that has recently made fair use a subject of greater interest than ever: the *de minimis* rule and the rule of private or noncommercial use, the market failure theory, and the transformative use argument.

De minimis Use and Private Use

There is a commonly held view that minimal uses of copyrighted works are just not significant or damaging enough to warrant the legal system's attention and/or to justify an exploration of copyright infringement. In normal, everyday life, we may copy and recopy e-mails that have been sent to us, read someone else's writing aloud, or make ad hoc audiovisual recordings of copyrighted works (Tehranian). The blogosphere is filled with multiple replications of fragments of the words and/or images created by people other than the blogger posting the material. For a range of reasons—from the sense that these personal uses are protected under the law, as the *Sony/Betamax* case found, to the anticipated difficulty and expense of identifying and tracking such uses—copyright holders have traditionally not bothered much with minimal personal uses.

Likewise, there is an established legal principle, the *de minimis* rule, that regards some activities as beneath the interest of the law. Literally translated, the Latin phrase "de minimis non curat lex" means "the law does not concern itself with trifles" (Ponte). For example, if the use involves a miniscule portion of a work, a potential copyright action might be rejected in light of the *de minimis* principle; the copying is trivial and does not warrant the court's interest. As we observed earlier with the development of the Gentlemen's Agreement of 1935, however, this disposition toward personal and trivial uses has a tendency to be reevaluated and may shift over time. As Hirtle says, "Private actions that had needed no defense in the past came to be viewed as potential infringements of copyright that needed the permission of the copyright owner" ("Research, Libraries and Fair Use" 4). As we experience significant changes in technology and our ability to make use of others' works, old customs and ways of viewing the law are revisited. This is happening again, both for personal and *de minimis* uses. "If personal use was once lawful solely because of enforcement difficulties, the easy enforcement of copyright prerogatives against individuals for unlicensed personal uses is yet another benefit of technological progress" (Litman, "Lawful Personal Use" 1874). Some of the changes to the *Copyright Act* include personal use exemptions like the *Audio Home Recording Act* (Title 17, sec. 1008) and the *Family Movie Act* (Title 17, sec. 110–11). By specifying exemptions rather than assuming that private, noncommercial, previously non-infringing uses may proceed without permissions seeking or special exemption, there may be an increasing confusion over which private uses are allowed (Madison 395).

An interesting fair-use issue touching on the *de minimis* principle is the question "how much of a musical recording can be digitally sampled without rising to the level where it may be considered an exercise of a copyright holder's exclusive rights"? According to the judge in *Bridgeport Music v. Dimension Films*, even if the amount taken is so small (in this case, three notes) and so altered that it is not recognizable by someone very familiar with the original work (in this case, in a sequence that made the notes almost unrecognizable as the original), if the sampler acknowledges he has taken it, he has exercised the exclusive rights of the copyright holder and is subject to an action for copyright infringement. In its decision, the Court wrote: "To begin with, there is ease of enforcement. Get a license or do not sample" (*Bridgeport* 20).

Market Failure

One hears this comment about licensing with increasing frequency in an era of rapidly expanding technological capabilities: "Copying is so easy to do that if you must copy, do so, but pay a small license fee whenever you do." Licenses are not a new thing; in various forms they have been around for some time. [See the discussion of compulsory licenses in Chapter 1] Licensing lies at the heart of another theory about fair use: it should only apply when the market has failed to support the desired use by *not* offering the wanted item for sale, or, in this case, for license. This market failure theory as applied to copyright argues that the societal goal of maximizing the exchange of goods and services in the open marketplace for money should be paramount, and that only when a desired good fails to make itself available—that is, when the incentive is too low for the copyright holder to make the item available—should an unauthorized use be permitted as fair. In her description of the market failure test, Boston University Law Professor Wendy Gordon observes:

> If the work is socially more valuable in the buyer's hands, then the economic model has suggested that he will be able to raise sufficient funds to purchase permission from the owner. In other words, to propose that fair use be imposed whenever the "social value

. . . outweighs any detriment to the artist" would be to propose depriving copyright owners of their right in the property precisely when they encounter those users who could afford to pay for it. Though a transfer to such user might be socially desirable, there is no need to compel it through fair use. (1615)

Market failure theorists generally define the market to include not just the original sale of the work or the unbundling and selling off of primary rights (e.g., derivative work rights such as screen adaptation rights for a novel), but any secondary revenue streams that might be created for partial, one-time, or otherwise constrained uses, such as a license to sample or to copy for use in support of classroom teaching.

Expressing a contrary view, however, Lewis and Clark University Law Professor Lydia Loren explains:

> A permission system only remedies the market failure that occurs because of high transaction costs. A permission system does nothing to cure the kind of market failure that is more central to the purpose of fair use and the constitutional purpose of copyright: the market failure that occurs when there are significant external benefits associated with a particular use that cannot be internalized in any bargained-for exchange. (6)

Applying a strict market-failure test in evaluating fair use may not take into account the wide variety of potential uses, their distance from the owner, the relative ability to pay market rates, or the fact that the proposed use may be vastly more beneficial to society at large than any incentive restricting the use could create for authors. An external benefit, such as use in an educational setting, would be such an example.

Transformative Use

Another yardstick sometimes used in evaluating fair use is the transformative or productive use test. Pierre Leval, the New York District Court judge whose finding of fair use in the Salinger case was overturned, wrote a key article for the *Harvard Law Review* (1990) introducing the term "transformative use," in which he noted that "the question of justification turns primarily on whether, and to what extent, the challenged use is *transformative*. The use must be productive and must employ the quoted matter in a different manner or for a different purpose from the original" (1111). Although Leval's transformative test is often quoted by those who would seek to quash any direct copying, the argument that he makes in the article is that the quotations from Salinger's letters *ought to have* met the transformative standard and been found to be a fair use, since the purpose of including direct quotations in the biography was not to merely reprint them but to employ them to advance a new, critical purpose. It is clear from his discussion that Leval intended transformation to apply not only to the form—that is, whether the new use included an exact copy of the original—but also to the environment and setting in which the work was used. Over time Leval's original meaning has been muddied, however, and we sometimes find "transformative" erroneously used as a synonym for "no exact copying took place."[1] As with some of the cases we discussed earlier, there is some evidence to suggest that the transformative evaluation sometimes rules all, that it is applied either as a trump to the four factors, or that it is so woven throughout the factor discussion that it is obvious how dispositive it is to the overall treatment of any particular case.

In our re-mixable culture, where social Web sites, podcasts, and video mashups enjoy skyrocketing popularity, how are we to apply the transformative standard? Clearly, many of these works are highly creative in their own right and might well satisfy a test for parody or even for a work that would qualify on its own for copyright protection.[2] Where there is measurable and significant copying involved, however, is the use fair? Has the work been sufficiently transformed if a person makes a video of her/himself singing and dancing along to a copyrighted song? How about if he/she keeps the musical parts but replaces the singing parts with new lyrics about a current election campaign? What if the animation is an entirely new work but periodically flashes stills from the latest *Star Wars* movie? If the *Star Trek* (*Paramount Pictures Corporation v. Carol Publishing Group*) and *Seinfeld* book cases (*Castle Rock Entertainment v. Carol Publ'g Group*) are any guide, the mere presence of copied elements, even within a much broader and original context, could be misinterpreted as non-transformative use and therefore without grounds for a fair-use finding.[3]

Perhaps Written Guidelines Are the Answer

And so what are we to do, we ordinary people who wish to avoid costly and unpleasant litigation but who also find it necessary or preferable, from time to time, to copy a painting, to share a magazine article with classmates, or to include a short clip of audio or video on a blog entry? Even though fair use was designed for judicial case-by-case evaluation of the facts and weighing of the exact circumstances, in reality this approach is far from practical, since users need to determine the status of their use *before* publishing material (and, one hopes, before litigation ensues).

Filmmakers, reporters, teachers, and librarians (among others) all regularly encounter situations in which the circumstances of potential use—and very likely the nature of the works being borrowed—are largely the same from case to case, and so over the years they've taken to writing guidelines for themselves and for their clients. There was something of a mania for guidelines in the early-to-mid-1990s, with the largely failed Conference on Fair Use (CONFU) launching attempts to develop guidelines for educational uses of multimedia, visual works, distance learning, and electronic reserves. Those attempts built in part on the guidelines developed much earlier for classroom copying, off-air videotaping, and interlibrary loans.[4] In leaning a bit too much to one side (users) or the other (copyright holders), most of these guidelines failed to attract broad support. As negotiated statements, we might have expected a little compromise on either side, as in the Gentlemen's Agreement of more than seventy years ago. As long as the purpose of the guidelines is clear (to establish some safe minimum ground on which to function), they create space in which a more conservative or risk-averse institution can operate alongside one that might wish to take a more expansive view of the law and its proscriptions. In reality, however, guidelines have not been seen either by those who would employ them or by the courts as a floor, but are very often interpreted as a ceiling, in effect, a set of rules dictating the absolute boundaries of acceptable use (Crews). Turgid, poorly written, or overly specific guidelines are virtually guaranteed to confuse and mislead instead of to simplify and liberate.

> Court interpretations of fair use are many and varied. Although knowing both the rules and laws is important, careful examination of case history reminds one that fair use is an elusive area with many twists and turns. The Stanford University Libraries provide excellent reference material concerning intellectual property law. A particularly helpful resource is their "Summaries of Fair Use Cases" Web page, which is governed by the notion that "the best method of understanding the flexible principle of fair use is to review actual cases decided by the courts." The case summaries and examples are found at <http://fairuse.stanford.edu/Copyright_and_Fair_Use_Overview/chapter9/9-c.html>.

Public Domain

When the term of copyright for a work expires, all restrictions on its use are lifted, and it may be copied, published, reworked, displayed, and performed by anyone for any purpose. The work has entered what is commonly known as the public domain (sometimes called the commons), that is, it becomes a free public good, and the use rights belong to no one and to everyone. Term expiration maintains one of the fundamental balances in US copyright law: the works are secured exclusively to the creator so that she may enjoy a reward for her work, but the term is limited so that others can exploit the work and thereby increase the number of artistic and scholarly works that society may enjoy. As American University Law Professor Peter Jaszi told Congress in 1995, "The enrichment of the public domain through the expiration of the term of protection is one of benefits for which we look to the institution of copyright" (Jaszi, "Copyright Term Extension Act of 1995" 6).

In reality, however, major changes to the law over the last century have tipped it in favor of exclusivity, with fewer and fewer works entering the public domain. Some of the most significant changes have occurred in the area of copyright renewal rules, copyright formalities, and copyright terms. Before the law was revised in 1976, creators were required both to register their copyright by filing official paperwork with the US Copyright Office and to renew it after an initial twenty-eight-year term. The term of protection for newly created works—life of the author plus fifty years for works created by individuals— was further extended to life of the author plus seventy years with the passage of the *Copyright Term Extension Act* (*CTEA*) of 1998 (the "*Sonny Bono Act*"). A work of corporate authorship now has a term of 120 years. According to the rules under which we live now, if such a work were published in the year 2005, the copyright would not expire until the year 2125. Hirtle notes that, thanks to the various changes in terms over just the relatively recent history of US copyright law, a full set of reference tools is necessary but often not sufficient to determine whether or not a given copyright has expired ("Copyright Term and the Public Domain").

Earlier, creators had also been required to place a clearly visible copyright statement on the work in order to qualify for protection. When the United States became a signatory to the *Berne Convention for the Protection of Literary and Artistic Works* in 1989 (World Intellectual Property Organization), the requirement that authors place a visible notice of copyright on the work was removed. A formal copyright notice is no longer required, and all registration-renewal requirements were removed.

The term public domain is also used to define another class of works, those that do not meet the originality requirement. Facts, systems, lists of ingredients, and other such information (US Copyright Office, *Copyright Office Basics* 3) cannot be claimed as original expression and are not eligible for protection under US copyright law. In the United States, publications of the federal government are also exempted from protection and become public domain the instant they are created.

Determining whether or not a work is still subject to copyright protection is challenging. The US Copyright Office has developed a nine-page guide to getting started but cautions: "This circular offers some practical guidance on what to look for if you are making a copyright investigation. It is important to realize, however, that this circular contains only general information and that there are a number of exceptions to the principles outlined here. In many cases it is important to consult with a copyright attorney before reaching any conclusions regarding the copyright status of a work" (US Copyright Office, *How to Investigate the Copyright Status of a Work* 1). Even if a potential user could clearly understand the basic rules for new works set forth in US law itself, she would have to take into account at least the following:

- Whether any special rules apply for the type of work. Sound recordings (*Copyright Law of the United States* 301I), for example, are subject to slightly different rules than are print works.
- What year the work was created, what the term rules were at that time regarding renewal, publication, and notice of copyright, and whether any later changes to the law retroactively adjusted either the term or the conditions of protection (Hirtle, "Copyright Term and the Public Domain").
- If the work was published abroad, whether it was published in a country that is also a signatory to the *Berne Convention*, and if so, if the work had expired in that country, and if so, whether the United States restored copyright when it signed the *Uruguay Round Agreements Act (URAA)* in 1994 (US Copyright Office, *Highlights of Copyright Amendments Contained in the URAA* 2).

The complexity of these rules and the potentially serious consequences of running afoul of them illustrate the value of a large store of public domain works that may be freely exploited and reused. Particularly for the smaller or poorer creator, the cost of investigating copyright status may in itself be a significant deterrent to reuse. As we will discuss in later chapters, the exemptions set forth in the *Copyright Law* are also not particularly reassuring, since many also require a judge's ruling to demonstrate eligibility with any absolute certainty.

The Creative Commons project, started by Stanford University Law Professor Lawrence Lessig and a group of like-minded individuals, seeks to attach explicit terms for use that come into being when the object is created, travel with it, and—indeed—travel with other, derivative works that are created "downstream." While not, strictly speaking, an alternative to copyright, Creative Commons is a greatly simplified license that can confer, for example, the right to exercise all of your exclusive rights as long as the user gives you credit (Creative Commons, "Creative Commons Attribution 3.0 United States"). This approach attempts to remove the doubt and fear typically associated with assessing whether or not a work has safely fallen into the public domain.

Much about the concept of the public domain depends on notions about "the commons" (the vast range of resources that the American people collectively own). David Bollier is one of the leading intellectuals pursuing ideas about the commons, writing numerous books and articles and making countless public presentations about the loss of these resources in the current age. Though his focus is broader than intellectual property alone, he has a keen interest in digital materials. On his Web page, "Reclaiming the Commons," he writes:

> Many of the resources that Americans own as a people—forests, minerals, government R&D, the broadcast airwaves, public schools, cultural spaces—are increasingly being taken over by private business interests, often with the full complicity of our government. This trend represents a modern-day "enclosure of the commons"—a vast appropriation of common assets that is siphoning revenues from the public treasury, shifting ownership and control from public to private interests, and eroding democratic processes and shared cultural values.

The page then lists a number of his most important presentations on the matter, most with downloadable files <http://www.bollier.org/reclaim.htm>.

Orphaned Works

The recognition that the public domain has ceased to grow (Jaszi; *Eric Eldred et al. v. John D. Ashcroft*, Petition for *Writ of Certiorari*, Brief of *Amici Curiae* by American Law Library Association et al. 10) has motivated interesting projects about, and a certain amount of support for, adjustments to the law for the use of works that are orphaned. The term "orphaned works" refers to material for which the copyright owner cannot be located.

Should the creator of a new work desire to re-use the work of another, his problems are not necessarily at an end even if he has the means, ability, willingness, and tenacity to seek permission. Materials fall into orphaned status for a wide variety of reasons. It may happen that the creator cannot be located. The original work may have lacked sufficient identifying information. Creators or their heirs may have moved from their original address without clear "forwarding" indications. Companies may have gone out of business, and the trail of asset acquisition may have gone cold or become so intricately complex that identifying the legally responsible party is impossible. In such cases, what should be done? Sometimes there do not appear to be any viable economic interests or creativity potentials for copyright protection to protect. In these circumstances, protecting the potential interests of unknown and unidentifiable parties can only be accomplished by forbidding the use of the material (to others) despite the fact that its use would be creative and worthy (for the new user), while the protection would be afforded to parties unknown. In such cases, the value of the protection, both to the public domain and the unknown rights holder, would be speculative at best and, at worst, might not rise to the level of value that making new use of the material might accrue.

Responding to calls for action on the issue of orphaned works, the Register of Copyrights, in 2005, commissioned a study and issued a call for public comment on the problem. The resulting report (US Copyright Office, *Report on Orphan Works: A Report of the Register of Copyrights*) recommended a number of specific changes to the law, all of which found their way into both the House and Senate versions of the law:

- In order to use an allegedly orphaned work, some kind of "reasonably diligent" search for the author must be performed and documented.
- If a search was attempted and failed, and the work was used without permission but a copyright holder later surfaced, there would be a limitation on that copyright holder's remedies for infringement.
- Clear attribution of the work used without permission would be absolutely necessary. (8–9)

A number of other conditions and remedies were proposed by commentators but rejected by the Register of Copyrights in her report:

- A requirement that the potential user file a public notice in a centralized system prior to using an allegedly orphaned work.
- Payment of a statutory licensing fee or creation of an escrow scheme.

The Register predicted that most owners would never surface, and thus the scheme, which would require significant resources to implement and maintain, would not actually serve its purpose.
- Registration or renewal by authors: The Register rejected this proposal largely out of concern about possible conflicts with the *Berne Convention* and the 1976 revision to the *US Copyright Law*.

Over the past few years a number of movements have sprung up whose goal is to make a change to the law itself in order to remedy this problem. One such remedy is a so-called "Orphan Works" bill, first introduced in the US Congress in 2006 and reintroduced in 2008 (*Shawn Bentley Orphan Works Act of 2008*; *Orphan Works Act of 2008*). If we believe that every new creator is a potential genius and every new work a potential masterpiece, as orphaned works supporters argue, uncertainty that chills creation is a societal evil and should be addressed. Furthermore, there's an argument that this uncertainty puts the works themselves at risk. "The costs of an inadequate system of access to orphaned works are huge: needlessly disintegrating films, prohibitive costs for libraries, incomplete and spotted histories, thwarted scholarship, digital libraries put on hold, delays to publication. In the cases where the work is truly an orphaned work, those costs are tragic because they are completely unnecessary" (Center for the Study of the Public Domain, Duke Law School 3).

It remains to be seen whether an orphaned works amendment will be adopted and what the effects of a new law would be. For the time being, the only guaranteed protection from a suit of infringement is clear-cut permission from a copyright holder.[CS]

Summarizing Special Issues in Copyright and New Media

As shown by our two-chapter treatment of copyright, including its historic legislative and case-based development as well as particular special issues and circumstances surrounding its implementation, copyright plays a very important role in the deployment of new media content. Often, when we raise the topic of intellectual property in new media, folks respond as though copyright is the only significant issue at hand. Hopefully, these chapters have both highlighted its importance and indicated some of the complexities raised by copyright issues.

In particular, digital media and the laws that have been implemented in order to control it (for example, the *DMCA* and *"Sonny Bono Act"*) have deeply compromised traditional user protections provided within copyright law. Loss of the public domain is perhaps the single most serious challenge to the founders' intent that copyright laws would encourage creativity. Without materials entering the public domain, the entire system is tilted to the advantage of large corporate content holders and against the common citizen-artist/creator. The ability to copy and remix is a defining element of digital media, but *DMCA* limitations on copying based on mandates by the rights holder often limit the legitimate use of the materials. Ruling out *de minimis* use as justification for fair use moves one in the direction of "pay per click," which would find everyday users assessed micro-fees for virtually every creative computational keystroke. It is no wonder that copyright and the issues surrounding the bundle of rights attendant to it are often characterized as the most important intellectual property issues on the digital landscape.

Stanford University law professor and practicing attorney Lawrence Lessig is usually a strong advocate of changing current copyright laws <http://www.lessig.org/blog/>. A prolific author and speaker, he is one of new media's most progressive lawyers. However, when it comes to proposed legislative changes to the orphaned works provisions of copyright law, Lessig articulates a powerful argument against legislation that is not demonstrably helpful. His argument points out the difficulties with revising copyright law: the complexities hiding within even simple changes that seem to be useful and straightforward weigh heavily against the full-scale reforms that Lessig and others often advocate. Lessig's argument against one such reform may be found in a May 20, 2008, *New York Times* op-ed piece entitled "Little Orphan Artworks."

As indicated in the Introduction, copyright is only one of many ways to protect the intellectual property that is involved in new media. Chapter 3 takes up patents, another major instrument in the suite of protections.[ELL]

Discussion Questions

1. One way to solve the orphaned work problem is to re-establish re-registration requirements. Doing so is expensive for large content holders in terms of time, effort, and money. But if they could afford the cost, would the benefits to the public domain and copyright system merit

the expense?

2. The World Wide Web introduces enormous complexities for fair use in educational settings. Discuss giving educational entities wider latitude with regard to fair use on the Web. For example, student work that includes protected materials is fair use if it is only turned in to the teacher or is arrayed on a password-protected site for a short time. Should fair use be expanded such that these works could be displayed on the Web without restriction?

3. Discuss *de minimis* usage. Should the courts re-invigorate the four-part test rather than taking the position that all copying requires permission?

4. Discuss sampling (more broadly than merely *de minimis*). How can a copy and re-mix culture be legally aligned with copyright requirements for licensing every sample? What are the values of transformative use in creativity?

5. Discuss the lack of alignment between terms for patents and copyright. Are there justifications (other than the mere history of developments) for extremely long copyright terms in the face of relatively short patent terms?

CHAPTER THREE

Patent

Let's begin this chapter by considering another conundrum. The case at hand is based on real events, with the specifics changed somewhat to protect identities and ideas.

The final project in the introductory Multimedia Production course at Bradley University (MM 113) requires students to combine the work they've done and skills they've learned throughout the semester into a substantial Web-based presentation. The students compile text, illustrations, graphics, photographs, sound, motion video, and animation with user interfaces to encourage and guide user-based engagement and activities. The topics are up to the students; they prepare a number of preliminary exercises and assignments as they work toward the final project.

During a recent semester, a student proposed the development of a piece of software as his final project. The student had written software code that enables Apple computer users to coordinate a number of software activities simultaneously and efficiently. The student's final project for the class "rolled out" the product and illustrated its functions and uses via a Web-based presentation featuring the various media types represented in the course.

Teacher and student discussed the project as follows:

Teacher: This is a really cool tool. What do you plan to do with it?

Student: My brother and I are polishing it, and then we are going to sell it on our Web site.

Teacher: Have you done a patent search to see if anyone already holds a patent on it?

Student: No. We're thinking that we're going to do it like shareware; we'll offer it as open source and then see if we can make some money by getting users to make contributions. We'll also have multiple versions available so that first we can "hook them" with the shareware version, then later offer to upgrade them to a more complete version for an additional cost.

Teacher: What if someone already holds a patent on this?

Student: Well, we did a search and we don't think anyone has a patent. Plus there's a lot of stuff like this out there, so we think that there must be so much prior art floating around that no one could hold a patent, including us. Plus, we're not sure if we can even get a patent on the software. And besides that, wouldn't copyright protection for our intellectual property be enough protection?

Teacher: Why not hire a patent lawyer to do a search anyway, just to be safe before you move forward?

Student: That's pretty costly. We don't really have the money for that. And besides, if we found that someone has a patent, we'd have to stop. We've looked, haven't found one, and so we're just going to push ahead and assume that even if someone holds a patent on some of this, they won't find us or won't care about us, if they do find out.

This instance points to many of the issues associated with patents in the new media era.

First, as noted in this volume's Introduction, work in the patent arena is extremely specialized, requiring highly technical legal study and endorsement. In addition to law school and bar exam, patent lawyers must pass a specialized program of study and the "patent bar" exam. Patent lawyers argue cases before a special court of appeals (the Court of Appeals for the Federal Circuit—CAFC). Patent law entails an exceedingly complex and global range of entanglements, as both by practice and by multiple treaties, the United States cooperates with foreign governments in the mutual and global protection of patent claims.

Second, the costs of not doing proper patent searches are potentially high. Inventors who infringe on patents face injunctions (court rulings that stop them from producing or distributing the item) and penalties that can run from hefty fines to millions of dollars in damage payments.

As a result of the complexities, the idea that inventors can discover whether or not their invention is already patented without paying for highly technical legal advice is deeply problematic. In the decade of 2000, the US Patent Office alone received approximately 350,000 patent applications each year and granted as many as 175,000 patents in an approval process that can take from between two and four years to complete.[1] Any given piece of technology might entail multiple aspects that are available for patent protection. And defending an infringement claim can be hugely expensive: defending large claims (those with more than $25 million at risk) can cost as much as $4.5 million; defending small claims (less than $1 million at risk) can cost between $300,000 and $750,000 (or about half the amount in dispute).[2] Although legal fees vary wildly by enterprise, time, and effort, many sources propose that sound, basic, and uncomplicated patent search and application procedures cost approximately $10,000 per application. In short, the costs for proper searches and articulate applications are high, but the risks surrounding not doing proper searches are even higher, and patent search work is not an arena for the untrained.

Third, patents have become such big business in and of themselves that infringers are likely to be found by professionals tasked to look for them. Since the formation of the CAFC in 1982, many large companies have formed sub-units within their legal departments with the specific purpose of investigating, exploiting, and litigating the company's patent portfolio. In some cases, these activities provide a revenue stream that is as large (or larger) than any other business/product activity in which the company engages. The purpose of the sub-unit is to find potential infringers and either (a) exact from them a licensing arrangement, (b) issue a cease-and-desist letter advising them to stop the potential infringing activity, or (c) begin litigation against potential infringers.[3] Further, many large corporate owners of patented intellectual property participate in cross-license agreements with other companies. In a cross-license, each company lists all its patents and agrees to share them with the other, meaning that both then hold the combined total. These arrangements are often multi-organizational and further enable large IP holders to find and prosecute infringers due to the assembly effects of their pooled resources.

Patent law shares a number of features with copyright law, such that material we've already covered helps orient our view. As is the case with copyright law, US patent law drew from European patent law, especially that of Britain, in its formative stages. US patent law takes its formal start from the same constitutional clause that gave birth to copyright law. Patent law is complex and professionalized to the extent that specialized legal practices are virtually required for expert navigation in its waters. Patent law both protects and constrains technological innovation. When it protects the process, it encourages improvements, thereby furthering the interests of consumers, citizens, and corporate investors. When it constrains the process, it can block (sometimes without merit or benefit) innovation and progress, quite to the detriment of citizens, consumers, and investors, not to mention innovators themselves.

Patent law develops along the same three tracks introduced through copyright law: legislation, the courts, and technological progress. There is at least one form, however, in which one encounters troublesome patent issues in a way that is opposite from similar considerations when dealing with copyright. In the new media age of copyright, a wide range of problems with enforcing laws finds everyday users as the disadvantaged set. Because of the influence/control over the process played by large, corporate, IP holders and interests, end users feel the brunt of copyright laws that seem out of reach and reason. In circumstances relating to patent law, inventors/innovators themselves are somewhat more impacted than are end users. That is to say, the very people who are supposed to be protected and encouraged by the law are those who are most negatively impacted by aspects of patent law practices that do not seem wholly functional and efficient. Innovation itself is at risk over patent law issues.

Another difference between copyright and patent protection is the degree to which intellectual property must qualify for protection of each type. Innovators' work is protected by copyright when the innovation is committed to form; work is only protected by patents after application and submission to, and review and approval by, the Patent Office. That approval requires successful matriculation through a number of rigorous qualification tests before the patent is issued. This is another reason to hire a good patent lawyer, as a well-drawn application may have a higher probability of success in the lengthy approval process than one generated by a novice or non-specialist lawyer. Additionally, there are controversies in the patent business that apply particularly to new media. Most important, the history of software patents is a topic of intense debate and is crucial to new media interests.

Types of Patents

In defining the topic of this chapter, the Patent and Trademark Office (PTO) notes that a patent

> for an invention is the grant of a property right to the inventor, issued by the United States Patent and Trademark Office. Generally, the term of a new patent is 20 years from the date on which the application for the patent was filed in the United States or, in special cases, from the date an earlier related application was filed, subject to the payment of maintenance fees. US patent grants are effective only within the United States, US territories, and US possessions. Under certain circumstances, patent term extensions or adjustments may be available.

The right conferred by the patent grant is

> the right to exclude others from making, using, offering for sale, or selling the invention in the United States or "importing" the invention into the United States. What is granted is not the right to make, use, offer for sale, sell or import, but the right to exclude others from making, using, offering for sale, selling or importing the invention. Once a patent is issued, the patentee must enforce the patent without aid of the USPTO.[4]

There are three basic types of patents: utility, plant, and design. A utility patent provides protection for useful inventions such as processes (including business methods), machines, articles of manufacture, or compositions of matter. Software, under certain configurations and presentations, may be patented as a kind of utility or process, but there are many controversial aspects to software patenting. A plant patent provides protection for new types of asexually reproducible plants. A design patent provides protection for novel, non-functional design elements. In order for an invention to be patentable it must be new or novel, non-obvious, useful, and must satisfy a variety of statutory requirements.

Although there are many questions surrounding software patents, a crucial issue is the uniqueness and non-obviousness of the innovation. The PTO has had difficulty keeping up with the many new media/digital applications, so some questionable practices have received protection. For example, take the case of "1-click online shopping," a practice that many argue is neither unique nor non-obvious (but has nevertheless been protected through a patent held by Amazon.com).

Colin Barker reports, on CNET News.com, about actions to challenge the "1-click" patent taken by actor Peter Calveley. Calveley wants to narrow the patent and uses his blog as a forum for raising money to support his efforts in the suit. Calveley convinced the PTO to reexamine the patent on the grounds of earlier, patented, art.

Legislative Development of US Patent Law

It is almost certainly the case that the monopolistic functions of patents were considered in ancient Greece. For example, Aristotle mentions that Hippodamus of Miletos proposed a system of rewards for the discovery of useful things (Merges et al. 123). However, most histories locate the fifteenth century as the starting point for the modern conception of patents.

Patent Legislation, 1400–1780

Early Influences

In Venice in 1443, Antonius Marini "requested the right to build flour mills for each of Venice's 24 boroughs, with nobody else permitted to build a flour mill that operated without water for 20 years" (Hovey 48). In 1474 the *Venetian Act* was passed, the first law regularizing the practice of granting patents (Merges et al. 124).

> Although it is certain that the genesis of the patent system originated in Italy, there is some ambiguity as to whether it began in Venice or Florence as Filippo Brunelleschi of Florence had invented a new kind of boat in which heavy loads could be effectively hauled over the river. In 1421, the Gentlemen of the Works requested from the Lords of the Council of Florence grant an exclusive privilege for Filippo Brunelleschi to make and use his invention on the waters of Florence for three years. Quite a few patents had already been granted prior to 1474 when Venice came up with its first patent statute. (Devaiah, I: Early Patents)

Early England

The first known English patent was issued in 1449 to Flemish-born John of Utynam for protection of a stained glass manufacturing method previously unknown to the English. The patent lasted for twenty years, and the stained glass process was used to make the windows of Eton College (biojudiciary.org, paragraph 3).

As we saw with copyrights, the earliest uses for patents in England were at the behest of royalty and served as much to encourage loyalty by handing out monopolistic favors and riches as to encourage invention. Many of the grants went to individuals in businesses in which they were not the lead innovators and did not, therefore, reward original invention. There were a number of different types of royal decrees carrying the weight of patent-type monopoly: royal charters, letters close (to instruct private persons), and letters patent (to instruct the public). "All the instructions and directives were recorded in rolls. Charter Rolls, Close Rolls and Patent Rolls were used to record the various types of state papers. Records suggest that Patent Rolls have been used since 1202" (Devaiah, II: UK Patents). Patents were also often used as trade incentives for businesses to engage favored foreign entities.

The Crown so abused the granting of exclusive rights that in 1624 Parliament tried to discipline the administrative use of exclusive grants by asking the courts to review all such grants to be sure that the item for which protection was sought was really unique and first. The Parliament also suspended all grants that had been issued that were still in effect and set the period of protection for new patented items to fourteen years. By the mid-1700s, English law required that applications for patents include specifications of the invention. America adopted many of the principles and practices found in English law, as did much of Europe, though France promoted a natural property rights foundation that suggested that inventors had natural rights to monopoly on their inventions. Most colonies with early patent laws rejected this idea in favor of a government-granted right based on application and review, as did the eventual national law enacted by the US *Constitution* (Devaiah, Procedures to Grant a Patent).

Colonial America and Early United States

Practices in many of the colonies preceded the eventual federal patent laws and state statutes. Grants were issued as early as 1641 in Massachusetts. Some colonies, however, limited or forbade the practice of patent-based monopoly, and many early leaders, Jefferson foremost among them, strongly opposed patents.

The Constitutional Convention in 1789 resolved to put patents into the Constitution by reversing Article II of the Articles of Confederation that had precluded Congress from issuing patents. The Patent Commission was formed in 1790, and the first patent was issued that year after the development of the *Patent Act of 1790*. The *Patent Act of 1790* followed British law and included both specification and examination requirements. It established and utilized the principle of "first to invent" rather than "first to patent." The initial *Act* was replaced by the *Patent Act of 1793* that added an aspect that soon became a serious impediment to the administration of patent law. The *Patent Act of 1793* added "judicial construction," whereby a court could grant a patent "on the face of it" without ascertaining novelty and utility. Many subsequent court cases were forced to deal with this articulation.

As was the case with copyright law, English law was not the only model that American lawmakers could follow. In 1791, French legislators passed the French patent law. Similar to the French/European (non-English) preference, the French law stresses the moral rights of authors via a natural law perspective not adopted by the Americans.

Nineteenth-Century America

In 1802, the Patent Office became distinct from the Trademark Office; in 1849 the office was placed in the Department of the Interior. The *Patent Act* of 1836 constructed the modern system of technical examination of patents as part of the process. That procedure was strengthened in 1861 when examiners were added to the staff of the office. In 1878 and 1887, respectively, the US patent process (1) aligned its patent timetables with many foreign practices and (2) joined the *Paris Convention for the Protection of Industrial Property*, thereby making effective dates in one country apply in others. In 1893 the Federal Court of Appeals system for patent cases replaced the state-based court appeals systems.

Twentieth-Century America

By the turn of the century, big business figured out how to leverage the patent system against individual inventors and in favor of corporations (Jaffe and Lerner 92). The *Sherman Anti-Trust Act* of 1890 was in part an attempt to address this issue. While the twentieth century would generally feature continued expansion of corporate control over patent-protected intellectual property, court application of stringent anti-trust enforcement, especially from the 1930s on, put a damper on the corporate use of patents as part of an aggressive business strategy until the early 1980s (Rivette and Kline 37–38).

The federal system underwent numerous changes during the first half of the century. In particular, control over the Patent Office was once again transferred in 1925, this time to its current location in the Commerce Department. A significant change in the court structure regarding patents took place in 1929 when the appeal process was moved from the appellate court of Washington, D.C., to the Court of Customs and Patent Appeals.

The middle of the century saw two especially significant changes to the patent law. In 1930, the *Plant Patent Act* went into effect, opening up an entirely new area of inventions meriting protection. In 1939, the two-year grace period regarding certain statutory bars was reduced to one year; in 1940, the two-year grace period relating to acts of prior use or prior publication was likewise reduced to one year (biojudiciary.org). In 1946, the law was amended to confine the "first to invent" principle to discoveries within the United States. Importantly for new media, through the 1950s and early 1960s "the Patent Office [said]: whatever software is, it is definitely *not* patentable subject matter" (Merges et al. 1007).

1952 saw a significant revision of the law that included provisions defining infringement (biojudiciary.org) and specifying novelty as a critical criterion for protection. The law that is in place at the current time owes its basic structure (sans later revisions) to the 1952 iteration (Ladas & Parry). There were a number of additional revisions through the 1950s and 1960s.

In 1968, the *Patent Cooperation Treaty* was signed; it went into effect in 1970 and enabled international patent protection among cooperating countries with a single application. In 1970, the name of the office responsible for patents changed again to the Patent and Trademark Office.

Throughout the 1970s, the Patent Court worked to differentiate between claims that mathematical formulae could be patented as part of software development and claims made for the inventions that implemented or applied the formulae (Merges et al. 1015). Throughout the decade, the patent status of software remained murky. (This subject will be covered in more detail in the patent litigation section below.)

Perhaps the most important changes in modern times took place in 1982 when the Court of Appeals for the Federal Circuit Court was created specifically to deal with patent appeals. This court became the arbiter of all disputes for patent infringement or validity and was peopled with patent specialists. One of the principal effects of the establishment of the Court appears to have been directly related to its nature as a specialist enterprise: the number of patents issued and contested virtually doubled within the decade following the establishment of the Court (Rivette and Kline; Jaffe and Lerner). Further, with increasing frequency, the Court found in favor of patent holders and against accused infringers such that by the 1990s corporations had fully turned toward patents as an aggressive strategy for wealth creation (Rivette and Kline). This refinement in the court process, mandated by legislative modifications, combined with the explosive increase in new computational technologies to change, perhaps forever, practices surrounding patent enforcement in America.

In effect, the changes led to a swamping of the patent office to the extent that while the office encouraged patent filings (due to administrative changes that turned the office into a governmental profit center) at the same time it found itself unable to adequately cope with the avalanche of applications. Most pundits in the new century, and many Congressional leaders, lament the understaffed and underfunded status of the office; at the time of this writing, Congress is investigating changes to the office and its procedures.

As noted in Chapter 1, many of the recommendations of the CONTU group began to become law in 1980, so that during that decade the courts started hearing the first generation of cases examining the implications of copying computer software. The first cases involved copyright. As will be shown by the patent cases discussed below, the courts made mixed rulings concerning patent rights and software through the 1970s and 1980s, until *State Street Bank & Trust v. Signature* in 1998 established the patentability of software.

In 1984, the *Semiconductor Chip Protection Act* blended copyright and patent protection as a way to protect the proprietary architecture of computer chips. As software inventors/authors continued to file applications that showed their work to be associated with some process (rather than merely pure code), the patent system continued moving toward protecting software. "By 1994, there were an estimated 14,000 issued software patents in the United States. Nevertheless, the Federal Circuit continued to debate the patentability of software" (Merges et al. 1016).

The General Agreement on Tariffs and Trade (*GATT*) *Uruguay Round Act* of 1994 and the 1995 World Trade Organization *Trade Related Aspects of Intellectual Property* (*TRIPS*) law included a change from a seventeen-year patent term to a twenty-year patent term (starting with the patent application's filing date). The debate that surrounded this modification to patent law created much upheaval that later led to passage of the *American Inventors' Protection Act of 1999* (biojudiciary.org).

In 1996 the PTO issued *Examination Guidelines for Computer-Implemented Inventions*, which reiterates the concept that code itself is not substantial so cannot be patented—it is not descriptive material nor a physical thing so is not statutory—while "a claimed computer-readable medium encoded with a computer program defines structural and functional interrelationships between the computer program and the medium which permit the computer's program's functionality to be realized, and is thus statutory" (Merges et al. 1029).

Controversies fomented by this rule and the continued explosion of software technology and efforts to protect it came to a head in *State Street Bank & Trust v. Signature Financial Group* (1998), a case in which the courts validated the patentability of business processes that were enacted via software. This case will be covered in the litigation section below.

In 1999, the *American Inventors' Protection Act* (*AIPA*) was passed to shield inventors from deceptive practices while also lowering US Patent and Trademark Office (USPTO) fees and clarifying and simplifying various administrative procedures of the office. The year 1999 also saw the passage of the *Anticybersquatting Consumer Protection Act*, an amendment to the *Lanham Anti-Trust Act*, as an effort to curtail URL abuse and cybersquatting on the World Wide Web. The *AIPA* is a form of trademark protection, to be further discussed in Chapter 4. [ELL]

The outcome of patent disputes is often an agreement between the companies wherein the patent holder licenses the technology to the infringer, usually following a damages payment, either on the way to, or after, a court finding that establishes the proper rights holder. For example, *New York Times* reporter Laura M. Holson describes a settlement between Vonage and SprintNextel that includes Vonage's payment and agreement to license Sprint's Internet-calling technology.

Traditional Media Patent Cases with New Media Implications

Graver Tank & Mfg. Co. v. Linde Air Products, Co., 339 U.S. 605 (1950)

Graver Tank is the first Supreme Court case to squarely address patent infringement under what is known as the "doctrine of equivalents." It is now commonly recognized that there are two types of patent infringement: literal infringement and infringement under the doctrine of equivalents. To prove literal infringement, a patentee must prove that the words of the claims of the patent "literally" read on the accused device. Alternatively, as set forth by the Court in *Graver Tank*, in order to prevent an infringer from making minor changes that would place the accused device outside of the literal words of the claims, a patentee may prove equivalent infringement by showing that the accused device "performs substantially the same function in substantially the same way to obtain the same result." Here the Court agreed with the trial court, which determined that a patent that claimed a welding composition having a combination of an alkaline earth metal silicate (e.g., magnesium) and calcium fluoride was infringed under the doctrine of equivalents by a welding composition having silicates of calcium and manganese (which is not an alkaline earth metal).

A simple example illustrates the difference between the two types of infringement. Suppose a patent claims a baking composition comprising butter, eggs, salt, sugar, flour, baking power, vanilla, and milk. If someone comes along with the same recipe but substitutes Splenda® for sugar, has this person committed patent infringement? There cannot be literal infringement because the patent claim does not literally read on the allegedly infringing recipe. There can, however, be infringement under the doctrine of equivalents. Even though this minor change places the accused recipe outside of the literal words of the patent claim, the accused recipe performs substantially the same function in substantially the same way to obtain the same result.

Graham v. John Deere, 383 U.S. 1 (1966)

Graham is the first modern Supreme Court case to address the critical issue in patent law of "obviousness." As previously discussed, to secure a patent on an invention, the invention must be new, useful, and non-obvious. Before Congress revised the *Patent Act* in 1952, obviousness was a creature only of the common law. *Graham* was the first case after the 1952 revision in which the Supreme Court heard a case involving the obviousness standard.

In *Graham*, the Court set forth the test that is still used by courts today. Under *Graham*, courts look at four factors (often called the "*Graham* factors") to determine if an invention would have been obvious at the time the invention was made to a person of ordinary skill in the art to which the subject matter pertains. These factors are: the scope and content of the prior art; the differences between the prior art and the claims at issue; the level of ordinary skill in the art; and, finally, secondary considerations of non-obviousness, such as commercial success, long-felt but unsolved need, and the failure of others.

The patent at issue in *Graham* covered a device that was "designed to absorb shock from plow shanks as they plow[ed] through rocky soil [which] prevent[ed] damage to the plow." The Court determined that this invention was obvious, because it was not sufficiently different from the prior art. Thus, the Court affirmed the finding of the lower court that the patent was invalid.

Markman v. Westview Instruments Inc., 517 U.S. 370 (1996)

Markman was the most important patent case of its decade. In a unanimous opinion, the Supreme Court affirmed the Federal Circuit and held that determining what the claims of a patent mean is a task for the courts to decide as a question of law, not a question for juries to decide as a question of fact. Before this case, determining what the claims of a patent meant (often called "construing the claims") was a task for a jury, which often led to unpredictable outcomes after years of litigating the patent.

Now, common practice is for District Courts to hold *Markman* hearings, where the words of the claims that are disputed by the parties are construed by the Court. Determining whether an accused product infringes a claim of a patent is thus a two-step process. First, the Court construes the claims; second, a jury determines whether the claim fits the accused device.

In *Markman*, the patent at issue was directed at managing inventory at a dry cleaner. Claim 1 of Markman's patent stated that the claimed product could "maintain an inventory total" and "detect and localize spurious additions to inventory." Thus, the term "inventory" was a disputed term. The jury found infringement of Claim 1, but the District Court subsequently granted the defendant's motion for judgment as a matter of law based upon the Court's own construction of the term "inventory." Markman appealed this ruling, but both the Federal Circuit and Supreme Court affirmed, holding that it is within the province of the Court to construe the claims of a patent.

Warner-Jenkinson Co. v. Hilton Davis Chem. Co., 520 U.S. 17 (1997)

Warner-Jenkinson is another very important patent case decided by the Supreme Court in the 1990s. In *Warner-Jenkinson*, the Court reaffirmed that the doctrine of equivalents outlined in *Graver Tank* is still good law. Here, the Court was faced with the issue of determining how an amendment to the claims during prosecution affects the scope of the claims during litigation. In other words, the Court had to determine whether or not there was infringement under the doctrine of equivalents when the patentee narrowed its patent claims during prosecution of the patent in the US Patent Office.

In *Warner-Jenkinson*, the plaintiff developed an ultrafiltration process to purify dyes. During prosecution of the patent, the patent examiner rejected the patent claims as originally written in light of prior art that disclosed an ultrafiltration process that operated at a pH of over 9.0 (pH is a measure of the acidity or alkalinity of a solution; water has a "neutral" pH of 7.0, whereas carbonated water has an acidic pH of 3.0, and concentrated hydrochloric acid has a pH approaching 0.0; on the other end of the scale, milk of magnesia has a pH of 10.0, whereas household ammonia has a pH of 11.9). In response to the Patent Office rejection, the patentee amended the patent claims to maintain that the process operated at a pH from 6.0 to 9.0.

After the patent was issued, the patentee sued the defendant, which had a process that operated at a pH of 5.0 and thus did not literally infringe the claimed process having a pH of 6.0 to 9.0. While it was undisputed that the upper limit of 9.0 was added in order to distinguish the prior art during prosecution of the patent, the reason for adding the lower limit of 6.0 was unclear from the record. The lower limit certainly did not serve to distinguish the prior art, which said nothing about pH levels below 6.0. Thus, while a lower limit of 6.0, by its mere inclusion, became a material element of the claim, that aspect did not necessarily preclude the application of the doctrine of equivalents as to that element.

The Court in *Warner-Jenkinson* held that there is a presumption that a change to a patent claim during patent prosecution is related to patentability, and that the patentee bears the burden of rebutting this presumption. If the patentee cannot rebut the presumption, then "prosecution history estoppel" applies as to surrendered subject matter, and the patentee cannot claim as an equivalent in litigation what it surrendered during prosecution. The Court sent the case back to the lower court to determine whether the patentee could rebut the presumption; if not, there could not be infringement of the claimed process operating at a pH of 6.0 to 9.0 by the accused process operating at a pH of 5.0.

State Street Bank & Trust Co. v. Signature Financial Group, 149 F.3d 1368 (Fed. Cir. 1998)

State Street Bank is an important Federal Circuit decision because it establishes that "business methods" can be patented. A business method patent, as its name implies, is a patent that covers a way of doing something in a business or transactional setting. The Federal Circuit held that as long as the way of doing something produces a "useful, concrete and tangible result," then the invention is patentable subject matter under section 101. To be patentable, the business method must also meet the other criteria for patentability, namely, it must still be new and non-obvious.

The patent at issue in *State Street Bank* was for a "Data Processing System for Hub and Spoke Financial Services Configuration." The "spokes" that the patent was concerned with were mutual funds that pooled their assets into a central "hub." This method produced a share price that was used for several things. Because this process produced a "useful, concrete, and tangible result," namely, a share price, the Federal Circuit held that the patent was not invalid for failure to claim statutory subject matter as required by section 101. Since the *State Street Bank* case, the US Patent Office has issued numerous business method patents, many of which are Internet-related.

Festo Corp. v. Shoketsu Kinzoku Kogyo Kabushiki Co., 535 U.S. 722 (2002)

In *Festo*, the Supreme Court further refined its *Warner-Jenkinson* holding regarding the interplay of the doctrine of equivalents and prosecution history estoppel. The Federal Circuit had held that any amendment to a claim during prosecution results in a complete bar to the patentee claiming as an equivalent the subject matter surrendered. Thus, under the Federal Circuit's holding, if a claim of a patent initially required a "metal wire," and during prosecution the patentee changed this claim language to a "copper wire," the patentee would be estopped from arguing during litigation that a device with a steel wire infringed the patent. In this example, the patentee surrendered the equivalent (the steel wire) when it amended its claim.

The Supreme Court, however, reversed the Federal Circuit and held that the bar is not an absolute bar but rather is a flexible bar. As set forth by the Court in *Warner-Jenkinson*, when a patentee amends a claim, there is a presumption that the amendment relates to patentability, and here the Court reaffirmed this principle. The Court also named three types of amendments that do not surrender subject matter, i.e., three ways that a patentee can overcome the presumption of subject matter surrender. First, the equivalent was unforeseen at the time the patent application was filed. Second, the reason for the change to the claim bears only a "tangential relation" to the equivalent. Third, and acting as a catch-all, "there may be some other reason suggesting that the patentee could not reasonably be expected to have described the insubstantial substitute in question."

In *Festo*, the asserted patents involved covered magnetic rodless cylinders for a piston-driven device. During prosecution, Festo amended its claims to include two limitations: a pair of sealing rings and the requirement that the sleeve be made of a magnetizable material. The defendant sold a competing product that was similar but that had a different type of sealing ring and a sleeve that was made of a non-magnetizable alloy. The Court held that because Festo amended its claims for reasons relating to patentability, prosecution history estoppel applied. Ultimately, the Court sent the case back to the lower courts to determine exactly whether the narrowing amendments surrendered the equivalent at issue.

Phillips v. AWH, 415 F.3d 1303 (Fed. Cir. 2005) (en banc)

Phillips was a decision that was heard *en banc* (i.e., by all the judges on the Federal Circuit), as opposed to the typical panel of three judges that usually hears an appeal. The issue before the Court in *Phillips* was the role that extrinsic evidence should play in construing a claim. There are two categories of evidence that courts look to construing a claim. The first is intrinsic evidence, which consists of the claim itself, the specification, and the prosecution history. The second is extrinsic evidence, which consists of dictionaries, encyclopedias, expert testimony, and anything else that is not intrinsic evidence.

In *Phillips*, the Federal Circuit set forth that extrinsic evidence is useful, but that it is less significant than intrinsic evidence. Thus, *Phillips* generally requires a District Court to consult extrinsic evidence only if the intrinsic evidence is insufficient to construe a claim. Nonetheless, the Court, in rather murky fashion, also explained that extrinsic evidence can play a role in claim construction, depending on the specific facts of a case.

The patent in *Phillips* was for a type of vandal-resistant wall that contained "internal steel baffles." The Federal Circuit looked to the intrinsic evidence, i.e., the claims, the specification, and the prosecution history and construed the disputed term "baffles." The Court reached a different construction for the term "baffles" than the District Court and accordingly sent the case back to the District Court for further proceedings.

KSR Int'l Co. v. Teleflex Inc., 127 S. Ct. 1727 (April 30, 2007)

In *KSR*, the Supreme Court rejected the "rigid approach" of the Federal Circuit in favor of an "expansive and flexible approach" on whether a patent claim was obvious in view of prior art. In *KSR*, the patentee sued the defendant for infringement on a patent claiming an adjustable vehicle control pedal connected to an electronic throttle control. The defendant argued that it was merely obvious, and therefore not patentable, to combine these elements. The defendant's win in the district court was overturned by the Federal Circuit. The Federal Circuit held that there was no teaching, suggestion or motivation (TSM) to combine prior art that in combination disclosed the claimed invention. The Supreme Court rejected the Federal Circuit's rigid TSM application.

The Supreme Court stated that "[a] person of ordinary skill is also a person of ordinary creativity, not an automaton." The Supreme Court held that the "obviousness analysis cannot be confined by a formalistic conception of the words teaching, suggestion, and motivation, or by overemphasis on the importance of published articles and the explicit content of issued patents." The Supreme Court stated that "[i]n many fields it may be that there is little discussion of obvious techniques or combinations, and it often may be the case that market demand, rather than scientific literature, will drive design trends." Thus, the Supreme Court noted, "[g]ranting patent protection to advances that would occur in the ordinary course without real innovation retards progress and may, in the case of patents combining previously known elements, deprive prior inventions of their value or utility."

Turning to the facts in *KSR*, the Supreme Court held that the district court was correct to conclude that, as of the time of the alleged invention, "it was obvious to a person of ordinary skill to combine [a pivot-mounted pedal] with a pivot-mounted pedal position sensor." Indeed, "[t]here then existed a marketplace that created a strong incentive to convert mechanical pedals to electronic pedals, and the prior art taught a number of methods for achieving this advance."

New Media Cases and Patent Law

Amazon.com v. Barnesandnoble.com, 239 F.3d 1343 (Fed. Cir. 2001)

In this Internet technology case, Amazon.com (Amazon) brought a patent infringement lawsuit against Barnes & Noble (BN) based on its business method patent for its 1-click® ordering method, which Amazon still uses today. Based on prior use of the Amazon.com Web site, the Web site "remembers" a user's information so that shipping address, billing address, and the like do not need to be re-entered to order an item. Thus, as the feature's name implies, a user simply clicks the 1-click® button, and the item is scheduled to be shipped.[5]

BN, on its Web site, installed a similar feature to Amazon's 1-click® button, which it called "Express Lane." This feature allowed a user to click one button to order a product. Amazon brought suit against BN, alleging that the Express Lane feature infringed its patent.

The trial court agreed with Amazon and granted a preliminary injunction in its favor (effective November 4, 1999—during the winter holiday shopping season), prohibiting BN from using the Express Lane feature. To grant a preliminary injunction in a patent infringement case, a court must determine that it is likely a patentee will prevail on its claim of patent infringement. The trial court determined that it was likely that the Express Lane feature infringed Amazon's patent, and thus it granted the preliminary injunction (upon Amazon's filing of an undertaking of $10 million to be awarded to BN should it be determined later that the preliminary injunction should not have been granted).

On February 14, 2001, the Federal Circuit, however, reversed. It found that while Amazon was likely to prevail on its claim of infringement, BN presented prior art evidence sufficient to cast doubt on the validity of Amazon's patent, and the Court reversed the preliminary injunction. Ultimately, the parties reached a confidential settlement, and the validity of Amazon's patent was never determined.

Rambus Inc. v. Infineon Techs. AG, 318 F.3d 1081 (Fed. Cir. 2003)

Rambus is an important case in the field of standard-setting organizations. Standard-setting organizations ensure that certain technical standards are agreed upon so that electronic devices can be designed to communicate and work with other electronic devices in accordance with those technical standards.[6] For several years in the 1990s, Rambus was a member of the Joint Electron Devices Engineering Council (JEDEC). JEDEC is a standard-setting organization that develops standards for semiconductor technologies, and it is composed of numerous competitors in the semiconductor industry. Importantly, JEDEC required its members to disclose patents and patent applications that related to the standards JEDEC was setting.

In this case, Rambus brought a patent infringement suit against Infineon based on its patents for dynamic random access memory (DRAM) technology. Infineon counterclaimed for fraud, based on allegations that Rambus failed to disclose certain patents and patent applications to JEDEC. In order to prove fraud, Infineon had to prove that Rambus made a false representation or an omission when it had a duty to disclose. Although a jury found that Rambus was liable for fraud, the Federal Circuit reversed, agreeing with Rambus that no reasonable jury could find that Rambus breached a duty to disclose to JEDEC.

The Federal Circuit first determined what duty to disclose Rambus owed JEDEC. The Court thoroughly reviewed JEDEC's disclosure policy and determined that the policy required patents and patent applications to be disclosed only where they were needed to practice under the standard. The Court then looked to whether Rambus violated this duty and determined that the adopted standards did not cover Rambus's patents or patent applications. Thus, the Federal Circuit reversed the jury's finding of fraud against Rambus.

Eolas Techs. v. Microsoft Corp., 399 F.3d 1325 (Fed. Cir. 2005)

This case involved technology relating to Internet browsers. The patentee, Eolas, sued Microsoft on its patent described as a "distributing hypermedia method for automatically invoking external applications providing interaction and display of embedded objects within a hypermedia context." As explained by the Federal Circuit, Eolas's claimed invention "allow[ed] a user to use a Web browser in a fully interactive environment." Eolas alleged that certain aspects of Microsoft's Internet Explorer (IE) infringed Eolas's patent.

The importance of this case lies in its analysis of one of the lesser-used sections of the patent code that defines infringement. Under 35 U.S.C. § 271(f), an entity commits patent infringement if it ships from the United States a substantial portion of a patented invention in uncombined parts and actively induces the combination of such components outside of the United States. Eolas claimed damages for domestic sales of Windows with IE, as well as for foreign sales under § 271(f).

One of the ways in which Microsoft exported Windows was by exporting a small number of golden master disks that contained Windows code. Companies abroad then used the disks to replicate the code and place it onto computers for sale outside of the United States. Thus, the Federal Circuit was faced with determining whether Microsoft's shipping of these golden master disks constituted infringement under § 271(f). After reviewing the precise language used in § 271(f), the Court held that software code is a patentable invention under § 271(f) and that the golden master disks are components of the computer program invention. Thus, Microsoft's activities constituted infringement under § 271(f).

NTP, Inc. v. Research in Motion, Ltd., 418 F.3d 1282 (Fed. Cir. 2005)

This case is, of course, the famous "BlackBerry" case. The case is noteworthy not only for its legal holdings but for the impact it threatened to have on the nation and the saga that it became. The case began in 2001 when NTP, a patent-holding company based in Virginia, sued Research in Motion (RIM), a Canadian company. NTP claimed that RIM infringed NTP's method and system patent claims covering wireless e-mail technology.

In 2002, the jury found for NTP. The total damages were calculated at $53,704,323. RIM appealed, and the trial court stayed an injunction pending an appeal. The Federal Circuit reversed in part and affirmed in part, sending the case back to the trial court. In March 2004, NTP and RIM announced a settlement wherein RIM agreed to pay $450 million, but the settlement fell apart. The case went back up on appeal, and in August 2005 the Federal Circuit issued its second opinion setting forth important legal principles regarding the extent to which an accused method or system must be practiced within the United States in order to infringe under 35 U.S.C. § 271.

The Federal Circuit held that in order for RIM to infringe the asserted method claims, each of the steps had to be performed within the United States. Because the method claims involved the use of hardware located in Canada, the Federal Circuit held that RIM could not infringe the method claims. As to the system claims, however, the Federal Circuit affirmed the jury's finding of infringement. The Court held that the accused system was used within the United States as long as the United States "is the place at which the system as a whole is put into service, *i.e.*, the place where control of the system is exercised and beneficial use of the system is obtained." The Federal Circuit held that the system was effectively located in the United States, even if some of the hardware was located in Canada.

In 2005 and early 2006, the case gained national attention as it looked like the District Court might enter an injunction, which would have shut down service to all "BlackBerry" users (at the time around four million people in the United States). Following this threat, the case ultimately settled in March 2006 for $612,500,000.

eBay, Inc. v. MercExchange, 126 S. Ct. 1837 (2006)

The *eBay* case is significant because in this case the Supreme Court rejected the general rule that, absent exceptional circumstances, a permanent injunction restraining further infringements should issue once patent validity and infringement have been determined. In doing so, the Supreme Court held that a permanent injunction should be granted only "in accordance with the principles of equity" as applied in non-patent cases.

The *eBay* case stemmed from a long-running dispute between eBay and MercExchange involving eBay's popular online auction site. At issue in the case was eBay's "Buy It Now" feature, which allows customers to purchase items listed on eBay's Web site for a fixed, listed price, bypassing the bidding process. In 2000, MercExchange had entered into licensing negotiations with eBay relating to its three business method patents. Those negotiations broke down, and in 2001 MercExchange sued eBay.

After a five-week trial, a jury found eBay and Half.com liable for patent infringement and awarded damages totaling $35 million to MercExchange. Both sides filed post-verdict motions, including a motion by MercExchange for a permanent injunction restraining future infringement by eBay. The District Court denied MercExchange's motion for a permanent injunction, holding that issuance of an injunction following a verdict of infringement is not automatic but instead is governed by traditional equitable principles, which require consideration of a four-factor test: (1) whether the plaintiff will suffer irreparable harm if an injunction does not issue; (2) whether the plaintiff has an adequate remedy at law; (3) whether granting the injunction is in the public interest; and (4) whether the balance of the hardships tips in favor of the plaintiff.

On appeal, the Federal Circuit reversed the District Court's denial of MercExchange's motion for a permanent injunction, applying a "general rule that courts will issue permanent injunctions against patent infringement absent exceptional circumstances."

In a unanimous decision, the Supreme Court held that the Federal Circuit erred in its categorical grant of injunctive relief. Noting that the *Patent Act* expressly provides that an injunction "may" issue in accordance with the principles of equity, the Court held that the traditional four-factor test applies to disputes arising under the *Patent Act* and must be used to determine when injunctive relief is appropriate.

The Supreme Court concluded that although the District Court recited the proper four-factor test, it erred in applying that test. More particularly, the Supreme Court held that neither a patentee's willingness to license its patents nor its lack of commercial activity in practicing the patents is sufficient to preclude a finding of irreparable harm. The Court recognized that some patent holders, including universities and "self-made" inventors, might reasonably choose to license their patents rather than practice the invention themselves, and that such actions should not categorically preclude them from satisfying the four-factor test and obtaining an injunction.

Without taking any position on whether a permanent injunction should issue, the Court thus vacated the judgment of the Federal Circuit and remanded the case to the District Court for a determination of whether MercExchange would be entitled to an injunction under a proper application of the four-factor test.

Two decidedly different concurring opinions, one authored by Chief Justice Roberts and the other by Justice Kennedy, demonstrate a fundamental disagreement among the justices regarding whether and when an injunction should issue against an adjudged infringer. Chief Justice Roberts admonishes against the District Courts' exercising their equitable discretion on "a whim" and observes that when applying the four-factor test, "a page of history is worth a volume of logic." In other words, even if the four-factor test is applied, a permanent injunction should follow a finding of patent infringement in most cases. Justice Kennedy takes a more restrictive view of a patentee's right to an injunction. Justice Kennedy thus instructed the lower courts to consider "the nature of the patent being enforced" and "the economic function of the patent holder" in evaluating the traditional four-factor test. In doing so, he cautioned against granting injunctive relief to patentees who "use patents not as a basis for producing and selling goods but, instead, primarily for obtaining licensing fees," i.e., today's so-called "patent trolls." Justice Kennedy added that the consequences of injunctive relief for business method patents must be considered, and the "potential vagueness and suspect validity" of some of these patents also may affect the calculus under the four-factor test. He further observed that where the patented invention is merely a small component of a larger product, monetary damages may well adequately compensate the patent holder, while an injunction may not serve the public interest. Thus, in Justice Kennedy's view, a lower court evaluating the traditional four-factor test will be faced with considerations not present in some earlier cases—considerations that may make an injunction more difficult for a patentee to obtain.

TiVo v. EchoStar, 516 F.3d 1290 (Fed. Cir. 2008)

Some EchoStar set-top boxes have DVR capabilities. Both EchoStar and TiVo devices use multimedia time warping system technology that allows DVRs to record live television while the owner watches a pre-recorded program. TiVo filed suit against EchoStar in 2004, alleging that its use of that technology infringed a TiVo patent. A jury awarded TiVo $73.9 million in damages.

On appeal, the Federal Circuit held that there was a failure of proof of literal infringement and reversed the judgment of infringement of the hardware claims with respect to all of the accused devices, and remanded for any further proceedings that may be necessary with respect to those claims. The Federal Circuit affirmed the judgment of infringement of the software claims with respect to all of the accused devices. Because the damages calculation at trial was not predicated on the infringement of particular claims and because the Federal Circuit upheld the jury's verdict that all of the accused devices infringe the software claims, the Federal Circuit affirmed the damages award entered by the district court.

The Federal Circuit noted that the district court's injunction was stayed during the course of the appeal, and the stay would dissolve when this appeal became final. The Federal Circuit stated that when the appeal became final, the district court could make a determination as to the additional damages, if any, that TiVo has sustained while the stay of the permanent injunction has been in effect.

This case illustrates an application of the Supreme Court's decision in *eBay* and that some courts will still enter a permanent injunction even though a defendant has a significant number of customers who will be impacted by the injunction.

IBM Corp. v. Amazon.com, Inc. No. 06–452 (E.D. Tex. filed Oct. 23, 2006)

This recently filed case illustrates that a large company such as IBM will assert its patent(s) against others, even though the asserted patent(s) is/are not part of the large company's business.

Here IBM asserted infringement by Amazon of two patents. One patent is directed to a system for ordering items using an electronic catalog. The patent discloses steps for searching a catalog database for information on a customer-selected item where the catalog database resides on a public computer. Information on the customer-selected item is downloaded to a Customer/Requestor computer system. The second asserted patent is directed to a system for adjusting hypertext links with weighed user goals and activities.

IBM asserted that Amazon "has built its business by infringing IBM's patents." On May 8, 2007, it was announced that the parties had settled all patent lawsuits between them for an undisclosed amount of money paid to IBM and a long-term patent cross-license agreement.

Amazon stated that the company's license to IBM's portfolio and specifically to its Web technology patents, "gives us greater freedom to innovate for our customers." IBM stated that it was glad the matter had been resolved through negotiation and licensing, and it looked "forward to a more productive relationship with Amazon in the future." [7] [RR]

Summarizing Patents and New Media

A number of aspects in the patent arena have problematic implications for new media. To begin, the high costs and time-intensive nature of the patent process work against the largely entrepreneurial nature of the development of new media. Small-volume and/or less-than-wealthy inventors struggle with the cost of patent searches and applications. Further, small or independent operations are in competition with huge multinational corporations, not only in the process of developing and implementing innovations (where small, quick, and nimble can be an advantage) but also in the legal arena where stables of highly paid corporate lawyers operate on a playing field that is anything but level and where scale can overwhelm potential competition.

The application process can take from three to five years for completion; the pace of developing new media far outstrips the ability of the patent application process to keep up. Once again, the large, corporate entity is advantaged in that it can afford to wait patiently through the long approval process as its many holdings and diverse products turn profits, while the entrepreneur needs a quick return on investment and capitalization.

Especially since business process and software patents were ruled acceptable, the Patent Office has been swamped far beyond capacity and reason. Patent approval work is so specialized that the office has difficulty retaining employees, since private pay outstrips government levels and specialized Patent Office employees are highly sought after in private enterprise. The enormous number of applications has challenged the office well beyond its limits and abilities to respond. Thus the application process takes even longer than ever. Conversely, new media innovations happen more quickly than ever.

Perhaps even more worrisome is the fact that early on in the process (just after the office began approving process and software patents) there was a general lack of deep expertise among regulators and examiners about the new digital media elements included in filings. At the same time, mountains of applications involving newly emerging, esoteric digital processes encouraged hasty and sometimes unwise patent approvals. For example, some patents issued in the early stages of the Internet now appear to be overly broad and perhaps spectacularly inappropriate. As illustration, one merely needs to do an Internet search of the term "patents for online video." The search returns numerous instances of claims of infringement involving companies holding patents related to transmitting, storing, and playing video over the Internet. Some early recipients of such patents claim that they should benefit—through license and royalty—each and every time a video is played using the Internet. Video is not the only instance of such broad claims based on approved patents, but it is a good example of the difficulties with many patents issued early in the Internet age.

Despite the difficulties, the patent system is alive and well in the United States and around the world. As already noted, a tremendous number of applications are filed, and the disputes that are regular fare in the courts are big business for corporations and legal firms. Patents and the processes used to establish them are not going away merely because of their shortcomings and challenges to them from new media. Understanding the fundamentals of the patent system can help new media participants steer clear of legal entanglements and infringements as they work to develop innovation and express digital creativity. [ELL]

Discussion Questions

1. Many people oppose software patents on the principle that they stifle innovation and are frequently spurious. Discuss pros and cons of software patents.
2. Should the government develop a two-tier patent system that would provide a low-cost and faster approval process available only to small businesses and individuals?
3. Should the government outlaw domain commerce (other than initial purchases for registration)?
4. How should the government remediate the difficulties in the Patent Office?
5. Discuss the twenty-year patent term. Is it the correct length? Refinements?

CHAPTER FOUR

Trademarks

A new teaching initiative finds author Dr. Ed Lamoureux entering the virtual world of *Second Life* as Professor Beliveau in order to teach classes and perform (by singing and playing guitar) as "the Professor." Moving into these new roles garners some online press attention. Lamoureux posts his syllabi and other plans to a blog, he is interviewed for an online podcast, and a number of bloggers post stories about his class offerings. The work seems worthy of special treatment on Lamoureux's personal Web pages, so he decides to add links to the activities.

All of the major category headings indicating links on Lamoureux's homepage <http://slane.bradley.edu/com/faculty/lamoureux/website2/index.html> feature a word mark as a visual indicator as well as a line of text describing the material to which the link is set. The first draft of the addition of the *Second Life* (*SL*) material featured the *SL* banner as the visual marker, with the text "to my *Second Life* Activities." The link goes to a page <http://slane.bradley.edu/com/faculty/lamoureux/website2/slstuff.html> that explains the activities and links to a number of files/pages that further describe the work.

However, on reflection, Lamoureux wonders if using the *SL* logo in this fashion might present a problem. For example, the text elements of the banner (the *SL* title) carry with them the registered trademark symbol [®]. Now, on the one hand, one can use the term *SL* in reference to the site/world without asking for permission or paying royalties as long as the use is covered by fair use. Further, courts have allowed the use of thumbnail images as parts of links to other sites. And clicking on the link takes one to a page about Lamoureux's *SL* activities. Is this use fair or a trademark violation? After all, when one clicks on the logo, one is not taken to the *SL* site but rather to another of Lamoureux's pages.

In response to this conundrum, and the implications of potential infringement, Lamoureux devises a new logo for the link (using a picture of his *SL* avatar posed within *SL*). However, he retains the *SL* banner, placing it on the second page of the set (the page that explains his activities) and setting its link to the *SL* site (thereby coming closer to the usually protected thumbnail/link exception). However, he does not resize the banner as a thumbnail but instead leaves it roughly the size one sees on the *SL* site. At the bottom of the page he also posts the disclaimer suggested/required by Linden Lab for use of the term *SL*.

Was Lamoureux's initial use of the logo/wordmark misguided and a violation? Was his solution to the problem strong enough protection against trademark violation? Over the period of time in which this book was written, Linden Lab came to appreciate the significant degree to which its trademarks were being misappropriated across a wide range of media. As a result, they updated their policies and issued extensive materials to guide one in the use of their intellectual property. Their changes and policies can be found at <http://secondlife.com/corporate/brand/>. As an introduction to some of the issues raised in this chapter, one can examine that new policy and note the ways that Lamoureux now displays affiliation with Linden Lab/*Second Life* on his Web pages.

This chapter examines both the development of traditional trademark law as well as a number of refinements that have taken place in the new media age.

Legislative Development of US Trademark Law

Early History of Trademarks

Trademarks may well be the oldest form of intellectual property protection. The earliest forms of trade, as far back as ancient China, India, Persia, Egypt,

Greece, and Rome, show evidence of trademarks on goods, as producers and merchants marked their wares with identifying symbols (Merges et al. 557). Marks on ancient products identified the producers (a form of advertising), indemnified the quality of the merchandise, and helped owners keep track of their property. Cattle (and slaves) were branded, medieval guilds marked their products with a guild identifier, metal workers were allowed or required to mark their work to identify the maker, bread-making recipes were specified such that batches could be marked for following the law, and wines and other agricultural by-products were often marked for their source and type (Paradise 14–15).

Trademark disputes come in all shapes and sizes and may occur at different stages in the life cycle of a trademark. For example, a recent dispute in the Trademark Trial and Appeal Board (the administrative body at the Patent and Trademark Office that handles conflicts that arise during the trademark application process) involves the question of whether and—if so—who may lay claim to trademark ownership in the "Happy Face" ☺. The ubiquitous yellow circle with two dots for eyes and an upturned, curved line for a mouth finds itself at the center of a battle between an entrepreneur, Franklin Loufrani, who registered the trademark in various countries around the world, and Wal-Mart Stores, Inc., the largest retailer in the world. Mr. Loufrani has argued that the icon has been used so widely in America that no single entity or person should be able to lay claim to exclusive trademark rights in it. Wal-Mart, on the other hand, has argued that as a result of its extensive use of the icon in its advertising campaigns, it has demonstrated "secondary meaning" in the minds of consumers, who associate the logo with Wal-Mart, at least for retail store services. At the same time, Wal-Mart has opposed Mr. Loufrani's efforts to register the word mark SMILEY on the grounds that the word has become generic or descriptive of the icon. At press time, the case remains pending (*Loufrani v. Wal-Mart*, Opposition Nos. 91/150, 278, 91/154, 632 and 91/152,145). One of the co-authors of this book represents Mr. Loufrani in the dispute.

As with other forms of intellectual property law, US practices followed early English models. Trademark protection was contained in English common law until the early 1800s. That common law referred to trademark counterfeiting as "palming off" a bogus item as bona fide (Paradise 1). Under that law, trademark owners with valid infringement cases were entitled to prevent others from use of the same mark in sales (Merges et al. 558). There were no recorded cases in US trademarks before 1824; the first successful infringement case was 1844.

US trademark law was slow to develop, largely because trademarks were not mentioned in Article 1, Section 8 of the Constitution, the portion of the federal law that became a mandate for the development of patent and copyright law. Since no mention was made of trademarks, the federal government did not develop laws. However, in the absence of federal law, the various states issued their own trademark laws (Seidel 2). This led to a number of inconsistencies and conundrums in trademark legislation over time, as the state statutes featured a variety of issues and contrasting interpretations, both among the states as well as with the eventual federal statutes. Two of the principal differences are (1) many of the early state laws addressed the issue of trademark dilution while the early federal legislation (*Trademark Act of 1881*) did not; (2) the states varied among themselves as to whether registration of a specific mark, rather than simple use of it in commerce, was required for protection. Jefferson recommended registration, and since there was no federal system, many of the states adopted his advice.

Early trademark legislation took a fairly limited view of the power of trademarks. In order to violate most of the early common law interpretations, infringers had to copy an existing mark in such a way as to be said to be copying the mark for the intention of misleading the public about the nature of the goods. The principal recipient of the protection, then, was actually as much the consumer as it was the original rights holder. Further, early interpretations of the protection did not so much protect the mark (the intellectual property) as they protected the commerce (the use of the mark in business). State statutes did not start protecting trademarks as a form of property until roughly the 1840s (Merges et al. 560).

The first US (federal) trademark statute, the *Trademark Act of 1870*, was enacted in response to the lack of federal legislation. The *Act* was grounded in Article 1 of the Constitution. However, as a result of Northern post-Civil War complaints about lawless counterfeiting in the South, the *Act* was revised after 1876 to make trademark counterfeiting a crime. This change led to the downfall of the law, and it was struck down by the Supreme Court in the *Trade-Mark Cases*, 100 U.S. 82 (1879) for exceeding the powers granted Congress by the patent and copyright clause of the Constitution. The ruling set the precedent that trademarks do not protect new ideas or creations but rather protect interstate commerce (Paradise 17).

Congress responded with the *Trademark Act of 1881*, which was based more firmly within Commerce Clause powers (Merges et al. 558). However, that revision left out the trademark counterfeiting provision; such protection would not reenter the law until 1984.

Modern Trademark Legislation and Development

The 1905 revision of the *Trademark Act of 1881* was both practically and conceptually important, as it replaced the requirement that infringements be both identical and intentional with the threshold that they present and encourage the likelihood of confusion (Merges et al. 560). The current federal trademark statute is the *Lanham Act of 1946*, codified in Title 15 of the *United States Code*. The *Lanham Act* specifies terms for establishing trademarks, trade names, and service marks, and for registering trademarks and service marks (trade names cannot be registered federally though some states allow the registration of company names). The *Lanham Act* specifies the different kinds of marks and sets up their classifications according to relative "strength" (as noted in Chapter 1, p. 14).

Under state common law, trademarks are protected as part of the law of unfair competition, with procedures that vary by state. As noted, many states also established trademark laws prior to the *Trademark* and *Lanham Acts*, and most states maintained their statutes after the enactment of federal legislation. In order to establish some sense of consistency across state lines while maintaining wanted balances both among the states and between the state and federal practices, two important policies have guided the formative standardization of state statutes.

First proposed in 1964 and then revised in 1966, the *Uniform Deceptive Trade Practices Act* (*UDTP*) was developed by the National Conference of Commissioners on Uniform State Laws. Additionally, the *Model State Trademark Bill* (*MSTB*) fostered uniformity among existing state trademark statutes and addressed proposals mandating compulsory registration statutes. Since its inception, the *MSTB* has been adopted in forty-six states and is used as the basis for state trademark statutes. The practice was proposed in 1949 and is supported by the International Trademark Association (INTA). The *MSTB* was revised in 1992 and 1996.

The *Lanham Act* went largely unchanged until 1984, when Congress passed the *Trademark Clarification Act* and the *Trademark Counterfeiting Act*. The *Counterfeiting Act* re-instituted many of the protections that were found in the 1876 amendment to the original *Trademark Act* by specifying the fines and penalties (both criminal and civil) associated with convictions for fraudulent use of trademarks (Paradise 18). The *Clarification Act* addressed the relationships among trademarks, branded goods (for example, *Kleenex*-brand tissues) and generic goods (tissues). The amendment put into legal practice standards for examining the extent to which a trademarked name had passed so far into the public consciousness as to no longer designate the brand, but rather to designate simply the general category of goods or services. For example, one is not able to register a trademark for terms such as "service stations."

The *Lanham Act* was revised in 1988 via the *Trademark Law Revision Act*. The revision changed the term for registration and renewal from twenty years to ten years. An "intent-to-use" system was added that enabled a company to reserve a mark with the evidence that the trademark will be used in the future. Thus, the mark can be applied for, but it cannot be registered or granted until the actual use of the trademark.

The *Federal Trademark Dilution Act of 1995* added a dilution statute to the *Lanham Act*. Dilution can be found whenever a "famous mark" is used by another, "if such use begins after the mark has become famous and causes dilution of the distinctive quality of the mark" (15 U.S.C. § 1125I). In 1999, Congress revised the law through the *Trademark Amendments Act*, which included a series of provisions that specifically targeted new-media-related issues such as cybersquatting and domain piracy. These will be addressed in the next section.

At the time of this writing, there are three proposals for legislation pending in Congress: H.R. 32, *Stop Counterfeiting in Manufactured Goods Act*; H.R. 683, *Trademark Dilution Revision Act*; H.R. 784, to clarify that service marks, collective marks, and certification marks are entitled to the same protections, rights, and privileges of trademarks.

Special Trademark Issues in New Media

In addition to the usual issues concerning the use of trademarks in analog media, new digital media environments present a number of special challenges to historic practices. The range of issues includes cybersquatting (and other domain-name-related activities), spam e-mail, misappropriation of hyperlinks, use of banner and pop-up ads, meta-tags, keywords and search engine manipulations, and questions related to page design (especially framing practices). However, most of these potential abuses have been addressed primarily through the courts; federal legislation regarding these new media questions has so far been scant.

The *Anti-Cybersquatting Consumer Protection Act* was enacted in 1999 as a *Lanham Act* amendment. The amendment provides trademark owners with a civil remedy against cybersquatting—the registering of others' trademarks as domain names and profiting from the sale of those domain names or traffic through the site. Cybersquatting can result in consumer fraud and public confusion as to the true source or sponsorship of products and services and thereby damage commerce and deprive consumers of their rights.

Between 1999 and 2000, the Internet Corporation for Assigned Names and Numbers (ICANN) worked to develop the *Uniform Domain-Name Dispute-Resolution Policy* (ICANN, Timeline). Fully implemented by ICANN, as mandated by the World Intellectual Property Organization (WIPO), the policy specifies that

> most types of trademark-based domain-name disputes must be resolved by agreement, court action, or arbitration before a registrar will cancel, suspend, or transfer a domain name. Disputes alleged to arise from abusive registrations of domain names (for example, cybersquatting) may be addressed by expedited administrative proceedings that the holder of trademark rights initiates by filing a complaint with an approved dispute-resolution service provider. (*Uniform Domain-Name Dispute-Resolution Policy*)

Although not US legislation, this policy is used by courts to determine the outcomes for cases involving claims of cybersquatting or other trademark-related conflicts involving domain names and addresses on the World Wide Web. Further examination of other trademark issues related to new media will be addressed in the case-analysis section below.

Cybersquatting cases can be very complex, involving claims and counterclaims across wide geographical regions and multiple countries ignored by the "place-less-ness" of cyberspace. Incidents such as the one between Indigo Networks and OnePhone Holding AB provide evidence of why WIPO and other international entities provide special tribunals for cyber disputes. *Computerworld's* Jaikumar Vijayan reports on the latter case, in which a domain-name holder accused of cybersquatting actually prevailed in a dispute with the party that filed the complaint and then also won a counterclaim of attempted reverse domain-name hijacking.

Traditional Media Trademark Cases with New Media Implications

Polaroid Corp. v. Polarad Electronics, Corp., 287 F.2d 492 (2nd Cir. 1961)

Polaroid held various US trademarks related to the term "Polaroid" dating back as far as 1936. Polaroid had become a well-known name for sheet polarizing material, products made from such material, optical desk lamps, and stereoscopic viewers well before Polarad was organized in 1944. Polarad was primarily in the business of microwave generating, receiving, and measuring devices, and television studio equipment. Polaroid brought suit in 1956, alleging that the use of the name Polarad infringed Polaroid's trademark rights and constituted unfair competition. In the case, a well-known judge, Judge Henry J. Friendly, stated a non-exclusive multi-factor test for determining whether there is a "likelihood of confusion" when analyzing trademark infringement: (1) the strength of the mark, (2) the similarity of the two marks, (3) the proximity of the products, (4) actual confusion, (5) the likelihood of plaintiff's bridging the gap, (6) defendant's good faith in adopting its mark, (7) the quality of defendant's products, and (8) the sophistication of the consumer. The Court ultimately found for Polarad, because it concluded that Polaroid had unreasonably delayed filing its suit for approximately ten years.

Big O Tire Dealers, Inc. v. Goodyear Tire & Rubber Co., 561 F.2d 1365 (10th Cir. 1977)

Big O Tire Dealers was a small tire-buying company worth approximately $200,000 in the mid-1970s. Big O's business included selling tires through independent tire retailers, and in the fall of 1975, Big O started marketing some tires under the name "Bigfoot" in fourteen states. In July 1974, Goodyear decided to use the name "Bigfoot" to promote a new tire and planned to launch a massive advertising campaign on September 16, 1974. When Goodyear discovered Big O's "Bigfoot" tires in late August, Goodyear contacted Big O. After various meetings, Big O made it clear to Goodyear that it was not interested in selling the rights to use the "Bigfoot" name, and Goodyear made it clear that it was going to use it, notwithstanding Big O's objections. Big O sued Goodyear in a Colorado District Court on November 27, 1974.

The jury found that the mark "Bigfoot" was not descriptive in nature as applied to tires and that Goodyear's adoption of the mark would be likely to cause confusion among ordinary customers or prospective customers as to the source of the goods. In addition to dismissing Goodyear's claims that certain jury instructions were inappropriate, the 10th Circuit also noted that this case was different than most regarding confusion in that it involved "reverse confusion." The Court explained that, generally, a trademark infringement suit results from a plaintiff having "a substantial investment in a well established trademark" and seeking lost profits/damages based on the second user's attempts to trade on the goodwill of the mark of the first user. In *Big O*, with a case of "reverse confusion," the second user (Goodyear) merely causes confusion as to the source of the goods but is not trading on the goodwill developed in the mark ("Bigfoot") by the first user (Big O).

Zazu Designs v. L'Oreal, 979 F.2d 499 (7th Cir. 1992)

Zazu Designs brought a trademark infringement suit against L'Oreal for using the name "Zazu" for a hair-coloring product sold by L'Oreal's subsidiary, Cosmair. L'Oreal conducted a search on the mark Zazu and acquired a covenant not to sue from a clothing manufacturer with the only federally registered trademark for "Zazu." L'Oreal was also aware of Zazu Designs' state service mark registration. After starting its national marketing of the new coloring product, L'Oreal sent representatives to visit Zazu Designs three times, at which point there still were no products being sold under the "Zazu" name.

The 7th Circuit found that Zazu Designs' minimal shipments of its product were merely an attempt to reserve a mark for intended use and that Zazu Designs' initial shipments were insufficient to establish trademark rights. The Court found that the District Court was incorrect to equate "a use sufficient to support registration with a use sufficient to generate nationwide rights in the absence of registration." The Court therefore held that Zazu Designs' sales of its hair product bearing the "Zazu" mark were insufficient, as a matter of law, to grant Zazu Designs national trademark rights in the mark at the time that L'Oreal began selling its coloring products. The Court held that L'Oreal did not infringe a mark held by Zazu Designs because L'Oreal was the first to market with a product bearing the mark and that Zazu Designs' intent to use the mark was irrelevant. Therefore, the Court vacated all damages awarded and remanded to the District Court to decide whether sanctions should be issued based on counsel's misconduct at trial, apart from any issues regarding trademark infringement.

Two Pesos, Inc. v. Taco Cabana, Inc., 505 U.S. 763 (1992)

In this case, Taco Cabana sued Two Pesos for trade dress infringement of the interior design of a Mexican restaurant under the *Lanham Act*. The jury found that, although Taco Cabana's trade dress had not acquired secondary meaning, it was inherently distinctive, and the Court therefore awarded damages to Taco Cabana. The Court of Appeals upheld the District Court's ruling, finding that the instructions to the jury were adequate and that there was enough evidence to support the jury's findings. The Supreme Court reviewed the provisions of the *Lanham Act* and found that there was nothing in the language of the act that would lead to a difference in analysis between inherently distinctive verbal or symbolic trademarks and inherently distinctive trade dress. The Supreme Court therefore upheld the lower courts' findings that trade dress could be inherently distinctive and that Taco Cabana should prevail, notwithstanding a finding that its unique trade dress had not acquired secondary meaning.

Qualitex Co. v. Jacobson Products Co., 514 U.S. 159 (1995)

In *Qualitex*, the Supreme Court held that a color could meet the legal requirements for trademark registration under the *Lanham Act*, provided that it has acquired secondary meaning in the market. Qualitex used a green-gold color for its dry cleaning press pads. Jacobson, a competitor of Qualitex, started selling its own dry cleaning press pads in a similar green-gold color. Qualitex then sued Jacobson for unfair competition and, after registering the green-gold color of its pads as a trademark, added a trademark infringement claim to its lawsuit. The District Court found for Qualitex, but the Court of Appeals set aside the judgment, stating that color alone could not be registered as a trademark. The Supreme Court, however, unanimously determined that the *Lanham Act* was broadly worded such that nothing prevented a color from being a descriptive trademark that could acquire secondary meaning over time. The Court found that a color could therefore come to indicate the source of the product, the primary goal of trademarks. The Supreme Court also addressed the functionality doctrine, essentially dismissing the idea that such a doctrine would create a general bar from obtaining trademark protection for a color, while acknowledging that if a defendant could prove that only limited colors could be used for the product, the functionality doctrine would then apply.

Wal-Mart Stores, Inc. v. Samara Brothers, Inc., 529 U.S. 205 (2000)

In *Wal-Mart*, the Supreme Court addressed the circumstances under which a product's design is distinctive for determining whether there can be infringement of an unregistered trade dress under the *Lanham Act*. Samara makes children's clothing sold by various stores. Wal-Mart, a large, well-known retailer, sells many things, one of which is children's clothing. Wal-Mart photographed clothes from Samara's line of clothing and hired a company to manufacture similar clothing. Wal-Mart sold the knockoffs of sixteen of Samara's designs and made over $1 million in profits. When Samara's attention was drawn to the fact that Wal-Mart and others were selling similar clothing below the price that Samara's distributors were allowed to charge, Samara sent cease-and-desist letters and eventually brought a lawsuit in the Southern District of New York. The suit alleged many counts, including infringement of unregistered trade dress under the *Lanham Act*. The District Court found in favor of Samara. After the 2nd Circuit upheld the decision, the Supreme Court granted certiorari.

The Court discussed the breadth of the language in the *Lanham Act* as covering not just words and symbols but also the design of a product. The Court also explained that product-design trade dress, like a color, can probably not be inherently distinctive, but that it can still attain distinctiveness through secondary meaning. The Court apparently narrowed its holding from *Two Pesos*, stating that the protection for inherently distinctive trade dress applied only to product-packaging trade dress and that product-design trade dress must acquire secondary meaning to be protected under the *Lanham Act*.

TrafFix Devices, Inc. v. Marketing Displays, Inc. 532 U.S. 23 (2001)

In this case, Marketing Displays owned a patent on a two-spring traffic sign design created to keep traffic signs standing in strong winds. After expiration of the patent, TrafFix started making signs using the same design, and Marketing Displays sued TrafFix for trade dress infringement, alleging that the design of the traffic signs was recognizable as belonging to Marketing Displays. The Supreme Court held that a functional design could not be trademarked and that a patented design was presumed to be functional. The Supreme Court explained that allowing trademark protection for something that is functional would be detrimental to competition based on something other than reputation and therefore improper.

The Court found that the fact that Marketing Displays' having obtained a patent on the design created a strong presumption that the patented features were functional and that Marketing Displays, as the patentee, had the burden of showing that the characteristic for which protection is sought is not functional. The Court stated that a design is functional if it makes the product work better or less expensive to produce, regardless of whether an alternative design is possible and unanimously held that the traffic sign design was clearly functional.

New Media Cases in Trademark Law

Panavision Int'l, L.P. v. Toeppen, 141 F.3d 1316 (9th Cir. 1998)

In *Panavision*, the 9th Circuit interpreted the *Federal Trademark Dilution Act* (*FTDA*) as applied to the Internet. Dennis Toeppen, a "cybersquatter," acquired domain names containing famous trademarks and attempted to sell them to the mark holders. One domain name that Toeppen acquired was Panavision.com, on which Toeppen displayed photographs of Pana, Illinois.

When Panavision attempted to register Panavision.com, it discovered that it already belonged to Toeppen. Panavision then contacted Toeppen, informing him of its trademark rights and requesting him to cease use of the mark and the domain name. In response, Toeppen stated that he had the right to use the domain name but that he would sell it and agree not to acquire other domain names that Panavision alleged to have rights to if Panavision paid him $13,000. Panavision refused Toeppen's offer, and Toeppen then acquired Panaflex.com. Panavision then brought suit against Toeppen in California under the *FTDA*, the California anti-dilution statute, and the *California Business and Professions Code*, alleging that Toeppen was in the business of stealing marks, registering them as domain names, and selling them to the rightful owners.

After determining that the District Court properly exercised personal jurisdiction over Toeppen, the 9th Circuit addressed the District Court's grant of summary judgment that Toeppen violated the *FTDA* and the California state laws. In order to prove a violation of the *FTDA*, Panavision had to "show that (1) the mark is famous; (2) the defendant is making a commercial use of the mark in commerce; (3) the defendant's use began after the mark became famous; and (4) the defendant's use of the mark dilutes the quality of the mark by diminishing the capacity of the mark to identify and distinguish goods and services. 15 USC. S 1125I." Toeppen did not dispute the first and third factors or that his use of the mark was "in commerce." However, Toeppen alleged that the District Court's findings that his use was commercial and that it diluted the quality of Panavision's mark were incorrect. The 9th Circuit agreed that case law supports Toeppen's claim that mere registration of a mark is not a commercial use as contemplated by the *FTDA*. However, the Court went on to note that Toeppen's business consisted of the registration and sale of the domain names, which is a commercial use. Next, the Court addressed the issue of dilution and discussed the idea that a domain name is more than an address and actually helps to identify the entity that owns the site. Additionally, the Court stated that Toeppen's registration of Panavision.com dilutes the capacity of the Panavision marks to identify goods and services, that potential customers visiting Panavision.com may be discouraged when finding that it is not Panavision's Web site, and that Toeppen's use of Panavision.com puts Panavision's name and reputation at the mercy of Toeppen. Therefore, the 9th Circuit upheld the District Court's finding of violation of the *FTDA*.

Bally Total Fitness Holding Corp. v. Faber, 29 F. Supp. 2d 1161 (C.D. Cal. 1998)

Bally sued Faber for trademark infringement, unfair competition, and dilution for his use of the phrase "Bally sucks" on a Web page. First, with respect to trademark infringement, the California District Court pointed out that the "likelihood of confusion test" applies to related goods, and that Bally is involved in the health club industry while Faber is involved in the design of Web pages. The Court clarified that the fact that Bally uses a Web site to communicate to its current and potential customers, while Faber used a Web site to communicate his criticisms of Bally to Bally's current and potential customers, relates to the medium used and "does not make the goods related." The Court found the goods unrelated as a matter of law but addressed the many factors considered in the likelihood of confusion test (strength of the mark, similarity of the marks, proximity of the goods, evidence of actual confusion, marketing channels used, degree of care likely to be exercised when purchasing the items, the defendant's intent in selecting the mark, and likelihood of expansion of the product line). The Court weighed the factors and found the primary purpose of the accused mark was criticism and not promotion of goods or services related to Bally. Therefore, the Court found that restricting the defendant from the use of the terms would limit the ability to publish critical commentary about Bally. Additionally, the Court found that there is little likelihood that Bally would expand its business to compete with Faber's anti-Bally commentary. Finding that the factors weighed in favor of Faber, the Court found that there was no likelihood of confusion of the marks and that Faber was therefore not infringing on Bally's rights.

Next, the Court addressed Bally's trademark dilution claim. The Court found that Faber's use of Bally's marks in the context of a consumer product review of Bally's services was not "in commerce." Furthermore, the Court held that even if Faber's use were commercial, it would not tarnish Bally's marks, since the marks are not tarnished or otherwise diluted, and Faber's use of the Bally marks in his criticism is protected by the First Amendment. Bally's unfair competition claim was based on dilution and trademark infringement. Therefore, the Court granted Faber's summary judgment motion with respect to all claims.

March Madness Athletic Ass'n v. Netfire, Inc., 2005 U.S. App. LEXIS 1475 (5th Cir. Jan. 24, 2005)

The term "March Madness" was first used by the Illinois High School Association (IHSA) to refer to its basketball tournament in the 1940s. It is thought that CBS broadcaster Brent Musberger first used the term "March Madness" in reference to the NCAA basketball tournament in 1982, after which the NCAA began licensing "March Madness" in 1988. The IHSA claimed exclusive rights to the mark and also licensed it to various entities including other state high school associations, Wilson, Pepsi, and *The Chicago Tribune*. After a lawsuit between the IHSA and one of the NCAA's licensees was adjudicated in 1996, the IHSA and NCAA eventually decided to jointly protect their rights in the mark. In 2000, following the filing of *March Madness Athletic Ass'n v. Netfire, Inc.*, the IHSA and NCAA formed the March Madness Athletic Association (MMAA), transferring each of their rights in the mark to the MMAA.

The defendants acquired the domain name marchmadness.com when one of the defendants falsely stated that Netfire was associated with the NCAA and was the rightful owner of the mark. The defendants then began developing content relating to the NCAA tournament for their site. After receiving a cease-and-desist letter from the NCAA in 1996 stating that the defendants were violating the NCAA's common law rights in the mark, the defendants decided not to operate their site for the 1996 tournament. Subsequently, in 1996, the IHSA sent a separate cease-and-desist letter, stating that the IHSA was the owner of all rights in the mark. Notwithstanding the two letters, the defendants operated their site from 1997 to 1999, when the domain registrar, NSI, took the domain name out of circulation at the IHSA's request. When NSI informed the IHSA that the hold on the domain name would cease absent court papers, the IHSA filed *March Madness Athletic Ass'n v. Netfire, Inc.*

The 5th Circuit upheld the District Court's rulings, which held that "March Madness" was a descriptive mark that had acquired secondary meaning and that marchmadness.com created a likelihood of confusion with the mark. The Court also upheld the District Court's rulings that the defendants' registration and use of marchmadness.com violated the *Anti-Cybersquatting Consumer Protection Act (ACPA)*, notwithstanding the defendants' lack of profit and that the plaintiffs were not entitled to damages because the defendants' registration and use of the Web site was prior to the enactment of the *ACPA*.

U-Haul Int'l, Inc. v. WhenU.com, Inc., 279 F. Supp. 2d 723 (E.D. Va. 2003)

This case involves pop-up advertising and plaintiff U-Haul's claim that defendant WhenU's pop-up advertising infringes upon U-Haul's trademark, constitutes copyright infringement, and amounts to unfair competition. U-Haul complains that WhenU's pop-up advertisements, which crowd the computer user's screen and block out U-Haul's Web site display, in effect, infringe on U-Haul's registered trademark and alter U-Haul's copyrighted advertisements.

WhenU distributes a software program that is generally co-distributed with other software programs, such as screensavers. WhenU's software is installed on a user's computer and uses common search phrases, Web sites, and keyword algorithms to scan the user's Internet activity to see if there are matches and, if so, displays pop-up advertisements of one or some of WhenU's clients, requiring users to navigate away from the advertisements to see the program they were viewing. The WhenU software does not use, alter or interfere with U-Haul's trademarks and copyrights. WhenU computer users must endure pop-up advertising along with her ugly brother, unsolicited bulk e-mail (spam), as a burden of using the Internet.

The issue that the District Court faced was whether WhenU's computer software was a form of trademark or copyright infringement or unfair competition. To prove trademark infringement, a mark holder must show that the defendant made commercial use of a valid mark in a manner that would be likely to cause confusion to consumers. Hence, a fundamental element of trademark infringement is that the defendant is using the plaintiff's mark in commerce. The Court found that WhenU was not copying U-Haul's trademarked material and that U-Haul could not establish how WhenU's advertisements "used" U-Haul's marks, because WhenU's advertisements were distinct from U-Haul's site, WhenU doesn't promote or advertise U-Haul's marks, and WhenU's software doesn't impede Internet users from accessing U-Haul's Web site by using U-Haul's marks. Therefore, the Court granted WhenU's summary judgment motion of non-infringement.

In order for a plaintiff to prove trademark dilution, the plaintiff needs to prove that the defendant is making commercial use of the plaintiff's mark(s) in commerce after the mark(s) became famous in a way that dilutes the distinctive quality of the mark. Once again, a key component for a finding that WhenU was diluting U-Haul's mark would be WhenU making a commercial use of that mark. The Court then pointed out that for the same reasons as with respect to trademark infringement, U-Haul could not show that WhenU was using U-Haul's marks and granted WhenU's summary judgment motion with respect to U-Haul's trademark dilution claim.

Playboy Enters., Inc. v. Welles, 279 F.3d 796 (9th Cir. 2002)

Former *Playboy* Playmate of the Year Terri Welles ran a Web site that used trademarked terms owned by *Playboy*. In particular, Ms. Welles's Web site included trademarked terms such as *Playboy* and *Playmate* in the metatags, which were used to identify Ms. Welles as a former Playmate of the Year. Additionally, each of the pages of the Web site used "PMOY '81" as a repeating watermark in the background. *Playboy* sued Ms. Welles, alleging that her use of the trademarked terms infringed and diluted its trademarks.

The court evaluated Ms. Welles's use of the trademarked terms and determined that the use of trademarked terms in metatags should be considered under the same test for nominative use, namely: (1) the product or service cannot be readily identified without using the trademark (i.e., trademark is descriptive of a person, place, or attribute); (2) only so much of the mark is used as is necessary for the identification (i.e., the words but not the specific font or logo); and (3) the user does nothing to suggest sponsorship or endorsement by the trademark holder—which applies even if the nominative use is commercial. Based on this test, the Court held that Ms. Welles's use of the terms in the metatags was nominative (the marks used were descriptive, only the terms were used, and nothing was done to suggest sponsorship) and therefore, by definition, could not dilute the trademark. [MC]

Web work implicates numerous trademark issues. The courts are not always clear as to the issues and how to resolve them equitably. This is another area in which the technology has gotten out front of the law in new media. Eric Goldman, on his Technology & Marketing Law Blog, discusses the details, results, and implications of *North American Medical Corp. v. Axiom Worldwide, Inc.* in which the 11th Circuit upheld a charge of trademark infringement related to metatags.

Summarizing Trademarks in New Media

As noted, illegal downloading of entertainment material, especially music and movies, captures the lion's share of attention in digital intellectual property law circles. However, as illustrated by the rampant illegal appropriation of trademarks in virtual worlds, trademarks, service marks, and word marks are ubiquitously distributed across the digital landscape. In many ways, major rights holders have as much or more at risk in the trademark area as they do with regard to content, as trademarks can sometimes be *the* principal element in economic exchanges. For example, shirts made at a factory can share every element from design to completion; however, applying various trademarks changes their value based on the relative "social ranking" of the "brand" attached by way of a logo.

In the digital world, marks can be reproduced easily and profusely. They can be appropriated and "applied" in obvious graphic display or hidden deep within metatags and other file or address information. Just as one point of view claims that "any sample," regardless of size or seemingly insignificant meaning, violates copyright law, one could claim that every use of a trademark by someone other than the legitimate rights owner dilutes the value of the mark. From this point of view, even use in non-commerical settings violates the rights of the trademark holder.

In the same respect, however, digital technologies "hyper-enable" the distribution of trademark items' identities far beyond the reaches of analog media. For example, many companies are giving careful consideration to the notion that use, by avatars, of branded items in virtual worlds encourages sales/purchases of those brands in real life (RL) by establishing deep bonds between the user and the brand. If so, even unauthorized use benefits rights holders. It is almost certainly the case that the intellectual property legal system will face vigorous challenges from digital media in the area of trademarks in the years to come. [ELL]

Discussion Questions

1. List and describe trademarks that are used so often that they are strongly headed toward passing into generic status.
2. Discuss the rampant use of unauthorized trademarks on the Web and especially in virtual worlds. In some ways, the use seems so ubiquitous as to be totally beyond the ability of the legal system to control it—almost worse than the illegal downloading of music. Implications? Outcomes? Solutions?
3. Where should one draw the line for fair use of trademarks? Generally, for example, one might settle on "commercial use" and the Court tests. However, "dilution" standards can find trademark holders taking offense and action over any and all non-licensed use of marks. Again, in a cut-and-paste culture, rampant use may indicate trouble afoot.
4. Discuss whether there should be term limits on trademarks. Under current law, regularly (re)registered trademarks are "forever," a status that keeps them out of the public domain. Would creativity be furthered by term limits?
5. A special adjunct of our court system was set up for patent work. In digital, adjudication of some cyber issues (domains, etc.) has been done in quasi-legal settings and over a narrow range of issues. Given the broad and specialized nature of new media issues in this area, should a special bar and court system be devised for URLs, domains, meta-tags, cyber crimes, and the rest? Why or why not?

CHAPTER FIVE

Trade Secrets

When teachers explain trade secret law to novice students, they almost always mention one or two particularly familiar brands. The secret recipes for Coca-Cola™ and Kentucky Fried Chicken™ are almost apocryphal exemplifications of the issues at hand. In both cases, the business information (the recipe and its application) is a tightly held and protected secret that is central to the mission of the organization. Steps are taken to protect the secrets; the number of people who know the recipes are limited in the extreme. If the secrets got out, the companies would be compromised, so they work diligently to protect the information. If it appears that information about the secrets is leaking, the organizations take rapid and effective steps to stem the informational tide. To date, apparently, neither secret has been compromised to the extent of entering the public domain.

For example, in 2007, a former secretary for Coca-Cola™ was convicted of selling trade secrets to people who were affiliated with rival Pepsi-Cola™. In the case in question, the recipe for Coke itself was not at risk; rather, the former employee took home product samples and documents and offered to sell, for $1.5 million, information about products that had not yet been launched. She was convicted and faced up to ten years in prison. The recipients of the information also pleaded guilty and at the time of this writing also await sentencing (*Wikinews*, "Woman Found Guilty"). Such an instance is the stuff of trade secret law throughout the history of the protection of analog materials.

The situation in the digital world provides a number of nuanced differences. Although the basic issues remain the same, the nature of digital information produces interesting variations. For example, in January 2007, the Apple Computer Company was ordered to pay $700,000 in legal fees incurred by bloggers who had spent time and money defending themselves against Apple's claims that the bloggers had compromised trade secrets in their online reporting of impending product developments at Apple. A California County court found that the bloggers were covered by First Amendment protections for journalists (*O'Grady v. Superior Court*). The ruling illustrates the complexities in both trade secret law as well as First Amendment issues in the digital age. In a time frame concurrent with the ruling, Apple sued another rumor site for the same claim, once again proposing that online bloggers were publishing leaked inside information in violation of trade secret law.

This chapter examines trade secret law, particularly with regard to the new complexities provided by digital technologies.

A particularly troublesome set of circumstances in trade secret cases involves former employees and the information they bring to new employers. It's difficult to know why an employee changed jobs and companies. In some cases, Business "B" might have "raided" employees from Business "A" specifically for their knowledge and experience in the business. In other cases, employees may simply have followed better opportunities. Likewise, it is very difficult to ascertain how much knowledge employees bring with them and apply in their new jobs, and which portion of information and experience constitutes trade secrets is often the ground for a court battle. Law firm Womble Carlyle's "Trade Secrets Blog" examines a contemporary case that illustrates the complexities of the new media employment environment related to trade secrets in its discussion of a complex employee case between MSC Software Corp. and Altair Engineering Inc. in which seven former employees at Altair became involved in similar software-related activities at MSC.

Legislative Development of US Trade Secret Law

Early Influences

Research suggests a number of situations in which the protection of trade secrets was manifest throughout the history of Western civilization. For example, ancient Roman courts mediated action relating to privacy expectations when slaves changed households; European societies that developed guild-based systems of training enacted privately executed standards and agreements protecting tradesmen from infringing on each other's practices as apprentices were trained and sometimes moved across cooperatives and companies; and the Industrial Revolution found both public and private sectors developing protections for the material and practices that enacted and furthered the rise of modern invention and manufacturing processes (Merges et al. 30–33). Protective legislation in the Anglo-American tradition did not come to the fore until the early 1800s. Trade secret law slowly developed out of common law, with the first cases of misappropriation of trade secrets being recorded in 1817 and 1837 (Merges et al. 33). A full, legal specification of trade secret law (at the federal level in a form that was generally followed by the states) was contained in the *1939 Restatement of Torts*.

Restatement of Torts, 1939

The first thing to understand about the *1939 Restatement of Torts* is that it does not actually comprise a law of trade secrets, per se. That is, these and a multitude of other "Restatements" are the work of the American Law Institute (ALI) and as such do not in themselves constitute formal laws. As noted at its Web site, the ALI

> [was] founded in 1923, [and] . . . has a membership consisting of judges, practicing lawyers, and legal scholars from all areas of the United States as well as some foreign countries, selected on the basis of professional achievement and demonstrated interest in the improvement of the law.
>
> ALI, through a careful and deliberative process, drafts and then publishes various Restatements of the Law, model codes, and legal studies to promote the clarification and simplification of the law and its better adaptation to social needs, to secure the better administration of justice, and to encourage and carry on scholarly and scientific legal work. (American Law Institute, "Overview, Institute Projects")

The *1939 Restatement of Torts* considered a range of intellectual property issues.

However, while other areas of IP law were codified via unified approaches by 1940, there was no unified federal (national) trade secret law at the time. The *Restatement*, then, was taken as an authoritative approach to standardizing the common law. According to the *Restatement*,

> A trade secret may consist of any formula, pattern, device or compilation of information which is used in one's business, and which gives him an opportunity to obtain an advantage over competitors who do not know or use it. . . .
>
> The subject matter of a trade secret must be secret. . . . Substantially, a trade secret is known only in the particular business in which it is used. . . . He may, without losing his protection, communicate it to employees involved in its use. He may likewise communicate it to others pledged to secrecy . . . a substantial element of secrecy must exist, so that, except by the use of improper means, there would be difficulty in acquiring the information. . . . Some factors to be considered in determining whether given information is one's trade secret are: (1) The extent to which the information is known outside of his business; (2) the extent to which it is known by employees and others involved in his business; (3) the extent of measures taken by him to guard the secrecy of the information; (4) the value of the information to him and his competitors; (5) the amount of effort or money expended by him in developing the information; (6) the ease or difficulty with which the information could be properly acquired or duplicated by others. . . . [1]

When the ALI published the *Restatement of the Law Second Torts*, the authors chose to leave out the sections relating to trade secrets "on the grounds that the law of trade secrets had developed into an independent body of law that no longer relied on general principles of tort law" (Merges et al. 34). The original *Restatement* was often adopted by courts and so remained influential.

Uniform Trade Secrets Act (UTSA) 1968–1985

In 1968, at the suggestion of the Patent Law Section of the American Bar Association, the executive committee of the National Conference of Commissioners authorized a committee to develop a uniform approach to trade secret law. The committee worked on the document through 1972, when it presented its first reading to the parent group. Further revision continued through 1979, when the bill was presented for a final vote. The *Act* was approved and recommended for enactment in all states.

In its 1985 revision, the National Conference of Commissioners on Uniform State Laws (NCCUSL) noted that:

> Notwithstanding the commercial importance of state trade secret law to interstate business, this law has not developed satisfactorily. In the first place, its development

is uneven. Although there typically are a substantial number of reported decisions in states that are commercial centers, this is not the case in less populous and more agricultural jurisdictions. Secondly, even in states in which there has been significant litigation, there is undue uncertainty concerning the parameters of trade secret protection, and the appropriate remedies for misappropriation of a trade secret. (*Uniform Trade Secrets Act*)

Further, the conference noted that the *Restatement of Torts, 2nd* omitted mention of trade secrets. The conference, then, set out "The Uniform Act [to] codif[y] the basic principles of common law trade secret protection, preserving its essential distinctions from patent law."

The *Uniform Trade Secrets Act* (*UTSA*) defines trades secrets as

information, including a formula, pattern, compilation, program, device, method, technique, or process, that: (i) derives independent economic value, actual or potential, from not being generally known to, and not being readily ascertainable by proper means by, other persons who can obtain economic value from its disclosure or use, and (ii) is the subject of efforts that are reasonable under the circumstances to maintain its secrecy.

The *Act* describes inappropriate behavior on the part of employees and competitors with regard to misappropriation of trade secrets as well as employer responsibilities for efforts to protect the information. [ELL]

Fine Points of the UTSA

The *UTSA* provides the following substantive provisions:

§1. Definitions

As used in this Act, unless the context requires otherwise:
(1) *Improper means* includes theft, bribery, misrepresentation, breach or inducement of a breach of duty to maintain secrecy, or espionage through electronic or other means.
(2) *Misappropriation* means: (i) acquisition of a trade secret of another by a person who knows or has reason to know that the trade secret was acquired by improper means; or (ii) disclosure or use of a trade secret of another without express or implied consent by a person who (A) used improper means to acquire knowledge of the trade secret; or (B) at the time of disclosure or use knew or had reason to know that his knowledge of the trade secret was (I) derived from or through a person who has utilized improper means to acquire it; (II) acquired under circumstances giving rise to a duty to maintain its secrecy or limit its use; or (III) derived from or through a person who owed a duty to the person seeking relief to maintain its secrecy or limit its use; or (C) before a

material change of his position, knew or had reason to know that it was a trade secret and that knowledge of it had been acquired by accident or mistake.

(3) *Person* means a natural person, corporation, business trust, estate, trust, partnership, association, joint venture, government, governmental subdivision or agency, or any other legal or commercial entity.

(4) *Trade secret* means information, including a formula, pattern, compilation, program device, method, technique, or process, that: (i) derives independent economic value, actual or potential, from not being generally known to, and not being readily ascertainable by proper means by, other persons who can obtain economic value from its disclosure or use, and (ii) is the subject of efforts that are reasonable under the circumstances to maintain its secrecy.

§2. Injunctive Relief

(a) Actual or threatened misappropriation may be enjoined. . . .

(b) In exceptional circumstances, an injunction may condition future use upon payment of a reasonable royalty for no longer than the period of time for which use could have been prohibited. . . .

(c) In appropriate circumstances, affirmative acts to protect a trade secret may be compelled by court order.

§3. Damages

(a) Except to the extent that a material and prejudicial change of position prior to acquiring knowledge or reason to know of misappropriation renders a monetary recovery inequitable, a complainant is entitled to recover damages for misappropriation. Damages can include both the actual loss caused by misappropriation and the unjust enrichment caused by misappropriation that is not taken into account in computing actual loss. In lieu of damages measured by any other methods, the damages caused by misappropriation may be measured by imposition of liability for a reasonable royalty for a misappropriator's unauthorized disclosure or use of a trade secret.

(b) If willful and malicious misappropriation exists, the court may award exemplary damages in the amount not exceeding twice any award made under subsection (a).

§4. Attorney's Fees

If (i) a claim of misappropriation is made in bad faith, (ii) a motion to terminate an injunction is made or resisted in bad faith, or (iii) willful and malicious misappropriation exists, the court may award reasonable attorney's fees to the prevailing party.

§5. Preservation of Secrecy

In action under this Act, a court shall preserve the secrecy of an alleged trade secret by reasonable means, which may include granting protective orders in connection with discovery proceedings, holding in-camera hearings, sealing the records of the action, and ordering any person involved in the litigation not to disclose an alleged trade secret without prior court approval.

§6. Statute of Limitations

An action for misappropriation must be brought within 3 years after the misappropriation is discovered or by the exercise of reasonable diligence should have been discovered. . . .

§7. Effect on Other Law

(a) Except as provided in subsection (b), this [Act] displaces conflicting tort, restitutionary, and other law of this State providing civil remedies for misappropriation of a trade secret.

(b) This [Act] does not affect: (1) contractual remedies, whether or not based upon misappropriation of a trade secret; or (2) other civil remedies that are not based upon misappropriation of a trade secret; or (3) criminal remedies, whether or not based upon misappropriation of a trade secret.

§8. Uniformity of Application and Construction

This act shall be applied and construed to effectuate its general purpose to make uniform the law with respect to the subject of this Act among states enacting it.

§9. Short Title

This Act may be cited as the Uniform Trade Secrets Act.

§10. Severability

If any provision of this Act or its application to any person or circumstances is held invalid, the invalidity does not affect other provisions or applications of the Act which can be given effect without the invalid provision or application, and to this end the provisions of this Act are severable. [RR]

Economic Espionage Act of 1996 (EEA)

In his book *Sticky Fingers*, Steven Fink retells the story of the Ellery Systems and Andrew Wang case as an illustration for why the federal government developed and enacted the *Economic Espionage Act of 1996*. Ellery Systems was a software developer working on large, Internet-related projects for numerous US companies. Wang worked for Ellery, then left to form his own firm,

"DC Nology." Later, the FBI charged Wang and his accomplice, Jing Cui, with stealing trade secrets from Ellery for the purpose of giving them to the Chinese. In short, Wang was accused of domestic economic espionage. However, the *Uniform Trade Secrets Act* was neither federal law nor articulate on such matters. In the end, the government's case against Wang went awry, and he was freed with much hoopla in the press. Partly as result of this case, and certainly under the influence of the growing global economy fostered by digitization and the Internet, the FBI encouraged willing lawmakers to press for and make new law. The *EEA* was the result.

The *Economic Espionage Act* formalizes the terms of the *UTSA* at the federal level, extends the *UTSA* in consideration of various sorts of economic espionage, and empowers the US court system with the ability to take action to protect important trade secrets when the need is proven. As federal law, the *EEA* carries criminal punishment, whereas the *UTSA* results in civil legal proceedings (McGonagle and Vella).

As is the case with other aspects of intellectual property law, there are a number of provisions within various international trade agreements that relate to trade secrets. In particular, *GATT* and *TRIPS* are implicated. This text will examine the implications of those laws in Chapter 7, which treats international IP law. [ELL]

Traditional Media Trade Secret Cases with New Media Implications

Kewanee Oil Co. v. Bicron Corp., 416 U.S. 470; 94 S. Ct. 1879 (1974)

In *Kewanee Oil Co. v. Bicron Corp.*, the US Supreme Court held that state trade secret law is not pre-empted by federal patent law. In *Kewanee*, the plaintiff was a leading manufacturer of a type of synthetic crystal useful in the detection of ionizing radiation. By 1966, this manufacturer had developed a novel, seventeen-inch crystal as a result of many processes and manufacturing techniques, some of which Kewanee Oil considered trade secrets. The individual defendants were former employees of Kewanee Oil who formed or later joined Bicron Corp. As a condition of their former employment with Kewanee Oil, they executed at least one agreement each requiring the signer not to disclose confidential information or trade secrets obtained as employees of Kewanee Oil. The Bicron Corp., formed in August 1969, was to compete with Kewanee Oil in the production of the crystals and by April 1970 had grown a seventeen-inch crystal. The plaintiff thereupon instituted an action in the US District

Court for the Northern District of Ohio seeking injunctive relief and damages for the misappropriation of trade secrets.

The District Court, applying Ohio trade secrets law, granted a permanent injunction against the disclosure or use by the defendants of twenty of the forty claimed trade secrets. Although holding that the District Court's findings of fact were not clearly erroneous, the Court of Appeals for the 6th Circuit reversed the District Court on the ground that Ohio's trade secret laws were in conflict with the patent laws of the United States (478 F.2d 1074).

The US Supreme Court reversed and remanded the case to the Court of Appeals with directions to reinstate the judgment of the District Court. An opinion by Chief Justice Burger, expressing the view of five members of the Court, held that state trade secret protection was not pre-empted by operation of the federal patent laws.

PepsiCo Inc. v. Redmond, 54 F.3d 1262 (7th Cir. 1995)

PepsiCo Inc. v. Redmond is an important trade secret case that affirms what is sometimes called the "inevitable disclosure" doctrine. In this case, PepsiCo sought a preliminary injunction against defendants William Redmond and the Quaker Oats Company to prevent Redmond, a former PepsiCo employee, from divulging PepsiCo trade secrets and confidential information in his new job with Quaker and from assuming any duties with Quaker relating to beverage pricing, marketing, and distribution. The District Court agreed with PepsiCo and granted the injunction. The Court of Appeals for the 7th Circuit affirmed.

This case involved fierce beverage-industry competition in the 1990s between Quaker and PepsiCo, especially in "sports drinks" (also called "isotonics") and "new age drinks" (such as non-carbonated drinks like tea and fruit drinks). In 1994, PepsiCo developed extensive plans to increase its market presence, while Quaker was trying to solidify its lead by integrating Gatorade and Snapple distribution.

William Redmond, Jr., worked for PepsiCo in its PepsiCola North America division (PCNA) from 1984 to 1994. Redmond's relatively high-level position at PCNA gave him access to inside information and trade secrets. Redmond, like other PepsiCo management employees, had signed a confidentiality agreement with PepsiCo. That agreement stated (in relevant part) that he would not disclose "at any time, to anyone other than officers or employees of [PepsiCo], or make use of, confidential information relating to the business of [PepsiCo] . . . obtained while in the employ of [PepsiCo], which shall not be generally known or available to the public or recognized as standard practices."

Shortly after Redmond told PepsiCo that he was joining Quaker in November 1994, PepsiCo filed suit against him, seeking an injunction to prevent Redmond from assuming his duties at Quaker and to prevent him from disclosing trade secrets or confidential information to his new employer. At a preliminary injunction hearing, PepsiCo offered evidence of a number of trade secrets and confidential information it desired protected and to which Redmond was privy, including PCNA's "Strategic Plan," an annually revised document that contained PCNA's plans to compete, its financial goals, and its strategies for manufacturing, production, marketing, packaging, and distribution for the coming three years. This strategic plan was developed with input from PCNA's general managers, including Redmond. Another alleged trade secret was PCNA's Annual Operating Plan (AOP), which was a national plan for a given year and guided PCNA's financial goals, marketing plans, promotional event calendars, growth expectations, and operational changes in that year. Another alleged trade secret was PCNA's innovations in its selling and delivery systems.

The district agreed with PepsiCo and entered a preliminary injunction. The Court of Appeals for the 7th Circuit affirmed. The 7th Circuit recognized that PepsiCo had not brought a traditional trade secret case, in which a former employee has knowledge of a special manufacturing process or customer list and can give a competitor an unfair advantage by transferring the technology or customers to that competitor. The Court, however, found no abuse of discretion in the District Court's holding that Redmond could not help but rely on PCNA trade secrets as he worked to plot Gatorade and Snapple's new course for Quaker, and that these secrets would enable Quaker to respond strategically and achieve a substantial advantage by knowing exactly how PCNA would price, distribute, and market its sports and new age drinks.

The 7th Circuit concluded that the District Court correctly decided that PepsiCo demonstrated a likelihood of success on its statutory claim of trade secret misappropriation based on the combination of (1) the demonstrated inevitability that Redmond would rely on PCNA trade secrets in his new job at Quaker, and (2) the District Court's reluctance to believe that Redmond would refrain from disclosing these secrets in his new position (or that Quaker would ensure that Redmond did not disclose them). Thus, the District Court's order enjoining Redmond from assuming his responsibilities at Quaker through May 1995 and preventing him forever from disclosing PCNA trade secrets and confidential information was affirmed.

In an industry side note, in March 1997 Quaker sold its Snapple business for $300 million, incurring a $1.4 billion loss from its purchase price of Snapple in 1994 for $1.7 billion. In August 2001, Quaker was merged into PepsiCo.

New Media Cases in Trade Secret Law

DVD Copy Control Assn., Inc. v. Bunner, 31 Cal. 4th 864, 889 (2003)

In *DVD Copy Control Assn., Inc. v. Bunner*, the California Supreme Court held that a preliminary injunction granted by a District Court did not violate the free speech clauses of the US and California Constitutions. In this case, the DVD Copy Control Association, Inc. (DVD CCA) sued defendant Andrew Bunner and others under California's *Uniform Trade Secrets Act* (*CUTSA*) (Civ. Code, § 3426 et seq.), seeking an injunction to prevent defendants from using or publishing "DeCSS," a computer program allegedly containing DVD CCA's trade secrets.

Recognizing the risk of widespread piracy, the motion picture industry insisted that a viable protection system be made available to prevent users from making copies of motion pictures in digital form. Without such protection, it would not have agreed to release movies on DVDs. To provide this protection, two companies—Toshiba and Matsushita Electric Industrial Co., Ltd.—developed the Content Scrambling System (CSS).

> CSS is an encryption scheme that employs an algorithm configured by a set of "keys" to encrypt a DVD's contents. The algorithm is a type of mathematical formula for transforming the contents of the movie file into gibberish; the "keys" are in actuality strings of 0's and 1's that serve as values for the mathematical formula. Decryption in the case of CSS requires a set of "[master] keys" contained in compliant DVD players, as well as an understanding of the CSS encryption algorithm. Without the [master] keys and the algorithm, a DVD player cannot access the contents of a DVD. With the [master] keys and the algorithm, a DVD player can display the movie on a television or a computer screen, but does not give a viewer the ability to use the copy function of the computer to copy the movie or to manipulate the digital content of the DVD. (Corley, supra, 273 F.3d 436–37)

The motion picture, computer, and consumer electronics industries decided to use the CSS technology to encrypt copyrighted content on DVDs and agreed that this content should not be subject to unauthorized copying or transmission, including making the content available over the Internet. To this end, they began licensing CSS technology in October 1996. Under the terms of the licensing agreement, licensees had to maintain the confidentiality of proprietary information embodied in the CSS technology, including the "master keys" and algorithms. The agreement also contained other terms and conditions designed to ensure the confidentiality of this proprietary information. These industries later established the DVD Copy Control Association, Inc. (DVD CCA) as the entity charged with granting and administering the licenses to the CSS technology.

Despite these efforts to safeguard the CSS technology, Jon Johansen, a Norwegian resident, acquired the proprietary information embodied in the technology—including the master keys and algorithms—by reverse engineering software created by a licensee, Xing Technology Corporation (Xing). Xing's software is licensed to users under an agreement that specifically prohibits reverse engineering. Using the proprietary information culled from this software, Johansen wrote a program called DeCSS that decrypts movies stored on DVDs and enables users to copy and distribute those movies. According to DVD CCA, DeCSS "embodies, uses, and/or is a substantial derivation of confidential proprietary information" found in the CSS technology. Johansen posted the source code of DeCSS on an Internet Web site in October 1999.

Soon thereafter, DeCSS appeared on other Web sites, including a Web site maintained by Andrew Bunner. Bunner posted DeCSS on his Web site allegedly because it would enable Linux users to use and enjoy commercial DVDs, thereby enhancing Linux's usability and popularity. Bunner also claimed that he wanted to be sure that programmers had access to information for improving the DeCSS program. Bunner and others were sued by DVD CCA after refusing to remove DeCSS from their Web sites.

The trial court granted DVD CCA's request for a preliminary injunction and entered an order prohibiting defendants from posting, disclosing, or distributing DeCSS or related proprietary material. Bunner appealed. His primary argument on appeal was that the injunction infringed his free speech rights under the state and federal constitutions. The California appellate court concluded that the injunction was an unconstitutional prior restraint and reversed.

The California Supreme Court granted review and held that the preliminary injunction did not violate the free speech clauses of the US and California Constitutions, "*assuming* the trial court properly issued the injunction under California's trade secret law." The Supreme Court remanded the matter to the California appellate court to determine whether the evidence in the record supported the factual findings necessary to establish that the preliminary injunction was warranted under *CUTSA*.

McRoberts Software Inc. v. Media 100 Inc., 329 F.3d 557 (7ᵗʰ Cir. 2003)

McRoberts Software Inc. v. Media 100 Inc. involved copyright infringement and misappropriation of trade secrets. A jury found in favor of the plaintiff on all three claims and awarded substantial damages. Upon motions by both parties for post-trial relief, the district judge (1) affirmed the jury's finding that Media 100 infringed MSI's copyright, misappropriated MSI's trade secrets, and breached their contract; (2) upheld the jury's award of damages to MSI for copyright infringement and breach of contract; (3) vacated the jury's award of damages to MSI for trade secret misappropriation, calling it duplicative of the copyright infringement award; and (4) awarded MSI attorneys' fees and prejudgment interest. On appeal, the Court of Appeals for the 7ᵗʰ Circuit reversed the District Court's order vacating the trade secret damages award and affirmed the remainder of the District Court's order.

In 1992 MSI developed a computer software program for character generation called Comet/CG. Character generation is the process of placing text over video and audio, as when words appear over images in a television ad or credits scroll at the end of a movie. Prior to MSI's inventing its software, character generation required specialized hardware that cost up to $100,000, but MSI's Comet/CG software provided similar character generation capability for users of Apple's Macintosh personal computers at around $1,300. Media 100 (formerly Data Translation, Inc.) manufactured video editing equipment, including the very expensive character generation hardware used by advertising agencies and television production studios. When Media 100 decided to enter the personal computing market, it turned to MSI to supply its Comet/CG software for use with its new "Media 100" line of personal video editing board hardware. MSI and Media 100 negotiated three separate licensing agreements, in 1993, 1995, and 1998.

Initially, Media 100's personal video editing boards functioned only on Macintosh computers through a video card component called a NuBus. Windows computers, in contrast, are compatible only with a video component called a PCI bus. Therefore, until Macintosh retooled its computers in 1995 to accept PCI bus hardware, video editing systems could only function on Macintosh or Windows machines but not both. The programming language for Macintosh and Windows machines was similarly incompatible, so MSI's Comet/CG source code could only be executed with Macintosh-compatible video editing boards. Early in the partnership between Media 100 and MSI, the Windows-versus-Macintosh debate remained on the distant horizon, at least in the video and graphic arts world. But it soon became clear that the personal computing market was going the way of Windows. By the time MSI and Media 100 negotiated their 1995 licensing agreement, both companies sensed that a profitable future had something to do with producing Windows-compatible products.

During negotiations for the 1995 agreement, MSI knew that Media 100 had developed a new video editing board based on the PCI bus architecture. While Media 100's new bus hardware made its products potentially compatible with Windows machines, the bundled video editing software (including Comet/CG) that Media 100 agreed to license from MSI still operated only on Macintosh machines. In 1998 Media 100 decided that it could no longer afford to ignore the Windows OS market, so it entered into an agreement with software development firm Vanteon (formerly Millennium Computer Corp.) to translate the Comet/CG source code from Macintosh to Windows (akin to translating English to Chinese, in the words of MSI owner McRoberts). Without MSI's consent or knowledge, Media 100 gave Vanteon a copy of MSI's confidential Comet/CG source code and paid Vanteon nearly $3.2 million to translate the code as quickly as possible. When Vanteon completed the task, Media 100 took the new code, put it into a Windows-compatible video editing system, and began selling it immediately. This new product line was named "Finish" and was essentially the same as the old "Media 100," except that Finish worked on Windows machines and Media 100 worked on Macintosh machines.

Soon after the Finish boards containing the translated Comet/CG code hit the market, MSI complained to Media 100 that it was not licensed to incorporate the Comet/CG software into its Windows-compatible product line, nor was it licensed to use any new version of Comet/CG that operated on PCI bus architecture rather than NuBus. Moreover, MSI demanded that Media 100 give it a copy of the translated Comet/CG code created by Vanteon as required by the licensing agreement. Media 100 refused to give MSI the translated code, but it removed all Finish products containing the translated MSI software from the market, licensed another company's Windows-compatible CG software, and reissued the Finish video boards with the new software.

MSI sued Media 100 in Federal District Court, claiming, among other things (1) copyright infringement under the *Federal Copyright Act* based on Media 100's unauthorized creation and distribution of the translated Windows-compatible Comet/CG software and (2) trade secret misappropriation under Indiana's *Trade Secret Act* based on Media 100's unauthorized disclosure of the confidential Comet/CG source code to Vanteon.

The jury awarded MSI $1.2 million for actual damages for copyright infringement, $900,000 in lost profits for copyright infringement, and $300,000 for trade secret misappropriation. In its cross-appeal, MSI claimed that the District Court erred by vacating the jury's award of $300,000 in damages for trade secret misappropriation. In granting Media 100's post-trial motion for judgment as a matter of law on this issue, the District Court ruled that MSI had failed to distinguish between its damages for copyright infringement and its damages for trade secret misappropriation, calling the trade secret damages duplicative and against the weight of evidence. The only explanation offered by the District Court for its decision was its belief that a successful claim for trade secret damages would have required MSI to argue and prove that it had suffered actual damages and lost unique ideas as a result of Media 100's breach of confidentiality.

Unlike the District Court, the 7th Circuit found that MSI presented ample evidence to support the jury's award of damages for trade secret misappropriation. The jury was clearly instructed by the Court as to how it should properly calculate damages for both trade secret misappropriation and copyright infringement. Because the Comet/CG source code represented both a trade secret and a consortium's copyright, much of the evidence presented at trial could have been used to substantiate damages for either one or both claims. Still, it was undisputed that the jury was instructed to consider different measures of damages in determining each award.

In calculating trade secret damages, for example, the District Court told the jury to consider either "the cost Media 100 would have incurred in acquiring the same information or trade secret through its own experimentation or through other lawful means," or "the actual value of what has been appropriated or the reasonable royalty at the time of the misappropriation." The jury was also reminded that MSI had the burden of proving its damages "for actual loss [proximately] caused by the misappropriation" by a preponderance of the evidence. In comparison, the instruction for computing copyright damages told the jury to determine "the amount of money adequate to compensate [MSI] for the reduction of the market value of the copyrighted work caused by the infringement," as measured by "the amount a willing buyer would have been reasonably required to pay a willing seller . . . for the use made by Media 100 of [MSI]'s Comet/CG source code." Although both instructions informed the jury that the value of the Comet/CG source code is relevant to determining damages, the value of the code is supposed to be measured differently in each instance. According to the 7th Circuit, it was neither surprising nor impermissibly duplicative for MSI to have presented numerous theories to the jury for calculating its losses.

The 7th Circuit noted that as a matter of law, it is possible to recover damages based on more than one legal theory in the same suit, provided the plaintiff provides sufficient evidence of his injuries. The evidence in this record suggested that had Media 100 lawfully gone about acquiring the rights to the Comet/ CG source code for the purpose of translating it into Windows, it either would have had to pay MSI to translate it or pay MSI for the right to hire someone like Vanteon to translate it. While Media 100 disputed this evidence, the jury was entitled to draw this inference from what it heard at trial. In particular, the jury learned that Media 100's customers wanted any new Windows hardware to be compatible with their Macintosh hardware running Comet/CG, which meant that Media 100 had a strong incentive to translate the Comet/CG code rather than incorporate Windows-based character generation software from a different company. Moreover, the jury heard evidence from MSI to suggest that the value to Media 100 of acquiring MSI's trade secret in the Comet/CG source code would have ranged from $383,000 to $1.3 million. MSI based these figures on (1) past software development contracts between Media 100 and MSI (as compared with software licensing contracts which the parties also entered into), (2) the profits realized by Vanteon in translating MSI's Comet/ CG source code, and (3) MSI's investment costs in the Comet/CG source code. Thus, the 7th Circuit held that the evidence showed that MSI suffered a measurable loss when Media 100 took its trade secrets in the Comet/CG source code and gave them to Vanteon, a competing software development company. The evidence also showed that this loss was different from the loss that MSI suffered when Media 100 incorporated the translated source code into Windows-compatible products and profited from its unauthorized distribution. For these reasons, the 7th Circuit held that it was an error for the District Court to vacate the jury's award of $300,000 to MSI for trade secret damages as duplicative of the copyright infringement damages.

IDX Systems Corp. v. Epic Systems, Corp., 285 F.3d 581 (7th Cir. 2002)

IDX Systems Corp. v. Epic Systems, Corp. highlights the importance of being able to specifically identify the trade secret(s) claimed to have been misappropriated by another. Both IDX Systems and Epic Systems make software for use in managing the financial side of a medical practice: billing, insurance reimbursement, collections, and the like. During the 1980s, IDX sold this software package to two medical groups that later merged into the University of Wisconsin Medical Foundation, which now comprises more than one thousand physicians. The foundation continued to use IDX software until December 2000, when it switched to software developed by Epic. IDX believes that Mitchell Quade and Michael Rosencrance, former employees of Epic who came to manage data processing at the foundation, not only instigated this change but also used their new positions to transfer valuable information to Epic. According to IDX's complaint, over the course of a year Quade and Rosencrance personally, and with the aid of other foundation employees, furnished Epic with details about how IDX's software works, enabling Epic to enhance its own package and ultimately take the foundation's business—and to match up better against IDX in the competition for other customers.

IDX's complaint under the diversity jurisdiction of 28 U.S.C. § 1332 charged the foundation, Quade, and Rosencrance with stealing IDX's trade secrets and breaking contractual promises of confidentiality. It also charged Epic with inducing the other defendants to do these things. The District Court dismissed the tort claims against Epic on the pleadings, observing that Wis. Stat. § 134.90(6)(a) overrides any theory that conflicts with the state's law of trade secrets. Later the District Court pared all contract-based claims out of the case, ruling that the confidentiality agreements were invalid under Wisconsin law (which the parties agree governs) because they do not contain temporal and geographic limitations. Finally, the Court granted summary judgment to the defendants on the trade secret claim, after concluding that IDX had failed to identify with specificity the trade secrets that it accuses the defendants of misappropriating (165 F. Supp. 2d 812; W.D. Wis. 2001).

To show that particular information was a trade secret, the 7th Circuit held that IDX had to demonstrate that it is valuable, not known to others who might profit by its use, and has been handled by means reasonably designed to maintain secrecy. The 7th Circuit agreed with the district judge that IDX failed to do this. The Court held that IDX had been both too vague and too inclusive, effectively asserting that all information on or about its software is a trade secret and did not match up to the statutory definition. The 7th Circuit noted that protective orders are available to make the process of identifying the alleged trade secrets less risky, and unless the plaintiff engages in a serious effort to pin down the secrets, a court cannot do its job.

The 7th Circuit held that a plaintiff must do more than simply identify a kind of technology and then invite the Court to hunt through the details in search of items meeting the statutory definition. The 7th Circuit stated that details such as the algorithms that the software uses to do real-time error checking (a vaunted feature of IDX's software), may be genuine trade secrets, but IDX did not try to separate them from non-trade secret elements such as its input and output formats. Nor did IDX contend that the defendants decompiled the object code or otherwise obtained access to the algorithms that power the program; instead, they alleged only that the foundation transferred to Epic those details that ordinary users of the software could observe without reverse engineering.

The 7th Circuit affirmed the judgment of the District Court to the extent that it granted judgment to the defendants on IDX's trade secret claims.

United States v. M.J. Trujillo-Cohen, CR-H-97–251 (S.D. Tex. 1997)

In *United States v. M.J. Trujillo-Cohen*, the US Attorney's Office in Houston, Texas, brought a two-count indictment under the *Economic Espionage Act of 1996* against Mayra Trujillo-Cohen for allegedly stealing proprietary software (specifically, the "4FRONT for SAP" and "FASTRACK 4SAP" programs) developed by Deloitte-Touche. According to the grand jury charges, Trujillo-Cohen, a former Deloitte-Touche employee, converted portions of the software programs, which she knew to be proprietary to Deloitte-Touche, by selling them to others for her personal benefit. In a plea agreement, Trujillo-Cohen pled guilty to one count under the *EEA* and one count of mail fraud. She was sentenced to concurrent terms of forty-eight months in prison on each of the *EEA* and mail fraud counts, followed by three years of supervised release. In addition, she was ordered to pay restitution in the amount of approximately $337,000, payable in full immediately.

EF Cultural Travel BV v. Explorica, Inc., 274 F.3d 577 (1st Cir. 2001)

EF Cultural Travel BV v. Explorica, Inc. involved application of the *Computer Fraud and Abuse Act* (*CFAA*) as well as misappropriation of trade secrets. EF and its partners and subsidiaries make up the world's largest private student travel organization and had been in business for more than thirty-five years. Explorica was formed in 2000 to compete in the field of global tours for high school students. Several of Explorica's employees were formerly employed by EF. Shortly after the individual defendants left EF in the beginning of 2000, Explorica began competing in the teenage tour market. The company's vice president (and former vice president of information strategy at EF), Philip Gormley, envisioned that Explorica could gain a substantial advantage over all other student tour companies—especially EF—by undercutting EF's already competitive prices on student tours.

Gormley considered several ways to obtain and utilize EF's prices: by manually keying in the information from EF's brochures and other printed materials; by using a scanner to record that same information; or by manually searching for each tour offered through EF's Web site. Ultimately, however, Gormley engaged Zefer, Explorica's Internet consultant, to design a computer program called a "scraper" to glean all of the necessary information from EF's Web site. Zefer designed the program in three days.

The scraper has been likened to a "bot," a tool that is extensively used on the Internet. Bots are used to gather information for countless purposes, ranging from compiling results for search engines such as Yahoo! to filtering for inappropriate content. The widespread deployment of bots enables global Internet users to find comprehensive information quickly and almost effortlessly.

Like a bot, the scraper sought information through the Internet. Unlike other bots, however, this scraper focused solely on EF's Web site, using information that other bots would not have. Specifically, Zefer utilized tour codes whose significance was not readily understandable to the public. With the tour codes, the scraper accessed EF's Web site repeatedly and easily obtained pricing information for those specific tours. The scraper sent more than thirty thousand inquiries to EF's Web site and recorded the pricing information onto a spreadsheet.

Zefer ran the scraper program twice, first to retrieve the 2000 tour prices and then the 2001 prices. All told, the scraper downloaded sixty thousand lines of data, the equivalent of eight telephone directories of information. Once Zefer "scraped" all of the prices, it sent a spreadsheet containing EF's pricing information to Explorica, which then systematically undercut EF's prices. Explorica thereafter printed its own brochures and began competing in EF's tour market.

The District Court granted a preliminary injunction against Explorica based on the *CFAA*, which criminally and civilly prohibits certain access to computers—see 18 U.S.C. § 1030(a)(4). The Court found that EF would likely prove that Explorica violated the *CFAA* when it used EF's Web site in a manner outside the "reasonable expectations" of both EF and its ordinary users. The Court also concluded that EF could show that it suffered a loss, as required by the statute, consisting of reduced business, harm to its goodwill, and the cost of diagnostic measures it incurred to evaluate possible harm to EF's systems, although it could not show that Explorica's actions physically damaged its computers. In a supplemental opinion, the District Court further articulated its "reasonable expectations" standard and explained that copyright, contractual, and technical restraints sufficiently notified Explorica that its use of a scraper would be unauthorized and thus would violate the *CFAA*.

EF alleged that the defendants knowingly and with intent to defraud accessed the server hosting EF's Web site more than thirty thousand times to obtain proprietary pricing and tour information, as well as confidential information about EF's technical abilities. At the heart of the parties' dispute is whether appellants' actions either were "without authorization" or "exceeded authorized access" as defined by the *CFAA*. The 1st Circuit concluded that because of the broad confidentiality agreement, appellants' actions "exceeded authorized access," and it did not need to reach the more general arguments made about statutory meaning, including whether use of a scraper alone renders access unauthorized.

The record contains at least two communications from Gormley to Zefer that seemingly rely on information about EF to which he was privy only because of his prior employment there. The documentary evidence also pointed to Gormley's heavy involvement in the conception of the scraper program. Furthermore, the voluminous spreadsheet containing all of the scraped information included the tour codes that EF claimed was proprietary information. Each page of the spreadsheet produced by Zefer included the tour and gateway codes, the date of travel, and the price for the tour. An uninformed reader would regard the tour codes as nothing but gibberish. Although the codes can be correlated to the actual tours and destination points, the codes standing alone need to be "translated" to be meaningful.

There was ample evidence that Gormley provided Explorica with proprietary information about the structure of the Web site and the tour codes. Manually gathering the various codes through repeated searching and deciphering of the URLs may theoretically be possible. Practically speaking, however, Explorica's wholesale use of EF's travel codes to facilitate gathering EF's prices from its Web site, if proven, reeks of use—and indeed abuse—of proprietary information that goes beyond any authorized use of EF's Web site.

Gormley voluntarily entered into a broad confidentiality agreement prohibiting his disclosure of any information "which might reasonably be construed to be contrary to the interests of EF." Appellants would face an uphill battle trying to argue that it was not against EF's interests for appellants to use the tour codes to mine EF's pricing data. Thus, the 1st Circuit stated that if EF's allegations are proven, it will likely prove that whatever authorization Explorica had to navigate around EF's site (even in a competitive vein), it exceeded that authorization by providing proprietary information and know-how to Zefer to create the scraper. The 1st Circuit held that the District Court's finding that Explorica likely violated the *CFAA* was not clearly erroneous. [RR]

Summarizing Trade Secrets in New Media

One of the key consequences of new media is the democratization of information. Stated in the extreme, when everyone is an investigative reporter, it's difficult to keep a secret. Although the situation has not yet reached the point where "everyone" is an investigative reporter, the number of blogs and bloggers is staggering, and the pace of new participants joining the fray seems unabated. Unique information exchange about new products can set a blog apart from competitors; the pressure to post timely and distinctive information in the blogosphere is strong. However, many (or most?) bloggers work without either substantial editorial constraints or legal counsel. Publication of information is in the hands of the author, and there is little reason to believe that "everyone" is familiar with trade secret law, one of the more esoteric aspects of the intellectual property suite.

As with everything about digital communication, the speed and ubiquity with which materials can be duplicated and the potential reach of networked duplication raise the intellectual property stakes above previous levels. In effect, the number of employees who can damage organizations has risen dramatically, not to mention the role of those outside organizations. Risks in the trade secrets area have increased exponentially in the digital age, while the legal system has (as with other areas in IP law) struggled, and largely failed, to keep up with technology. One suspects that massive changes in the system will be required very soon if trade secret law is to keep pace with change. [ELL]

Discussion Questions

1. Note Apple Computer's long-standing battles with bloggers over information they consider trade secrets. Discuss the ways the "blogosphere" impacts trade secrets.
2. With regard to bloggers, consider freedom of the press and freedom of speech issues. Should bloggers be treated as journalists?
3. Trade secret law became closely tied to espionage through the *Industrial Espionage Act of 1996*. Should a special court system be set up (like that for patents) to separate the handling of espionage cases from domestic trade secret cases?
4. Employee job change is one of the leading circumstances in which trade secret cases arise. Employment in new media industries is notoriously "fluid." What actions should employees and employers in new media industries take, on the trade secret front, in this environment?
5. What appear to be the principal areas in trade secret law (both in the laws and in the circumstances of execution surrounding them) needing revision in light of new media?

CHAPTER SIX

Rights of Publicity, Privacy, and Defamation[1]

Although it is not technically accurate to do so, it may be useful (at least as a starting point) to think about "rights of publicity" as most often involving "celebrities," "defamation" to be most often associated with "private citizens," and "rights of privacy" to be a highly complex set of features involving a broad range of topics that have seen radical changes, especially over the last decade. Many privacy laws have been added and/or changed of late; however, one would say in general that many of the expectations of privacy that Americans once held so dear have been muted either by the choices that individuals make that fail to protect their own privacy (such as using credit cards and posting to blogs) or the use that others make of information that is inaccurately assumed to be private (online availability and harvesting of information or identity theft and the like). As indicated, these categorizations are not absolute, as the issues can—and sometimes do—intermix.

Black notes five main phases in the development of privacy laws. First, historical periods prior to 1900 without specific laws; second, tort law that established damages for invasion of personal privacy; third, Supreme Court decisions recognizing a constitutional right of privacy; fourth, Supreme Court action balancing the public's right to know with law enforcement's need to counter the use of technology in crimes; and fifth, the public's expectation of privacy with technology (261–62).

Historical Touch Points

Unlike for copyrights, patents, and trademarks, early English common law did not offer examples of established legal principles for rights of publicity, privacy, and defamation. Although some of those rights can be implied from various protections of copyrights and trademarks, neither formal legislation nor sufficient numbers of cases established clear precedent prior to the end of the nineteenth century. In the United States, the issues rose to the level of judicial attention in 1890 when Samuel D. Warren and future Supreme Court Justice Louis D. Brandeis wrote an article in which they argued that the Constitution, though never stating so directly, offers a "right to be left alone." Thereafter, a number of privacy torts were developed (Warren and Brandeis).

Subsequently, courts have relied on aspects of the First, Fourth, Fifth, and Fourteenth Amendments to protect various aspects of personal autonomy. There is federal history with regard to various rights of privacy as they are often taken to stand as a Constitutional right (via inference). In each of the areas, there remains to this day, however, no *single* broad, federal law protecting rights of publicity, nor is there broad federal legislation against defamation of character. However, there are now a large number of federal laws dealing with specific aspects of many of the rights. Further, in the absence of unified and broad federal legislation regarding these points of law, much of the development of law in these areas takes place at the state level.[2] To date, twenty-eight states are on record as recognizing the right of publicity; of these, many do not recognize a right by that name but protect it as part of the right of privacy. In other states the right of publicity is protected through the law of unfair competition (Wex, "Publicity"). Minnesota and Virginia appear to be the only states that have rejected the right to privacy involving giving unreasonable publicity to an individual's private life. Because the rights are relatively new (as compared to the long history of the development of common law features such as copyright) and because the laws are primarily driven by state rather than federal law, there is much variety and unevenness in interpretation and application of these legal principles. By the 1970s, forty-nine of the fifty states had passed laws recognizing the invasion of privacy as a legal issue (Black 263).

Although these aspects were briefly defined in the Introduction to this book, a quick reminder of the privacy torts is useful here because of the overlapping and complex nature of the considerations. Individuals maintain control over the commercial use of their "persona" (name, image, etc.). Others cannot use one's image for commercial gain without permission. This right of publicity is most often invoked by celebrities, because in many instances, their personae are more recognizable and influential than that of everyman, and, therefore, the use of their personae entails higher commercial values than that of non-celebrities. However, the basic rights are accorded regardless of status.

Further, individuals are assumed to be able to control access to certain types of information about themselves, especially when the release of that information to others would cause the person to be seen or treated in a negative light or if making the information known would otherwise threaten or damage the source's reputation or put them at other kinds of risk. Various rights of privacy will be detailed in sections following treatment of the rights of publicity. Unfortunately, the digital age has found many Americans willing to compromise their privacy rights. Further, concerns over terrorism have increased the use of surveillance technologies in many communities. Some would go so far as to claim that privacy in America (as we once knew it) is effectively a thing of the past. Nevertheless, there are numerous laws still in place to protect privacy.

Laws against defamation protect citizens from slander and libel—false communication in word or print that purposefully damages the reputation of others. Since the threshold for defaming public figures is somewhat higher than in the case of innocent private citizens, laws against defamation can be seen as reaching down to the average citizen perhaps more thoroughly than rights of publicity.

As noted by Solove, a significant problem with relying on the privacy torts and with the lack of overarching covering law is that infringements based on single/isolated acts tend to miss current privacy problems of a more general nature. For example, "modern privacy problems are the product of information flows, which occur between a variety of different entities. There is often no single wrongdoer; responsibility is spread among a multitude of actors, with a vast array of motives and aims, each doing different things at different times" (61–62).

Rights of Publicity

Consider this hypothetical situation:

A friend who is a photographer for your student newspaper asks you to help him/her out with a photo spread for this week's issue. You are asked to meet at the practice facility used by both the men's and women's basketball teams, as the article will be about supporting the schools' sports teams. You arrive at the appointed hour and sit in the stands watching a practice while your friend shoots a large number of pictures. Come publication day, the spread runs and includes one of the pictures of you watching practice, shot from behind you, using your view of the court as point of reference. You are pleased to "make the paper" and get a load of positive comments from friends.

On the Web site for the paper, another picture of you, taken in the same location at the same shoot, is published. This time the picture is of you from the front. There is a banner behind you that was provided by the local car dealer who lends cars to the coaching staff. The banner identifies the dealer; the picture appears in an advertisement on the Web site of the student paper that focuses on the dealer as a strong supporter of the school, its sports program, and its students. You are not named in the ad, but the ad copy notes that: "our students are 'topnotch' in part due to the support of this gracious sponsor." When you call your friend and ask, he/she notes that you signed a release permitting the photo shoot and that the dealer relationship is a benefit to the school and the teams that you love very much. Should you be proud of your image being used in this fashion? What are your rights in this example? Have your rights been violated?

Although our rule of thumb at the start of the chapter suggested that rights of publicity most often apply to celebrities, the fact is, as exemplified by our hypothetical, every citizen maintains the right above and beyond copyright issues against the unauthorized use of their name and person (their persona, including name and image) in ways that might damage the commercial value of their good name (Smedinghoff 262). However, with regard to the commercial value of a person's image, celebrities have more at stake than do regular private citizens as their images are more marketable.

From the production side of the equation, though, everyone who publishes material must be concerned over aspects of rights of publicity, as one can get into loads of trouble by infringing on others' rights. And in this day of ubiquitous self-publishing on the Web, everyman becomes responsible for adherence to these principles.

Important Exceptions to Rights of Publicity

Perhaps the most "federal" of laws applying to questions concerning rights of publicity has to do with First Amendment protections of free speech. Communication with strong public interest is protected speech: news, commentary, satire, critique, and some other forms of speech are protected when the information can be interpreted to be within the public's right to know. News and information of public interest, even when about public figures with a lot at risk, are generally treated as outside the realm of protection under rights of publicity.

There are a number of situations in which materials used do not (in general and normal usages) constitute violation of rights of publicity. The use of images of buildings in public areas is not a violation, as rights of publicity adhere to persons, not buildings. However, talking pictures of corporate buildings may violate trademark, copyright, or privacy laws. Images of persons done in such a way as to hide the identity of the subjects of the images do not violate publicity rights. Images of persons present at newsworthy events, as long as the image is used as part of reporting about the event rather than used for other, more commercial purposes or for purposes that far exceed the role of the individual as mere spectator, do not violate rights of publicity (Hassett).

Additionally, artistic and literary uses of likeness, name, voice, and/or identity/persona are often protected by court interpretations of freedom of artistic expression. In some jurisdictions and cases, artistic expression using "identity imagery" is solidly protected; in others, those rights are hotly contested. Further, some states limit the full protection of rights of publicity laws to advertising; in others, additional commercial venues are considered. Generally, parodies are protected as a form of artistic expression/free speech, virtually regardless of the abuse to which the identity/image is put.

Foundations for Rights of Publicity

As noted, most of the developments for rights of publicity law are generally found in case law/judicial decisions in the courts of the various states. Some highlights will be noted later in this chapter. Legislative developments can be found in a number of places.

Some federal guidelines can be extracted from various sections of the *Restatement of the Law*. For example, section 46 of the *Restatement of the Law Third, Unfair Competition*, notes: "One who appropriates the commercial value of a person's identity by using without consent the person's name, likeness, or other indicia of identity for purposes of trade is subject to liability for the relief appropriate." Further, in section 652A of the *Restatement of the Law, Torts 2d*, one finds: "The right of privacy is invaded by: . . . (b) appropriation of the other's name or likeness . . . ; (c) unreasonable publicity given to the other's private life . . . ;" (Hassett). And, as Wex points out, "The Federal Lanham Act can also provide protection where a person's identity is used to falsely advertise a product or designate its origin."

As one might expect, given the nature of the entertainment industry, many of the developments in rights of publicity come from California and New York, two states in which celebrity rights have particular relevance. For example, the *Celebrities Rights Act* was passed in California in 1985. The act extended the personality rights for a celebrity to seventy years after his or her death (Find-Law). New York, for example, protects rights of publicity with privacy law such as the following: "Any person whose name, portrait or picture is used within this state for advertising purposes or for the purposes of trade without the written consent first obtained [from the person] . . . may maintain an equitable action . . . and may also sue and recover damages for any injuries sustained by reason of such use . . ." (*N.Y. Civil Rights Law* § 51; Satterlee et al.).

Generally speaking, the likeness, name, voice, and/or identity/persona cannot be used for advertising (and other commercial purposes) without explicit (written) consent. Further, the performances of actors may be used only with permission. Additionally, the usage agreements between producers and the "identity provider" should set the grounds for the uses to which the likeness, name, voice, and/or identity/persona may be put. Uses that exceed the agreement are often held as violations of the subject's publicity rights.

Another important area of consideration is the public distribution of information that could be construed to be private and of little public interest. Particularly in a global networked and mass media environment, information spreads at an astronomical rate of speed. The release of private information, even about public figures, has enormous potential for damage and harm. Since celebrities live very public lives, parsing the differences between material that is of public interest and material that is within their privacy rights is very difficult. The privacy aspect will be taken up later; for now, rights of publicity are in the forefront of our consideration. Even celebrities, and certainly private citizens, have a right to control the degree to which their most private information is put to use by others for commercial gain. The courts in California and New York are replete with examples of celebrity suits against tabloid publications for the wrongful distribution of private information, ostensibly (from the perspective of the celebrity) for the mere purpose of selling papers, as opposed to providing information that the public has a right to know about the figure.

Digital technologies and the Internet complicate rights of publicity issues in the extreme. The rapid and broad dissemination of materials raises the stakes in all areas of publicity, privacy, and defamation. Also, the overlap between the relationships among "news," "public information," and "private information" on the Internet are very complex and yet to be fully worked out by the courts. For example, some material that appears on blogs can be said to be newsworthy to the degree that it gains protections against violation of publicity rights. Other information on the same blog may well violate a person's publicity rights. And, of course, rights of publicity notwithstanding, the entire range of intellectual property rights is at risk (or at least, in play) in the Webbed/networked media environment. [ELL]

As noted, much law pertaining to rights of publicity is based on state statutes. However, federal law complicates an already diverse situation. Section 230 of the *Communications Decency Act (230 CDA)* grants ISPs immunity from prosecution for various IP violations that users might inflict on others. In *Perfect 10, Inc. v. CCBill LLC* (and similar cases), courts have ruled that federal immunity trumps state legislation. However, in a recent New Hampshire case, *Jane Doe v. Friendfinder Network*, a Federal District Court judge ruled that the immunity provisions in section 230 of the *Communications Decency Act (230 CDA)* do not bar a state law claim for a violation of a person's "right of publicity." This ruling opens the door to right of publicity claims based on state laws that might not be overruled by *230 CDA*.

Traditional Media Rights of Publicity Cases with New Media Implications

Haelan Laboratories, Inc. v. Topps Chewing Gum. Inc., 202 F.2d 866 (2nd Cir. 1953)

A baseball player endorsed the plaintiff's brand of chewing-gum. The player granted the plaintiff exclusive rights to use the player's photograph in connection with the sales of the plaintiff's gum. Later, Topps, Haelan Laboratories' competitor, induced the player to enter into a contract granting Topps the right to use the player's photograph for sales of Topps' gum during the term of the plaintiff's contract with the player.

Topps' principal argument was that a statutory right of privacy is personal and not assignable. If this argument had been accepted, it would have meant that the player could, at most, grant a release of liability for use of the player's photograph for a commercial purpose. Therefore, the defendant argued that defendant's conduct could not have invaded any right of the plaintiff.

The Court rejected the defendant's argument, concluding that "the ballplayer also promised not to give similar releases to others," and that inducing the player to breach that agreement would constitute tortuous conduct. Essentially, the Court held that in addition to a right of privacy, an individual has the legal right to grant exclusive use of one's image, likeness, or name. The Court found that whether or not such a right was a "property" right was immaterial and coined the term "right of publicity" to describe such a legal right. The Court found that such a right existed and remanded the case to the District Court to determine whether the defendant induced the player to breach a contract granting the right of publicity from the player to the plaintiff.

Zacchini v. Scripps-Howard Broadcasting Co., 433 U.S. 562 (1977)

Zacchini was a performer in a human cannonball act in which he was shot out of a cannon into a net hundreds of feet away. Zacchini sued Scripps-Howard, a television broadcasting company, to recover damages, because Scripps-Howard videotaped Zacchini's entire performance at an Ohio county fair and played the videotape on an 11 o'clock news program. The Ohio Supreme Court rendered judgment for Scripps-Howard on the grounds that the performance was a matter of public interest and therefore Scripps-Howard was constitutionally privileged to include the performance in its newscasts. The Court went on to state that because there was no intent to injure Zacchini, the right of publicity did not prevent Scripps-Howard from broadcasting Zacchini's performance.

The US Supreme Court granted certiorari and explained that prior federal case law involving the First and Fourteenth Amendment privilege exceptions cited by Scripps-Howard applied to cases where the press was reporting news events and generally involved defamation cases. The Court distinguished this case, stating that the Constitutional privilege should not be applied where the press is attempting to "broadcast or publish an entire act for which the performer ordinarily gets paid."

The Court then held that although Ohio could grant such a privilege as a matter of its own state law, there is no Constitutional requirement to allow the press to broadcast such a performance and that the right of publicity protects the proprietary interest of an individual to "reap the reward of his endeavors." The Court held that Ohio maintained its right to "protect petitioner's right of publicity" or to "privilege the press in the circumstances of this case," as its own state laws provided. To the extent that the Ohio Supreme Court based its finding for Scripps-Howard on the First and Fourteenth Amendments, the Court therefore reversed the Ohio Supreme Court's findings.

Henley v. Dillard Department Stores, 46 F. Supp. 2d 587 (N.D. Tex. 1999)

Don Henley, a musician, sued Dillard, a department store, for violating his right of publicity. Dillard ran a newspaper advertisement for a shirt styled as a "Henley." To catch consumer attention, the ad pointed to a model ostensibly named "Don" saying "this is Don's Henley." The Court reviewed the case law regarding the "three elements a plaintiff must prove to recover for the tort of misappropriation of name and likeness in Texas: (1) the defendant appropriated the plaintiff's name or likeness for the value associated with it, and not in an incidental manner or for a newsworthy purpose; (2) the plaintiff can be identified from the publication; and (3) there was some advantage or benefit to the defendant."

The Court found that Dillard intended to use the term "Don's Henley" for commercial advantage, believing that the expression would catch consumers' attention due to its similarity to Don Henley's name. The Court also found that the use of the term "Don's Henley" in the advertising was enough to identify Henley—the Court discussed the various cases, stating that an individual can be identified in many ways, including use of the individual's "name, nickname, voice, picture, performing style, distinctive characteristics or other indicia closely associated with a person." Finally, the Court held that Dillard obtained a benefit from the advertising. Here, the Court found that proving a profit is not necessary and that it is only necessary to show that the defendant received a commercial benefit from use of the plaintiff's name or likeness that the defendant would not otherwise have received. Dillard's experienced advertisement creators described the benefit that they intended to receive from associating "Don's Henley" with their shirts as "being able to catch the eye of the consumer and make the ad more interesting." Because of the decision by the advertising designer to run the advertisement, the Court found that the benefit of Henley's endorsement was obtained without Henley's consent, regardless of whether the advertisement was profitable. Therefore, the Court found that Henley's right of privacy was violated and granted his motion for summary judgment.

Abdul-Jabbar v. Gen. Motors, 85 F.3d 407, 415–16 (9th Cir. 1996)

Former basketball player and actor Kareem Abdul-Jabbar sued General Motors (GM) for trademark infringement and violation of his right of publicity under California's state law for the use of his former name, "Lew Alcindor," in a television commercial without his consent. The television commercial was for an Oldsmobile vehicle and included a trivia question to which the answer was

"Lew Alcindor, UCLA, '67, '68, '69." GM withdrew the commercial when Ab-dul-Jabbar complained after it had aired five or six times. The District Court, based on the fact that Kareem had abandoned his former name and that GM's use of his former name could not be construed as Kareem's endorsement of GM's product, granted summary judgment in favor of GM.

In addition to discussing aspects of Abdul-Jabbar's trademark claims, the Court addressed GM's primary argument that Abdul-Jabbar had abandoned the name Lew Alcindor with respect to the right of publicity claim. GM ar-gued that, because Abdul-Jabbar had not used the Alcindor name in over ten years and because the name was not in "common, present use," GM could not infringe Abdul-Jabbar's right of publicity by using the Alcindor name. Abdul-Jabbar countered, and the Court agreed, that a name cannot be abandoned and that in addition to a person's right to use his name or identity for commercial purposes, that person also has the right to *not* use the identity for commercial purposes. The Court therefore found that Abdul-Jabbar had alleged sufficient facts to state a claim and survive summary judgment, reversing the District Court's grant of GM's motion for summary judgment.

Cardtoons, L.C. v. Major League Baseball Players' Ass'n, 95 F.3d 959 (10th Cir. 1996)

Cardtoons filed a declaratory judgment action asserting that their parody base-ball trading cards did not infringe the baseball players' rights of publicity. An example was a card of a player dubbed "Treasury Bonds," a parody of San Francisco Giants' outfielder Barry Bonds. The card had a recognizable cari-cature of Bonds, "complete with earring, tipping a bat boy for a 24 carat gold 'Fort Knoxville Slugger.'" The card also contained a team logo for the "Gents" and other humorous text on the back. The District Court held that the First Amendment allowed for a parody exception to Oklahoma's statutory right of publicity, granting Cardtoons's declaratory judgment that the cards do not in-fringe Bonds' rights of publicity.

The 10th Circuit evaluated a potential right of publicity claim under Okla-homa law and found that the cards produced by Cardtoons did meet the three required elements—defendant's knowing use of plaintiffs' names or likenesses; on products, merchandise or goods; and without plaintiffs' prior consent—and therefore infringed Bonds' rights of publicity. The Court next addressed the "news" exception and a First Amendment-like "incidental use" exception of the Oklahoma statute. The "news" exception allows for use of a person's iden-tity for news reporting, public affairs, political campaigning, or sports broadcasting. The "incidental use" exception exempts uses in commercial media that are not "directly connected with commercial sponsorship or paid advertising." The Court found that neither exemption provided protection for Cardtoons, because Cardtoons' use of Bonds' likenesses is directly connected with a proposed commercial endeavor.

Although the Court held that the defendant's use of Bonds' likenesses in parody trading cards violated the right of publicity, the Court found that the First Amendment protects Cardtoons' right to publish its parody trading cards. The Court discussed the idea that parody is a humorous form of social commentary and that humorous as well as serious commentary on "an important social institution constitutes protected expression." Finally, the Court weighed the effects of limiting the rights of publicity versus the effects of limiting free expression and held that the effect of limiting the rights of publicity in this case were negligible, while limiting free expression would eliminate "an important form of entertainment and social commentary that deserve First Amendment protection." The Court therefore affirmed the grant of Cardtoons's declaratory judgment that its parody trading cards do not infringe Bonds' rights of publicity.

Toney v. L'Oreal USA, 406 F.3d 905 (7th Cir. 2005)

June Toney, a model, authorized Johnson Products Company to use photographs of her in connection with its hair-relaxing product, "Ultra Sheen Supreme," in national magazine advertisements for a limited time. When L'Oreal, a successor company to Johnson, later used the photographs after the expiration of the initial contract, Toney sued L'Oreal for violation of her right of publicity. The District Court dismissed Toney's claim, asserting that federal copyright law preempted her right of publicity claim.

The 7th Circuit reversed the District Court's holding, finding that Toney's right of publicity was infringed by the use of Toney's likeness in connection with the packaging and promotion of L'Oreal's hair-care product. The Court analyzed the *Illinois Right of Publicity Act* (*IRPA*) and the claims in the suit to determine whether copyright law preempted Toney's claims. The Court determined that Toney's identity was not fixed in a tangible medium of expression and that there was no work of authorship at issue because a person's likeness or persona is neither authored nor fixed. Furthermore, the Court found that the rights protected by the *IRPA*, which allow a person to control the commercial value of her identity, are not equivalent to any of the rights protected by federal copyright law.

Newcombe v. Adolph Coors Co., 157 F.3d 686 (9th Cir. 1998)

Don Newcombe is a former all-star baseball pitcher who played the majority of his career for the Brooklyn Dodgers and the Cincinnati Reds in the 1950s, with time taken out to serve in the Korean War. Newcombe, a well-known re-covering alcoholic who has been sober since 1967, has helped numerous people in their battles against substance abuse and has served as spokesperson for the National Institute on Drug and Alcohol Abuse. Killian's Irish Red Beer, owned by Coors, ran an advertisement in the *Sports Illustrated* swimsuit edition that featured a beer and some text on the right side and a drawing of an old-time baseball game on the right. Although the drawing did not depict a specific team or stadium, the drawing featured a pitcher in the windup position, a single in-fielder, and an old-fashioned outfield fence. Newcombe, his friends, family, and former teammates immediately recognized the pitcher as being Newcombe in his playing days. The drawing of the pitcher in the advertisement was based on a 1947 photograph of Newcombe on the mound. The District Court dismissed the suit, finding that the intent of the advertisers was to have a generic baseball scene and not to exploit Newcombe's image.

The 9th Circuit reversed the District Court's finding, holding that there was a "triable issue of fact" as to whether the plaintiff was "readily identifiable as the pitcher in [the] advertisement" and "whether the advertisement made use of Newcombe's likeness." The Court found that the stance of the pitcher in the advertisement was similar to that of Newcombe in the photograph and that none of the other pictures of record depicting pitchers in the wind-up po-sition included a similar stance. The 9th Circuit therefore reversed the District Court, holding that the jury may find that Adolph Coors used an image of Newcombe without his permission.

Carson v. Here's Johnny Portable Toilets, Inc., 698 F.2d 831, 835 (6th Cir. 1983)

Johnny Carson, the long-time host of *The Tonight Show*, sued Here's Johnny, a company involved in the sale and rental of portable toilets for trademark infringement and violation of the right of publicity. On *The Tonight Show*, each night, Mr. Carson was introduced with the familiar phrase "Here's Johnny." The District Court dismissed Carson's complaint. The 6th Circuit affirmed the District Court's finding that there was no likelihood of confusion, and thus the trademark infringement claim failed. However, the Court reversed the District Court's finding with respect to the right of publicity and found for Carson, holding that "if the celebrity's identity is commercially exploited, there has been an invasion of his right whether or not his 'name or likeness' is used. Carson's identity may be exploited even if his name, John W. Carson, or his picture is not used."

The Court summarized prior right of publicity cases, clarifying that use of a person's name or picture is not necessary to find that the person's right of publicity has been violated. The Court included references to cases finding infringement of people's rights of publicity when the infringer used the person's nickname, likeness, and, in at least one case, a car that was associated with the person who was a professional race car driver. The dissenting opinion attempted to distinguish between other cases finding a violation of right of publicity by stating that this case involved a phrase and did not involve the appropriation of a celebrity's "name, likeness, achievements, identifying characteristics or actual performances."

New Media Cases in Rights of Publicity Law

CBC. Distribution and Marketing, Inc. v. Major League Baseball Adv. Media, L.P., F.3d (8th Cir. 2007)

The plaintiff, CBC, brought this action seeking a declaratory judgment against the defendant, Major League Baseball Advanced Media, to establish its right to use the names of MLB players without any license. By selling subscriptions, the plaintiff provided a "fantasy" sports Web site that included a "fantasy" baseball league. The fantasy league used the names and performance statistics of actual MLB players. Up until 2005, the plaintiff had licensed the use of the names and statistics from the Major League Baseball Players Association. At the end of its agreement with the plaintiff, the Players Association decided to exclusively license MLB players' names and statistics to the defendant. The plaintiff thereafter initiated this action to prevent the defendant from suing to enjoin the plaintiff's continued use of the players' names and statistics. The District Court granted summary judgment to the plaintiff, holding that the plaintiff was not infringing any state-law rights of publicity that belonged to the players, and that even if it were, the First Amendment preempted those rights. On appeal, although the Court of Appeals for the 8th Circuit disagreed with the District Court that the plaintiff was not infringing the players' right to publicity, it nonetheless affirmed that the claims were preempted by the First Amendment.

The Court began its discussion by reviewing the District Court's findings regarding the right to publicity claims. The Court noted that the District Court was correct in determining that the plaintiff's use of the names and statistics was without consent. However, the Court disagreed with the District Court's finding that the plaintiff was not using the players' names as a symbol of identity. The Court explained: "The District Court did not understand that when a name alone is sufficient to establish identity, the defendant's use of that name satisfies the plaintiff's burden to show that a name was used as a symbol of identity." The Court also disagreed with the lower court's finding that the plaintiff's use of the players' names was not for a commercial advantage. The Court noted that although the plaintiff's use of the names for fantasy sports did not fall squarely within the recognized categories of commercial advantage, it was clear that the plaintiff used them for purposes of profit. Therefore, the Court found that the defendant did have a cause of action for violation of the players' rights to publicity.

The inquiry, however, did not end there. The Court determined that the right of publicity claims were preempted by the First Amendment. In so doing, the Court recognized that the plaintiff's use of the names in an "interactive form" was entitled to First Amendment protection. The Court then noted that the names and statistics were of public interest and value and that the states' interest in protecting an individual's right to privacy was not implicated because the players were handsomely rewarded for their participation in the actual games. Accordingly, the Court held that the defendant's claim for violation of the right to publicity was preempted. On June 2, 2008, the US Supreme Court refused to hear MLB's appeal, thereby maintaining the public domain status of statistics and players' names in the fantasy league context.

KNB Enters. v. Matthews, 78 Cal. App. 4th 362 (Cal. Ct. App. 2000)

The plaintiff, KNB, was the owner of a Web site that displayed erotic photographs. The plaintiff owned—by contractual assignment—the copyrights to several hundred photographs and occasionally posted some of these photographs to various Usenet newsgroups in order to promote its Web site. The defendant, Matthews, characterized Usenet as "a public forum on the Internet where individuals can participate in the open exchange of information." Essentially, plaintiff attempted to entice users on Usenet to subscribe to the plaintiff's Web site by uploading sample images to Usenet. The defendant used a software program that consolidated and copied erotic photographs posted on Usenet. The defendant, without the plaintiff's consent, displayed hundreds of copyrighted photographs on the defendant's Web site, "Justpics"—a Web site where customers pay a monthly membership fee to view erotic photographs taken from Usenet.

Plaintiff brought suit, however, not under federal copyright law, but rather under California state law covering commercial appropriation. Essentially, the plaintiff alleged that the models'—the women who posed in the pictures—right to publicity was violated. The linchpin issue for the Court, then, was to decide whether federal copyright law preempted the misappropriation claims.

The Court began its discussion on California's right of publicity law. The Court noted that although the models were not recognized celebrities, the plaintiff nevertheless was able to allege that the defendant profited by making sales, selling memberships, and saving time and money by "substituting a few moments of copying for what could have been days or weeks of work." After briefly reciting relevant copyright law, the Court acknowledged that the photographs themselves were copyrightable and that unauthorized display of the photographs was copyright infringement, but that the issue was not the photographs but rather the models' likenesses.

The Court continued, citing cases wherein copyright law and preemption of misappropriation claims were at issue. The Court distinguished cases in which copyright preemption was found based on the fact that in those cases, the models or actors were suing the entities that lawfully owned the copyrights to the models' or actors' photographs. Unlike those cases, the Court noted, the defendant was not lawfully entitled to distribute or use the photographs, and thus the plaintiff was not using the right to publicity to make up for its lack of copyright rights.

Moreover, the Court cited *Nimmer on Copyright* for the proposition that "right of publicity claims generally are not preempted by the *Copyright Act* [emphasis added]." Subsequently, the Court stated that while it would find a misappropriation claim preempted "where an actor or model with no copyright interest in the work seeks to prevent the exclusive copyright holder from displaying the copyrighted work," it would not do so "where . . . the defendant has no legal right to publish the copyrighted work."

Finally, the Court concluded that the two-part test for preemption—that (1) the subject of the claim must be a work fixed in a tangible medium of expression and be within the subject matter of copyright protection, and (2) the right asserted under the state law must be equivalent to the exclusive rights granted under copyright law—was not met because the subjects of the claims were the actual likenesses of the models, and accordingly were not copyrightable, and the right of publicity does not come within the subject matter of copyright. Therefore, the Court reversed the finding of summary judgment for the defendant and remanded the case.

Carafano v. Metrosplash.com Inc., 207 F. Supp. 2d 1055 (C.D. Cal. 2002)

The plaintiff, Christianne Carafano, was an actress who went by the stage name of "Chase Masterson." The plaintiff filed her lawsuit against the defendants, operators of the Web site Matchmaker.com, alleging, among other things, misappropriation of the right of publicity.

Matchmaker.com provided a Web service that allowed members to search a database containing profiles posted by other members. All a person had to do to join this online community was to fill out an application and a questionnaire. Eventually, after the running of a trial period, a user was required to pay a monthly fee to continue membership. In 1999, an unknown person created a trial account on Matchmaker.com under the name "Chase 529." The profile created by this anonymous user included four photographs of the plaintiff and the plaintiff's home address and an e-mail address. The user also filled out the online questionnaire using various lewd and licentious answers. As a result, the plaintiff received obscene phone calls, letters, and faxes. After learning of the existence of the profile, the plaintiff filed suit against the defendant. In turn, the defendant moved for summary judgment.

As an initial matter, the Court determined that the plaintiff's various causes of action were not barred by the *Communications Decency Act of 1996 (CDA)*—an act designed to protect "interactive computer services" from liability for third-party postings. While the Court agreed with the defendants that Matchmaker.com was an "interactive computer service" for purposes of the *CDA*, the Court nevertheless determined that immunity under the *CDA* was inapplicable because Matchmaker.com was an "information content provider"—an entity unable to find refuge under the *CDA*. The Court noted that Matchmaker.com was not simply a conduit of the information that was provided on its Web site. Rather, by requiring the users to fill out a questionnaire, it was an active player in developing the information that was ultimately posted. Therefore, the Court found that immunity from suit under the *CDA* did not extend to the defendants as a matter of law.[3]

The Court continued its discussion, addressing each of the plaintiff's causes of action. In one of her causes of action, the plaintiff alleged that the use of her photographs in the Matchmaker.com profile constituted an appropriation of her likeness. The defendants argued that summary judgment was appropriate because the plaintiff—a public figure—could not demonstrate that the defendants acted with the requisite constitutional malice. In response, the plaintiff argued that the actual malice standard did not apply because the Matchmaker.com profile constituted commercial speech—which, if classified as such, would allow the plaintiff to avoid having to prove actual malice. The plaintiff's contention rested, in part, on the basis that Matchmaker.com's business depended on getting free trial members to become paying customers by allowing them to access profiles such as the one at issue.

The Court rejected the plaintiff's argument, stating that "[t]he fact that Matchmaker makes a profit from selling memberships does not transform the speech at issue into commercial speech." The Court distinguished a case out of the Court of Appeals for the 9th Circuit (in which a company, without authority, used a photo of a surfer to promote its clothing) from the case before it, where the defendant allowed members to post information about themselves in an online profile. The Court ultimately concluded that the profiles on Matchmaker.com did not constitute commercial speech. Therefore, the Court granted the defendant's motion for summary judgment with respect to the issue of misappropriation of the right of publicity.

Perfect 10, Inc. v. CCBill LLC, 481 F.3d 751 (9th Cir. 2007)

The plaintiff, Perfect 10, the publisher of an adult entertainment magazine and the owner of the Web site Perfect10.com, filed suit against two defendants, CWIE and CCBill, alleging, among other claims, violation of the right to publicity. The plaintiff's Web site is a subscription-based site where members pay a fee so that they can gain access to thousands of images of models displayed on the Web site. Many of the models featured on the Web site signed releases of their rights of publicity to the plaintiff. The first defendant, CWIE, is a provider of Web hosting to the owners of various Web sites. CWIE ensures that its clients' service or Web site is connected to the Internet. The second defendant, CCBill, facilitated the ability of customers to use credit cards or checks to pay for subscriptions. The plaintiff began sending letters to the defendants alleging that the defendants' clients were infringing not only copyrights but also the state law right of publicity. Notably, the District Court found that the defendants were not immune from right of publicity claims under the *Communications Decency Act of 1996*. The Court of Appeals for the 9th Circuit, however, reversed this particular finding of the District Court.

In reversing the District Court finding regarding the right to publicity, the Court noted that the immunity created by the *CDA* was limited by another section of that act that requires courts to "construe [the act] in a manner that would neither 'limit or [sic] expand any law pertaining to intellectual property.'" The Court, accordingly, explained that the *CDA* did not shield service providers from laws dealing with intellectual property. The question remained, however, whether intellectual property encompassed federal intellectual property or state intellectual property or both. The Court noted that the scope of federal intellectual property laws, unlike that of the state intellectual property laws, was well established and uniform. The Court further explained that state intellectual property laws varied significantly from state to state. Because Internet Web sites have material that reaches many different states at any one time, the Court reasoned that to allow "any particular state's definition of intellectual property to dictate the contours of this federal immunity would be contrary to Congress's expressed goal of insulating the development of the Internet from the various state-law regimes." Therefore, the Court construed intellectual property as used in the *CDA* to mean "federal intellectual property." In a footnote, the Court explained that a number of state law claims, including right to publicity, could be classified as state intellectual property claims such that "an entity otherwise entitled to §230 immunity would thus be forced to bear the costs of litigation under a wide variety of state statutes that could arguably be classified as 'intellectual property.'" Consequently, the Court held that the defendants were eligible for immunity under the *CDA* for all of the state law claims—including the right to privacy—raised by the plaintiff.

Pesina v. Midway Mfg. Co., 948 F. Supp. 40 (N.D. Ill. 1996)

The plaintiff, a martial artist, brought suit against the defendant, Midway, alleging among other things that the defendant used his persona, name, and likeness without consent, and accordingly infringed his common law right of publicity. The defendant was in the video game business and created the popular martial arts games Mortal Kombat and Mortal Kombat II. In order to create characters and images for the game, the defendant hired models to perform movements that could be captured, edited, and transferred into the game. The plaintiff was one such model, and he claimed Midway improperly used his image in the home version of the two games. The defendant moved for summary judgment.

The Court granted the defendant's motion for summary judgment with respect to the plaintiff's right of publicity claim, because there was no evidence that the plaintiff's persona, name, or likeness had any commercial value and—even if it had any such value—the likeness was unrecognizable in the video game. The Court noted that the video images of the plaintiff "were extensively altered prior to being incorporated into the games," and thus, "after comparing Mr. Pesina and the game character, Johnny Cage, who allegedly resembles the plaintiff, only 6% of 306 Mortal Kombat Users identified Mr. Pesina as the model." The Court also dismissed any argument that the use of the plaintiff's name for only eight seconds in one of the games was actionable.

The Court intimated that the plaintiff may have been able to argue that he had become associated with the game character, Johnny Cage, such that the character invoked the plaintiff's identity, but that the Court would have nevertheless rejected this argument. The Court found that the evidence showed that the plaintiff was not a well-known martial artist and that the public did not "even recognize him as a model for Johnny Cage." Consequently, the Court granted the defendant's motion for summary judgment.

Ahn v. Midway Mfg. Co., 965 F. Supp. 1134 (N.D. Ill. 1997)

The plaintiffs—three models—filed suit against the defendant, Midway, alleging, among other issues, that the defendant used their personas, names, and likenesses without consent and accordingly infringed the common law right of publicity. The defendant was in the video game business and created the popular martial arts games Mortal Kombat and Mortal Kombat II. In order to create characters and images for the game, the defendant hired models to perform movements that could be captured, edited, and transferred into the game. The plaintiffs were such models, and they claimed Midway improperly used their images in the home video, home computer, and hand-held versions of the two games. The defendant moved for summary judgment.

The Court found that the plaintiffs' right of publicity claims were preempted by the federal copyright laws. The Court noted that preemption exists where the work was fixed in a tangible form and falls within the subject matter of copyright and where the right asserted is equivalent to any of the rights specified in the *Copyright Act*. The Court found that the plaintiffs' images had been videotaped and thus were fixed in a tangible form and that the substance of the videotaped images fell under choreographic works under the *Copyright Act*. Notably, the Court stated in a footnote that even if the plaintiffs had argued that their performance, rather than the videotape of the performance, was the work they were trying to protect, the argument would nonetheless fail because "the performances were embodied in copy and therefore, were 'fixed.'" The Court then determined that the right of publicity is equivalent to the rights of distributing, performing, and preparing derivative works under the *Copyright Act*. Accordingly, the Court granted the defendant's motion for summary judgment.

Michaels v. Internet Entm't Group, Inc., 5 F. Supp. 2d 823 (C.D. Cal. 1998)

The plaintiffs, Bret Michaels and Pamela Anderson Lee, who had intervened in the case, filed for a preliminary injunction against the defendant, Internet Entertainment Group, Inc., to prevent the dissemination of a videotape showing the plaintiffs engaged in sex acts together. The plaintiffs alleged, among other things, violation of the California statutory right of publicity. At the time of the suit, Bret Michaels was best known as the frontman for the rock band "Poison," and Pamela Anderson Lee was primarily known as a television and film actor. The defendant was a corporation in the business of distributing adult entertainment through the Internet and had obtained a copy of the video through a private investigator who maintained he had received the tape from a client claiming to be an associate of the plaintiffs. The Court, prior to issuing the injunction, determined that the plaintiffs would likely succeed on the merits in their claims of copyright infringement, violation of the right to publicity, and violation of the right to privacy.

In regard to the right to publicity claim, the Court, as an initial matter, rejected the defendant's argument that the plaintiffs' state claim was preempted by federal copyright law. The Court found that the plaintiffs had alleged that their names, likenesses, and identities had been used on the radio, television, and Internet to advertise the distribution of the videotape. Therefore, according to the Court, the defendant's conduct was "unrelated to the elements of copyright infringement, which are concerned only with distribution of the Tape itself."

The Court then recited the elements of both the common law right to publicity claim and the statutory right to publicity claim. The Court found that the first element—defendant's use of the plaintiffs' identities—was met, since the plaintiffs' names and identities were used to promote the videotape. Moreover, the Court found that the second element, requiring that the use be to the advantage of the defendant, was likewise met because the defendant used the identities and names to sell subscriptions to its Web site. Further, the Court determined that the plaintiffs never consented to the use of the tape. Additionally, the Court found that the defendant knowingly used the names for purposes of promotion and that there was a direct connection between the use and the promotion. Finally, the Court found that there was evidence to indicate that the plaintiffs would be injured by the defendant's exploitation of their names and identities based, in part, on the fact that the plaintiffs' images and careers would be damaged by being associated with the pornography trade. Therefore, the Court found that the plaintiffs had shown a likelihood of success on the merits.

Almeida v. Amazon.com, Inc., 456 F.3d 1316 (11th Cir. 2006)

The plaintiff, Almeida, brought suit against the defendant, Amazon.com—a recognized leading Internet retailer with a focus on online book sales—alleging, among other things, violation of her right to publicity under both Florida common and statutory law. The plaintiff had consented to being photographed for a photo exhibit and book. The resulting image was displayed at the exhibit and in the first edition of the book. Subsequently, the publishers of the book in which the plaintiff's image was displayed decided to publish a second edition. The second edition, although similar in many respects to the first edition, now displayed the plaintiff's picture on the book's cover. Further, the second edition was then offered for sale on Amazon.com's Web site. Frequently, when Amazon.com offers books for sale, it provides the user with a photo of the book cover. The plaintiff contended that this practice led to a violation of the plaintiff's right to publicity.

The Court began its discussion by explaining that the District Court determined that the plaintiff's right to publicity claim was preempted by the *Communications Decency Act of 1996*. The Court discussed the parties' various arguments concerning the scope of the *CDA* but ultimately found that it need not address whether the District Court erred, because the plaintiff's right to publicity claim would not survive a motion to dismiss in any event. The Court concluded that it was unnecessary for the District Court to recognize the preemption issue.

The Court then analyzed the plaintiff's right to publicity claim and determined that Amazon.com did not violate any publicity right because it did not use, as contemplated by the statute, the plaintiff's image for trade, commercial, or advertising purposes. The Court cited relevant case law for the proposition that use of an image in a publication is not commercial simply because that publication is offered for sale. The Court distinguished cases in which defendants affirmatively aimed at emphasizing the role of plaintiffs for marketing purposes, stating, "[I]n contrast, Amazon does not make editorial choices as to the book cover images it displays on its website." The Court concluded that Amazon.com's practice of putting up pictures of the covers of books it is selling was not an "endorsement or promotion of any product or service, but is merely incidental to, and customary for, the business of internet book sales." Essentially, the Court analogized Amazon.com's practice to that of a traditional bookstore having books on the shelf with the book covers facing out toward customers. Accordingly, the Court found no cause of action for right to publicity and, consequently, it affirmed the District Court's grant of summary judgment, albeit on separate grounds.

Bosley v. Wildwett.com, 310 F. Supp. 2d 914 (N.D. Ohio 2004)

The plaintiff, Catherine Bosley, a television news reporter who had achieved

regional celebrity, filed for a preliminary injunction against the defendants—
multiple companies—for violation of the plaintiff's right to publicity. The
plaintiff participated in a "wet t-shirt" contest that was filmed by one of the defendants, Dream Girls, to be part of a DVD called *Spring Break 2003*. Shortly
after the plaintiff was filmed, Dream Girls released a video from the contest.
Subsequently, Dream Girls released a second version of the video, this time
emphasizing the fact that the plaintiff appeared naked on the tape. Thereafter,
Dream Girls licensed the video of the plaintiff's performance to a second company, Marvad Corporation. Marvad owned the Web site "SexBrat.com," which
distributed adult entertainment over the Internet through a subscription service. Members of SexBrat.com who paid a subscription fee were, among other
things, allowed to see portions of the plaintiff's performance. The Web site and
video drew immense publicity, and the plaintiff eventually had to resign from
her new anchor position. The plaintiff filed for a preliminary injunction to prevent the distribution of her image via the defendants' businesses.

The Court began its discussion with an explanation of the relevant Ohio
and Florida statutory and common law claims for right to publicity. The Court
then rejected the defendants' argument that the use of the plaintiff's image
was not for a commercial purpose. The Court noted that the defendants used
the images of the plaintiff to directly promote the sale of videos and Web site
memberships. The Court further explained that the "prominent display" of the
plaintiff's name and image on the cover of the video and on the Web site constituted an advertisement for the Dream Girls video and that the use of the
plaintiff's image constituted direct promotion of the defendants' products and
services.

The defendants further argued that their use of the plaintiff's image fell
under the "public affairs exception." The Court cited case law for the proposition that the test of whether or not the public affairs exception applies turns
not on the type of media in which the image appears but rather on whether the
use of the image is a matter of legitimate public concern. The Court then noted
of the Internet, "In modern times, one could extend this analysis to conclude
that information relating to a legitimate public interest on an internet web
page is protected communication." The Court explained that images that are
otherwise newsworthy are not always protected in the context of advertising.
The defendants' use was, according to the Court, clearly advertisement.

The Court also rejected the defendants' argument that the First Amendment barred the plaintiff's right to publicity claim because, as the defendants
contended, their use of the plaintiff's image was protected speech. The Court
noted that because the defendants were using the plaintiff's image "solely for

the use of the purpose of commercially exploiting her fame" and because the use of the images lacked artistic expression and significant editorial comment, the case was distinguishable from cases in which First Amendment protections applied. The Court further found the defendants' prior restraint arguments unpersuasive, noting that the right to publicity bears close similarity to the goals of patent and copyright law and that the First Amendment "is not a license to trample on legally recognized rights in intellectual property."

Finally, the Court rejected the defendants' allegations that the plaintiff had consented to the taping. The Court noted that, at the very least, explicit oral consent was required and that all the defendants could allege was tacit consent. Ultimately, the Court issued the preliminary injunction.

Stern v. Delphi Internet Servs. Corp., 626 N.Y.S. 2d 694 (1995)

The plaintiff, controversial radio talk show host Howard Stern, brought suit against Delphi Internet Services Corporation, alleging commercial misappropriation of Stern's name and picture. Delphi sponsored an electronic bulletin board debating Stern's candidacy for office of governor of New York and included his name and picture as part of the bulletin board. The Court described Delphi as "an online computer network" that had "set up on its on-line electronic bulletin board, a subscriber participation debate on the merits of Stern's candidacy." It was undisputed that Delphi used Stern's name and picture without his permission in a full-page advertisement in *New York Magazine* and the *New York Post*. The ad read as follows:

> Should this man be the next governor of New York? You've heard him. You've seen him. You've been exposed to his Private Parts. Now he's stumping to be governor. Maybe it's time to tell the world exactly what you think. The Internet's the one frontier even the King of (Almost) All Media hasn't conquered. And Delphi's where you get aboard. The online service that "leads the way in Internet access." With Delphi, navigating the Net is as easy as falling down. Assistance is available at every turn. From help files, guides and books, to hundreds of online experts, including Wald Howe, Delphi's resident Internet guru and all around smart guy. So whether you think Howard-the-Aspiring-Governor should be crowned King of the Empire State, or just greased up and sent face-first down a water slide, don't put a cork in it. Sit down, jack in, and be heard.

Delphi's principal contention, however, was that its use of Stern's name and photograph fell within the bounds of the "incidental use exception." Delphi argued that because its advertisements were for a service related to news dissemination—the online forum to discuss Stern's candidacy—it is entitled to protection under the incidental use exception even though Delphi, as a company, was neither solely nor predominately engaged in the dissemination of news.

The Court agreed with Delphi. In so doing, it analyzed various cases dealing with the issue of the "incidental use exception." The Court noted that "New York courts have consistently held that the incidental advertising exception applies to all 'news disseminators,' not just newspapers and magazines." Further, the Court analogized Delphi's online forum—which is only a percentage of its entire business—to the traditional media, television networks. The Court noted that television networks engaged in both news dissemination and entertainment, but television was given the same privileges as other media where the statutory right to privacy is at issue. The Court concluded, "[b]ecause Stern's name was used by Delphi to elicit public debate on Stern's candidacy, logically the subsequent use of Stern's name and likeness in the advertisement is afforded the same protection as would be afforded a more traditional news disseminator engaged in the advertisement of a newsworthy product." The Court ultimately held that the use of Stern's name to advertise the subject—a debate of Stern's candidacy—on an electronic bulletin board fell within the incidental use exception.

Fox v. Encounters Intern., 318 F. Supp. 2d 279 (D. Md. 2002)

The plaintiff, Mrs. Fox, brought suit against the defendant, Encounters International, alleging (among other issues) misappropriation of likeness. The plaintiff was foreign-born and not a citizen of the United States. The plaintiff came into the United States on a consort's visa petition, applied for by the plaintiff's fiancé, a US citizen she had met through a marriage agency. Their engagement, however, fell through, and shortly thereafter the plaintiff met the defendant's president, Ms. Spicack. Ms. Spicack's company was a "mail-order bride service" that operated via an Internet Web site, "Encounter.com." American men could access the Web site and, after paying a subscription fee, create an online profile and upload pictures of themselves. Ms. Spicack introduced the plaintiff to another American gentleman, Mr. Fox, an Encounter.com member. Both parties disputed, however, when and whether the plaintiff became a client of the defendants. Shortly after they met, the plaintiff and Mr. Fox became engaged and wed. The marriage failed, in part, due to alleged domestic abuse. The plaintiff thereafter sued her husband, Mr. Fox, and the defendant, alleging—among other things—that the defendant had violated her right to publicity when the defendant featured the plaintiff's photo on its Web site without her consent. The defendant moved to dismiss all of the plaintiff's claims, including the misappropriation claim.

In regard to the plaintiff's misappropriation claim, the defendant argued that the plaintiff had failed to state a claim for which relief could be granted, since the photo of the plaintiff involved a public interest—thus invoking an exception to the requirement of consent under the Virginia statutory misappropriation claim—and the plaintiff had given consent to the photographs. The Court, however, found the defendant's argument unpersuasive. The Court noted that items used for advertising were expressly not included in the exception, and that Encounter.com was unquestionably "an engine to advertise [the defendant's] service to introduce Russian women to American men for marriage and permanent residency." The Court further rejected the defendant's assertion that there was a great public interest in romance, marriage, and "methods of dating prospective spouses," i.e., Web site dating services. Regarding the defendant's contention that the plaintiff consented, the Court explained that the defendant's argument had ignored the written consent requirement under the statute and further noted that there was no evidence that any written consent was given. Accordingly, the Court denied the defendant's motion to dismiss the misappropriation count.

Brown v. ACMI Pop, N.E.2d (Ill. App. Ct. Aug. 2, 2007)

The estate for the plaintiff, the late recording artist James Brown, brought suit against the defendant (stock image company Corbis), alleging—among other things—that the defendant infringed the plaintiff's right of publicity through the defendant's unauthorized commercial use of his image on the Internet. The defendant was in the business of licensing copyrighted photographs, doing so by displaying a catalogue of over two million photos on its Web site to facilitate the ability of customers to identify images they wished to license. The photos displayed on the defendant's Web site were obscured with a visible watermark or a very low resolution to preclude unauthorized use of the pictures prior to licensing. The plaintiff alleged that this use of his photo violated his right to publicity. The Circuit Court initially granted the defendant's motion to dismiss the claims, finding that the defendant's use was noncommercial, thus precluding a claim for right of publicity, and that in any event the federal *Copyright Act* preempted the claim. The Circuit Court, however, upon the plaintiff's motion for reconsideration, reversed all of its initial holdings and thereafter certified two questions regarding its right to publicity findings on appeal to the Illinois appellate court.

The Court of Appeals first analyzed whether the defendant's use of the plaintiff's images on the Web site could be considered commercial. The defendant argued that unlike the facts in cases cited by the plaintiff, the defendant's use of the images dealt with *intangible* property—the transferring of a legal right created by the *Copyright Act*—rather than *tangible* property, such as, for example, an image affixed to a t-shirt for sale. Essentially, the defendant argued that it was not selling a product but instead offering a license on the copyrights it owns. The Court found that because there was valid disagreement as to whether the use was commercial, the Circuit Court had not erred in denying the defendant's motion to dismiss.

As for the copyright preemption claim, the Court rejected the defendant's argument that the defendant was exercising its rights to reproduce and publish the plaintiff's images under the federal *Copyright Act*, and therefore any right of publicity claim was preempted by the *Act*. The defendant's contention centered on its belief that the use of the plaintiff's likeness on the Internet did not extend beyond the use of the copyrighted photos. Further, as the defendant argued, the copyrighted work was not used to endorse a product but rather was used to distribute a license. The plaintiff responded by arguing that the images advertised for sale on the defendant's Web site constituted a fixed work on the Internet because the "license" resulted in tangible property in the form of a photograph to the end user. The plaintiff further argued that he had never consented to any sale of his photos and never had any control over the copyright interest to release. The Court held that the Circuit Court had not erred in denying the defendant's motion to dismiss. The Court laconically explained that "where it is possible that the photos as displayed on [the defendant's] Internet Web page can be interpreted as tangible, the *Publicity Act* as applied here would not preempt copyrights."

In February 2008, the Illinois state legislature was presented with a series of amendments to the Illinois right of publicity statute by proponents of the business model at issue in the Brown litigation. The bill has been approved in the Senate and is set for a vote in the House. If passed, the new law would immunize corporations like Corbis from right of publicity suits and would obviate the return of *Brown v. ACMI Pop* to the trial court. Some see the success of that legislation as a blow to individual rights of publicity; others see it as crucial to the survival of an entire industry segment of the new media: image galleries. [MC]

Rights of Privacy

Rights of privacy are generally referred to as the right against unreasonable intrusion, rights against unreasonable public disclosure of private facts, rights against others presenting perceptions of one's person in false light, as well as the previously discussed appropriation of name or likeness. Considerations about privacy violations often circulate around the issue of consent and whether that consent was given explicitly or implicitly.

Foundational Legislative Developments in Privacy Rights

Arguments based on constitutional grounds are, of course, situated in judicial cases (to be described below). However, the foundational constitutional issues are a legislative matter. Some claims have been based on the Fourth Amendment: "The right of the people to be secure in their persons, houses, papers, and effects, against unreasonable searches and seizures." In *Olmstead v. United States* (1928), the Supreme Court affirmed that the privacy aspect is as important (or sometimes more important) than the property aspect (Legal Information Institute). However, through rulings in *Olmstead v. United States* (1928) and *Goldman v. United States* (1942), the Court found that privacy only related to physical entry into private premises and did not apply to the interception of communication (wiretapping). Wiretapping was not included in the expectation of privacy until 1967's *Katz v. United States* and *Berger v. New York*.

Some claims are based on Fifth Amendment protections against self-incrimination. In general, the Fourth and Fifth Amendments are interpreted as applying to actions the government takes against individuals rather than applying to the actions of private citizens.

Other claims are based on First Amendment rights. That the government has the power to protect the privacy interests of its citizens by penalizing publication or authorizing causes of action for publication implicates directly First Amendment rights (Legal Information Institute).

Further, in 1965 (*Griswold v. CT*, on birth control devices and advice; see Ferrera et al. 189; Black 265–66), the Supreme Court ruled for "zones of privacy" implicit in the *Bill of Rights*. The California Supreme Court later (1994) noted two kinds of protections: (1) rights of the individual to avoid disclosing personal matters, and (2) independence in making certain types of important decisions. However, "federal constitutional privacy rights only apply to prevent governmental or state action." Civil liberty claims based on federal constitutional rights of privacy are relatively recent developments. However, many states have added privacy rights to their state constitutions. *NAACP v. Alabama* (1958) established the inviolability of privacy in the freedom to associate with privacy in one's memberships/associations.

Statutory Privacy Developments

There are a number of federal laws addressed to protect privacy, especially on-line. One must keep in mind, however, that a number of the laws apply only to what the federal government may or may not do in the area of privacy. Since the early 1970s, "Congress has passed over 20 laws pertaining to privacy" (Solove 67).

The *Communications Act of 1934* provides for privacy in telephone and telegraph communications. This law was passed after *Olmstead v. United States* (1928), as Congress attempted to control wiretapping of telephone, telegraph, and radiographic communication. However, the impact of the law was obviated by *Goldman v. United States* (1942) and was not reestablished until 1967 and 1968.

The *Federal Records Act of 1950 (FRA)* calls for accurate documentation of government documents.

The *Freedom of Information Act (FOIA) 1966* (amended in 1996 and 2002) requires the publication of modes of access for citizens to review held information.

The *Omnibus Crime Control and Safe Streets Act of 1968* including the *Wire Tap Act of 1968* applies to both the interception and storage of electronic communications. Landline phones are protected as private; cellular and wireless phones are not.

The *Telephone Harassment Act of 1968* legislates against interstate harassment using phones.

The *Privacy Act of 1974* addresses government's protection of information held in government databases about individuals. The government may not hide the existence of databases and must publish that they exist, including details about how to access the database and information within it. The 1974 *Act* was modified in 1988 by the *Computer Matching and Privacy Protection Act* against the practice of cross-matching information in a variety of databases.

The *Privacy Protection Act of 1980 (PPA)* protects materials held in order to publish. In other words, authors often collect numerous materials, often through research of various kinds, preliminary to publishing articles and/or books. The *PPA* prevents the government from seizing those materials without proper court authorization.

The *Cable Communications Policy Act of 1984 (CCPA)* requires cable operators to inform subscribers about the nature of, and uses for, collected information and prohibits disclosure of viewing habits.

The *Electronic Communications Privacy Act of 1986 (ECPA)* legislates against unauthorized interception and disclosure of electronic communications. The *ECPA* updates the *Wiretap Act of 1968*. The *ECPA* excludes voice-over-Internet (VOI) protocols. The portion of the law dealing with e-mail was later clarified by the *Computer Matching and Privacy Act* of 1988 and 1989 that amended the 1974 *Privacy Act* against database matching. The *ECPA* provides protection for electronic mail and other "stored electronic communications." Operators of electronic communications services were barred from disclosing the content of a message in storage, except in authorized criminal cases. The *Act* expands privacy protection by including all providers, rather than just common carriers. The *Act* also narrows the definition of "content" so as to exclude protection of interception or disclosure of party identities or the existence of the communication (Black 274).

The *Video Privacy Protection Act (VPPA) of 1988* forbids video stores from divulging the titles of videos rented or purchased.

The *Computer Fraud and Abuse Act (CFAA)* of 1988 covers a wide range of acts in which offenders knowingly seek to defraud via electronic communications. Various types of spam, scams, "phishing," identity theft and other nefarious activities are referenced in the *CFAA*.

The *Telephone Consumer Protection Act (TCPA)* of 1991 legislated against certain advertising and solicitation practices (automated dialers, etc.) and prohibited some activities on cell phones and pagers. Spam via electronic mail was not yet covered by this action. The *Act* makes it illegal to use mechanical means to place toll/charged calls.

The *Driver's Privacy Protection Act (DPPA) of 1994* prevents the longstanding practice, in many states, of selling personal information in motor vehicle records. Marketers were often the recipients of this information.

The *Federal Information Infrastructure Protection Act (NIIPA)* of 1996 updates the *CFAA* (88) and further includes interstate and foreign communications. The *NIIPA* is the primary law against viruses, worms, and the like.

The *Children's Online Privacy Protection Act (COPPA)*, of 1998 sets standards for the treatment of children on sites targeted at them especially with regard to the collection of information. The *COPPA* sets aside a previously approved parental consent requirement under certain circumstances. The *COPPA* requires site managers to post clear and explicit notifications of the kinds of information that sites targeted at children collect (among other aspects).

The *Child Online Protection Act (COPA)* of 1998 updates the *Communications Act of 1934* prohibiting commercial online targeting of children with harmful materials. Both the COPA and the COPPA define children as thirteen years of age and under. In July 2008, the US Court of Appeals for the 3rd Circuit, for the third time, struck down *COPA*, with judges saying the law is a vague and overly broad attack on free speech.

The *Child Pornography Prevention Act (CPPA)* of 1996 was passed to deter the spread of so-called "kid porn." A particularly interesting aspect of this law is that it finds infractions when sites *use* minors in depictions *of* minors. In many countries, the depiction of child pornography constitutes a violation. For example, in the United States, "child-play" in *Second Life* is not illegal, as it is an activity in which adults wear avatar skins that cause them to *look like* children, sometimes for the purpose of engaging in virtual sex with other adults (using either adult or child-like avatars). Since the activity is between consenting adults and doesn't use minors in its production, US law does not constrain the activity as do the laws in some countries where depiction alone constitutes a violation.

The *Protection of Children from Sexual Predators Act (PCSPA)* of 1998 requires operators (ISPs) to report system use by known predators.

The proliferation of Web 2.0 technologies, especially in search, marketing, and social computing, have challenged everything we knew about privacy. One part of the problem clearly rests with users. In some ways, people who post a lot of personal information about themselves "deserve what they get" in terms of the dissemination and use of that information. In other ways, and from another point of view, one should be able to utilize computational communication technologies without thereby providing personal information to unwanted parties. *New York Times* contributor Adam Cohen confronts this dilemma in his 2008 article "One Friend Facebook Hasn't Made Yet: Privacy Rights," where he argues that "what Web sites need to do—and what the government should require them to do—is give users as much control over their identities online as they have offline. Users should be asked if they want information to be viewable by others, and by whom. . . ." Cohen adds that users should be consulted before their information about their behavior is disseminated, and they should be asked to "opt in" to the information exchange. Cohen's arguments speak strongly in favor of overturning the status quo, in which marketers and Web site operators wield strong, technological, hidden tools as the ultimate levers over users' private data, in favor of environments in which users are clearly informed and adequately empowered to make conscious decisions about the utilization of their data.

Traditional Media Privacy Cases with New Media Implications

Katz v. United States, 389 U.S. 347 (1967)

At the time of *Katz*, wiretapping had not yet been included in privacy expectations. Katz was convicted of illegal gambling based on wiretaps obtained by the FBI on conversations he had from a public telephone booth. Trial and appeal courts convicted and upheld based on excluding Fourth Amendment claims of protection from illegal search and seizure, finding that there was no physical entrance into Katz's private property. The Supreme Court overturned the conviction, finding that while the Fourth Amendment doesn't protect places (like a public phone booth), it does protect people and matters that they intend to keep to themselves. The Court, in *Katz*, set the requirement that the government must obtain a properly authorized warrant before wiretapping.

Berger v. New York, 388 U.S. 41 (1967)

As with *Katz*, *Berger v. New York* dealt with authorizations for wiretaps. Berger was indicted and convicted of conspiracy to bribe the chairman of the New York State Liquor Authority based upon evidence obtained via a wiretap. The surveillance was carried out under a New York state law allowing the authorized placement of a wiretap for up to sixty days (with renewal for sixty more, with cause). The Supreme Court found the law violated the Fourth Amendment in that the "authorization to eavesdrop for a two-month period is equivalent to a series of searches and seizures pursuant to single showing of probable cause."

Whalen v. Roe, 429 U.S. 589 (1977)

Although concerned with medical records and not "media/new media" as such, *Whalen v. Roe* dealt with important database issues. In 1972, the State of New York passed anti-drug regulation that required prescriptions for a class of "dangerous drugs" be written on an official form, in triplicate, with one copy going to the state for database entry. The information included names of doctors, patients, and medications. Sets of doctors and patients both challenged the statute on the ground that it violated Fourth Amendment privacy protections. The Supreme Court found in favor of the State of New York and ruled that the statute was not unconstitutional.

Nixon v. Administrator of General Services, 433 U.S. 425 (1977)

After former President Richard Nixon resigned from office, he executed an agreement with the administrator of the General Services Administration (GSA) to ship his private papers from Washington to California, where he was to retire and where he expected a presidential library to be built. As part of the agreement, Nixon mandated a process and time frame that would allow him to eventually destroy materials from the collection, particularly audio recordings. Of course the Watergate crisis had found audio recordings to be particularly damaging to the Nixon presidency.

When Congress learned of the agreement, it acted by passing the *Presidential Recordings and Materials Preservation Act* (*PRMPA*), legislation that put into practice procedures for handling the materials and protecting their integrity. The *PRMPA* obviated the previous agreement between Nixon and the GSA by mandating certain procedures for that agency. Nixon filed suit against the GSA and thereby challenged the *PRMPA*, claiming that the *PRMPA* violated a number of principles concerning the separation of powers, various presidential rights and powers, as well as the former president's First, Fourth, and Fifth Amendment rights. In this, Nixon "concedes that, when he entered public life, he voluntarily surrendered the privacy secured by law for those who elect not to place themselves in the public spotlight.... He argues, however, that he was not thereby stripped of all legal protection of his privacy, and contends that the Act violates fundamental rights of expression and privacy guaranteed to him."

The Court found against Nixon for a number of reasons. While noting that Nixon did retain some expectation of privacy for his personal and/or family matters, the bulk of the materials in question were public documents, and the procedures that had been set up to screen the documents before any of them would be made public were sufficient to protect the former president's privacy.

Times Mirror Company v. Superior Court (CA), 53 Cal.3d (1991)

Testing the California state *Freedom of Information Act,* the question in this case was whether the governor of California properly refused a request to disclose his daily, weekly, and monthly appointment calendars and schedules. In August 1988, a reporter for the *Los Angeles Times* wrote the governor requesting, under the *Act,* copies of his "appointment schedules, calendars, notebooks and any other documents that would list [the Governor's] daily activities as governor from [his] inauguration in 1983 to the present." The governor's legal affairs secretary responded that the information requested was exempt from disclosure under the *Act.* The state Supreme Court held that the information request was overly broad and that the government office was allowed to protect some of the private information that would be held within detailed daily records.

United States v. Smith, No. 91–5077 (5th Cir. 1992)

A neighbor of Smith's girlfriend has problems with break-ins and suspects Smith. He uses a scanner to intercept Smith's phone calls, learns that Smith is dealing drugs, and alerts police. The police use the tip and help the neighbor record phone conversations, then arrest Smith for drug activities. Smith argued that his phone conversations were intended to be private and that the use of intercepted phone messages was a violation of the *Omnibus Crime Control and Safe Streets Act of 1968* and the *Wire Tap Act of 1968.* The trial court threw out the claim and used the information to help with the conviction. The Court of Appeals upheld the conviction. However, in doing so, the Court opened the door for the application of privacy issues to cellular and wireless phone conversations.

In general, the reason that cellular and wireless phone conversations are not protected against unauthorized interception is that the technology is so easy to intercept. Because the signals are broadcast over open frequencies, the expectation of privacy is waived. The fine print on cellular phone contracts spells that out but, of course, most people don't read it. However, in *Smith* the Circuit Court noted that there are circumstances through which citizens could strengthen their privacy expectations when using wireless devices. If the user acquired equipment that specially protects the data transmission, say by encryption or by operating in a frequency not accessed by "normal" radios or scanners, the citizen could be "marking" his intention that the conversation be private. Further, if the interceptor has to go to extraordinary means to intercept the talk, once again, the circumstances might mark a violation of privacy expectations. However, this area of the law is murky, and *Smith* complicated rather than clarified the landscape.

McIntyre v. Ohio Elections Commission (1995)

In *McIntyre v. Ohio Elections Commission,* the US Supreme Court set aside an Ohio state law that prohibited the distribution of campaign literature that did not contain the name and address of the person or campaign official issuing the literature. McIntyre (deceased by the time the case reached the Supreme Court) had been cited and fined for distributing leaflets in opposition of a school levy. Some of the self-produced leaflets did not identify her as the author. The Court's decision upheld the First Amendment right to publish anonymously.

New Media-Related Rights of Privacy Cases

Steve Jackson Games v. U.S. Secret Service (1993)

Steve Jackson Games v. U.S. Secret Service tested the *PPA* of 1980 against seizure of work output prior to publication when a computer running an online bulletin board and books prior to their publication were seized. Steve Jackson Games published books and board games and operated an online bulletin board for conversations about various computer gaming activities. Due to a number of factors, including the activities of a business associate well known in the hacker community, the Secret Service came to suspect the company of involvement in hacking. A Secret Service-led raid on the company included the confiscation of computers and data files, thereby closing the bulletin board and taking materials being prepared for publication (a book). The US District Court of Texas, Austin Division, ruled that the Secret Service had violated Jackson's privacy rights under the *PPA*, and the US 5th District upheld the ruling on appeal.

State ex rel. Macy v. One Pioneer CD-ROM Changer (1993) and *Davis v. Gracey*, 111 F.3d 1472 (10th Cir. 1997)

In this case, an Oklahoma court and the US 10th Circuit Court of Appeals held that the *PPA* had *not* been violated by a seizure of 500 MB of material waiting to be pressed onto a CD for publication. In this case, Anthony Davis had been arrested for the computer-based distribution of pornography. In the process, computers and storage equipment were confiscated. Davis was convicted; he appealed on a number of factors, all of which were denied. The principle at interest here was that the confiscation of a small amount of material that was being prepared for legitimate publication could not "shield" the accused from the findings resulting from the legal seizure of the larger bulk of illegal materials.

CompuServe v. Cyber Promotions, Inc., 962 F. Supp. 1015 (S.D. Ohio, C2–96–1070, 1997)

Cyber Promotions, Inc. v. America Online, Inc., 948 F. Supp. 436 (E.D. Pa. 1996)

In both cases involving Cyber Promotions, a spam/bulk e-mail distributor, District Courts in Ohio and Pennsylvania, respectively, found that Internet service providers (ISPs) CompuServe and AOL, respectively, have the right to block spam/bulk electronic mail sent using their proprietary systems. In the CompuServe case, property tort law was at the core of the Court's finding in that Cyber Promotions committed a kind of trespass against CompuServe's property. In the AOL case, the Court found that AOL's action was not a violation of Cyber Promotions' First Amendment rights (and was a proper expression of AOL's rights).

Smyth v. Pillsbury Corp., 914 F. Supp. 97 (E.D. Pa. 1996)

Smyth v. Pillsbury Corp. helped establish the *lack* of privacy, for employees, in corporate electronic mail. Mr. Smyth worked for Pillsbury. Company policy promised that all electronic mail was private and would not be intercepted or used in action against employees. However, after a series of e-mail exchanges with a supervisor, Smyth was fired based on comments contained in his electronic mail. Smyth claimed that Pennsylvania state privacy law protected him; the Court found no such protection for e-mail.

Shoars v. Epson America, Inc., No. SCWI 12749, Cal. Sup. Ct., Los Angeles Cty. (1989)

Shoars worked for Epson, implementing electronic mail systems. Epson promised its employees that the e-mail system was private but instructed Shoars to monitor employee electronic mail. Shoars complained within the company and was fired as a result. Shoars sued, claiming that the company practice violated privacy law (and also that the firing was inappropriate). The Court upheld the termination, finding that the law did not protect electronic mail stored on the company servers.

Flanagan v. Epson America, Inc., No. BC007036, Cal. Sup. Ct., Los Angeles Cty. (1991)

In a case similar to *Shoars*, Epson was found to be reading the stored e-mail messages of its employees. A class action suit was filed on behalf of all the employees whose e-mail had been looked at. The California Supreme Court found that neither state nor federal law protected e-mail transacted or stored on company equipment.

Defamation and New Media

Because defamation law is wholly found in state statutes, no review of legislative developments will be attempted here. The speed and reach of online communication have greatly increased the risks inherent in, and costs as a result of, defamatory communication. And, of course, global jurisdictional variety greatly multiplies the challenges. This review considers the US context, but broader global aspects cannot be easily dismissed.

Most generally, defamation is taken to be communication that sheds false light on the victim. When done through writing or visual imagery, one is dealing with libel; when done through speech and sound, slander results. A statement can only be defamatory if it is false; therefore, true statements of fact about others, regardless of the damage rendered, are not defamatory (although such comments might represent other sorts of privacy or hate-speech violations). Defamation may occur when one party (the eventual defendant if a case goes forward) writes or says something that is false about a second party (plaintiff) such that some third party "receives" the communication, and the communication of false information damages the plaintiff.

Generally, individuals rather than corporations or groups are involved, though some hate-speech law invariably includes group aspects. However, the online environment has broadened somewhat the approach to "defamation via group association/factors." For example, the Online Policy Group defines digital defamation as "online hate speech, defamation and/or profiling of various minority groups including, but not limited to, the lesbian, gay, bisexual, and transgender community, youth, the elderly, disabled, racial, ethnic, or religious minorities, and other traditionally underrepresented groups" <http://www.onlinepolicy.org/defamation.htm>.

The damage done by the defamation might be to one's reputation alone or may involve more substantive outcomes (loss of job or future income, etc.). Remedies can include retractions and apologies and/or reparations for damages. There are significant differences as to how jurisdictions treat "opinions." In some courts/cases, giving one's "honest opinion," though perhaps representing a negative evaluation of others, is not the same (and is less forbidden by law) as is stating a falsehood as "fact." Other jurisdictions do not recognize a difference between "opinion-giving" and "stating facts," so disqualify that ground for defense.

The Internet has complicated these issues, not only due to its speed and reach but also due to philosophic perspectives about the degree to which "information is free" and the various degrees of anonymity found in cyberspace. Some take the 'Net to be a place of free information exchange, regardless of veracity. Cut-and-paste culture finds fragmentary information spread widely, often without proper attribution. The Internet challenges in-place defamation law although the courts have repeatedly validated the fact that the law does apply. Once again, everything has changed; nothing has changed.

> The Internet and cell phones have raised the stakes over defamation exponentially. Young people are particularly vulnerable. The Anti-Defamation League notes that "cyber-bullying is reaching epidemic proportions. Recent surveys reveal that 54 percent of young people have been its targets, and 80 percent have witnessed it online. Most harassment occurs via instant messaging (47 percent of incidents), followed by e-mail (13 percent) and chat rooms (11 percent)" (Boyette). The most prominent case may well be that of Megan Meier (nearly fourteen years old) of Missouri, who committed suicide after experiencing incidents of harassment/teasing online. Her story is fully documented at the Megan Meier Foundation Web site <http://www.meganmeierfoundation.org/>. In May 2008, a federal grand jury in Los Angeles returned a four-count indictment against one of the participants for using computational communication information to inflict emotional distress on Meier in violation of MySpace's terms of service (Patrick and Hunn).

Traditional Media Defamation Cases with New Media Implications

New York Times v. Sullivan, 39, 376 U.S. 254 (1964)

Consolidated and decided with *Abernathy v. Sullivan*, this case concerned a full-page ad in *The New York Times* that alleged that the arrest of the Rev. Martin Luther King, Jr., for perjury in Alabama was part of a campaign to destroy King's efforts to integrate public facilities and encourage blacks to vote. L. B. Sullivan, the Montgomery city commissioner, filed a libel action against the newspaper and four black ministers who were listed as endorsers of the ad, claiming that the allegations against the Montgomery police defamed him personally. Under Alabama law, and in state court in Mongomery, Sullivan did not have to prove that he had been harmed, and a defense claiming that the ad was truthful was unavailable, since the ad contained factual errors. Sullivan won a $500,000 judgment at the trial level. However, *The Times* appealed the ruling to the Supreme Court, and that body held that the First Amendment protects the publication of all statements—even false ones—about the conduct of public officials except when statements are made with actual malice (with knowledge that they are false or in reckless disregard of their truth or falsity). Under this new standard, Sullivan's case collapsed, the state judgment was overturned, and the ruling contributed to a positive climate for open public discussion, supported by the press, of issues of social importance regardless of whether they were "pleasant" for governmental leadership.

Hustler Magazine, Inc. v. Falwell, 485 U.S. 46 (1988)

In *Hustler v. Falwell*, the Supreme Court unanimously held that the First Amendment free-speech guarantee in most cases prohibits awarding damages to public figures to compensate for emotional distress intentionally inflicted upon them. In order to qualify for such damages, public figures would have to prove that the statements were false and that the person who made them either knew they were false or acted with reckless disregard for the truth. The Court ruled that *Hustler* Magazine's parody of Jerry Falwell did not reach either standard, and so reversed a jury verdict (and a $250,000 damage award) that had been in favor of Falwell.

Procter & Gamble Mfg. Co. v. Hagler, 880 S.W.2d 123, 128–29 (Tex. App. 1994)

In this case, the Texas Court of Appeals reversed a jury decision that would have awarded a Procter & Gamble employee over $15 million. Hagler, the employee and plaintiff in the case, claimed that the posting of his termination (for theft) on the company electronic bulletin board was defamatory. The Texas Court of Appeals reversed on the grounds that the posting was factual and lacked any actual malice on the part of Procter & Gamble.

Robert Thomas v. Bill Page et al., No. 04 LK 013, Circuit Court for the Sixteenth Judicial Circuit, Kane County, Ill. (2007)

In 2004, Illinois Supreme Court Chief Justice Robert Thomas, a former Chicago Bears place kicker, sued a newspaper for libel over a column (written by Page) that claimed the judge had traded a verdict/vote for political favors. A jury awarded Thomas $7 million after finding that the former columnist for the *Kane County Chronicle* had acted with malice when he wrote the article. Page claimed that the information had come from an anonymous source he would not identify, thereby making a defense based on the truth standard problematic.

New Media-Related Cases
in Defamation Law

Alexander G. Lunney v. Prodigy Services Company, &c., Respondent, et al., 99 N.Y. Int. 0165, no. 164 (Dec. 2, 1999)

Lunney v. Prodigy is an important pre-*DMCA* safe harbor case involving a claim of defamation arising out of a third party's offensive e-mail to a Boy Scout leader carried/delivered via Prodigy's network and services. The New York court found that, like a telephone carrier, Prodigy, as an ISP, is not a publisher and could not be held responsible for the effects of content negotiated through its systems.

Cubby v. CompuServe Inc. No. 90 Civ. 6571. USDC (S.D.N.Y. Oct. 29, 1991)

This action for libel, business disparagement, and unfair competition was based on allegedly defamatory statements made in a publication carried on a computerized database delivered via CompuServe. The "Rumorville" electronic forum was one of hundreds hosted on CompuServe. Cubby, Inc., had started a forum ("Skuttlebut") that was competitive with Rumorville. Cubby alleged that Rumorville defamed Cubby/Skuttlebut by publishing untrue claims about Cubby/Skuttlebut on Rumorville. The Court found that CompuServe enjoyed the full protection of safe harbor in this case, as they would neither have been aware of, or responsible for, materials published on sites they merely hosted.

Stratton Oakmont, Inc. v. Prodigy Services Co., 1995 WL 323710 (N.Y. Sup. Ct. 1995)

Stratton Oakmont, Inc. v. Prodigy Services provided an "alternative take" on the roles and responsibilities of ISPs. A poster to one of Prodigy's online forums made defamatory claims about the president (Daniel Porush) of the Stratton Oakmont securities firm. The Court found that Prodigy was liable for carrying the libel, largely because their promotional and marketing presentation of their online forum services carried an implied promise that they would monitor the sites they carried and would take down offensive materials. Despite the finding in the case, Porush was later found guilty (by the SEC and other agencies and entities) of a variety of illegal financial transactions, very much in support of the claims made in the defamatory comments. In this case, then, "truth" was not able to serve as defense against a claim of defamation; at the same time,

ISPs were forewarned about the risks in making claims about monitoring the content carried in their networks.

Zeran v. America Online Inc., United States Court of Appeals, No. 97–1523 (4ᵗʰ Cir. 1997)

Zeran had been the victim of a malicious Internet hoax in which his identity was connected to advertising for items glorifying the Oklahoma City bombing. Zeran sued AOL for not taking down the defamatory materials. The trial court's decision that AOL was protected by the safe harbor provisions of the *Communications Decency Act*, much of which sought to protect children in the online environment, was upheld by the appeals court.

Blumenthal v. Drudge, 992 F. Supp. 44 (D.D.C. 1998)

In *Blumenthal v. Drudge*, the US District Court for D.C. upheld the safe harbor provisions protecting ISPs from responsibility for materials provided through their networks. That protection was strengthened through the *Communications Decency Act*. Blumenthal, a Clinton White House operative, sued Matt Drudge and AOL for defamation over false claims about his marriage; Drudge retracted the claims two days after making them, claiming that his sources had misled him. The Court found in favor of Drudge and AOL, and Blumenthal eventually settled the matter by paying Drudge what was said to be a relatively small amount for having missed a deposition.

Dendrite International, Inc. v. John Doe No. 3, Superior Court of New Jersey, Appellate Division. 342 N.J. Super. 134 2001

Dendrite International, Inc. v. John Doe No. 3 was not, in itself, a defamation case. Dendrite, a financial services broker, wanted to sue three people who had been anonymous posters to an online message board. The messages brought into question the performance of Dendrite's stock. Dendrite sued to obtain the identities of the posters, particularly poster no. 3, against whom the company wanted to bring a defamation suit. The ISP Yahoo! provided the identities of nos. 1 and 2 but refused in the case of no. 3, as their policy specified that they would only give up identities in cases in which their terms of service were violated or harm had been done to users. The Court agreed with Yahoo!'s assessment that poster no. 3 had done no harm, so the motion to provide the identity was denied. The decision was upheld on appeal.

Elena Cisneros v. Robert Sanchez, 1:05-cv-00259, USDC (S.D. Tex. Dec. 7, 2005)

Cisneros had sued Sanchez for defamation (in Texas State Court), claiming that he had either authored defamatory materials about her anonymously or had allowed them to remain on a Web site that he maintained. Cisneros was the wife of a political opponent of Sanchez. Sanchez moved the case to Federal Court under a claim of safe harbor under the *CDA*. However, the Court found that as maintainer of a Web site, he did not qualify as an ISP, and since the case was about liability over the publication of defamatory statements, trying to claim federal protection under the *CDA* was inappropriate (as was the move to the Federal Court). The case was returned to state jurisdiction and Sanchez later settled out of court for $150,000.

Sue Scheff, Parents Universal Resource Experts vs. Carey Bock and Ginger Warbis, Case Number: 03–022937 (18), Circuit Court, Broward County, Fla. (Sept. 2006)

Bock hired Scheff as a functionary in Parent Universal Resource Experts— PURE—to help Bock remove her sons from a boarding school in Costa Rica. Scheff put Bock in touch with a third party for assistance. Subsequently, Bock published defamatory material about Scheff (and PURE). Scheff and PURE sued in Florida State Court. Bock appeared initially but then defaulted. The default judgment totaled $11.3 million.

Summarizing Personal Torts in New Media

The broad lack of national uniformity in rights of publicity, privacy, and defamation might have been somewhat more tolerable when disagreements were between neighbors or people living in the same state or were limited primarily to gossip columnists, tabloids, and celebrities. The courts have adjudicated, and will continue to settle, differences between parties claiming intrusion. Governments can (and sometimes do) use information against their citizens in ways that strike us as "un-American."

Privacy legislation has focused primarily on important and necessary constraints on the ability of the government to pry into citizens' private lives and leverage their data in unacceptable ways.

However, new media raise the stakes in these legal areas to unprecedented levels. The wide-ranging complexities in the set of "rights to be left alone" are further exacerbated by the speed, reach, and viral nature of new media.

Although concerns about government intrusion are still valid and in need of vigilant control, the commercialization of information has accelerated at breakneck pace in the age of digital information. Behavioral marketing and targeting promise streamlined information retrieval; the more marketers and information providers know about individual preferences, the more parsimonious and tailored to the consumer are their returns of information and services. The more information about themselves individuals are willing to release, the quicker the credit approval, the larger the discount on purchases, the better the free service add-on. To many, the age of information was once thought to be about increasing our ability to collect information about—and thereby understand elements within—our world. In contemplation and retrospect, the age of information now appears to be more about the collection of information about consumers than about products. In the digital age, we've become commodified in ways only dreamed of by Madison Avenue advertising executives operating in the classic mass media era of the twentieth century.

At one time there was significant concern on the part of privacy advocates about the amount of information that citizens were willing to give out in order to apply for credit, manage their money, subscribe to services, register their opinions via polls, and the like. In these instances, advocates cautioned that people were revealing too much information about themselves to companies that provided inadequate protections for and assurances concerning the further use of that information. Marketing firms were said to offer individuals very small rewards and advantages for the data, then profit wildly as they combined data collected from many to be resold to the highest bidder among businesses wanting information about consumers. These uses of information still abound; privacy advocates had little impact on behavior in comparison to the strong urge on the part of consumers for easy and quick credit, discounts, and for public ways to voice opinions.

However, the rise of the World Wide Web, personal sites thereon, and especially social media, have far outstripped concerns about information entered on credit applications or given to consumer pollsters. Americans now willingly post vast amounts of information about themselves, their habits, and their preferences as part of the everyday process of social interaction. The idea of keeping oneself in private is almost passé. In fact, some social pundits note that to *not* establish a Web presence in order to "tell the proper story" about oneself is to risk having others tell stories that are not true. Jason Frey made just this point in a 2008 *Wall Street Journal* column when he wrote: "Put it all together [the need to defend and define your own identity online; efforts to correct the record on something, or to clear up potential confusion between you and someone with the same name; the threat of dilution of your persona by spam bloggers, or sploggers] and bit by bit the case for having a page of one's own emerges—as one poster in a Slashdot conversation on the subject put it, 'Your name is essentially your very own brand; might as well try to paint it in a decent light.'"

Under such conditions, and given the enormous amount of content published by and about people in this new digital environment, legal practices in the privacy tort areas seem archaic and ineffectual. The raw amount of online defamation and invasion of privacy may well totally outstrip the ability of the legal system to even scratch the surface in response. Much like the case with copyright, the citizenry is generally almost totally unaware of the laws in these areas, yet is still accountable to them, and violates them with impunity. Are consumers merely unaware of the law, or are the laws in these areas so technically obtuse as to be largely beyond the reach of everyman? There is a tremendous lack of clarity concerning the status of bloggers in light of the constitutional protections afforded the press. Privacy law is very unclear as to the information management responsibilities of private industries. Rights of publicity laws have seldom been applied to common citizens. When they have, special circumstances have been in evidence, as opposed to the current situation wherein tens of millions of private citizens have very public claims to celebrity. As with the aspects of intellectual property law discussed previously in this volume, the law, and its just application, seems light years behind the technological advancements of the age of digital communication. [ELL]

Discussion Questions

1. Is everyman with a blog or personal Web site now like a celebrity with regard to rights of publicity?
2. Virtually no one reads terms of service or click wrap agreements. Yet most policies concerning software and/or online privacy are stated therein. Users click their agreement with and responsibility to those principles. Should government mandate that privacy terms be stated in more clear fashion? Are there circumstances that would convince consumers/users to take more care over privacy?
3. Had real estate ownership rights or free speech rights or freedom of religion rights been curtailed and compromised in the United States as quickly as have privacy rights, there might have been a citizen revolt. Why have US citizens so fully allowed/participated in the devaluation of their privacy rights?

4. The blogosphere can be a very nasty place. Discuss/describe instances that seem to you to be defamatory in nature and note reasons why cases have not been brought.
5. Social scientific researchers are held to strong practices that protect research subjects' identities and privacy. Data produced by subjects and used by researchers are strongly controlled. Contrast this with the publication and circulation of pictures, names, and text on blogs. On the one hand, subject protection (and protection of their data) seems a good thing and is an important part of overseeing social scientific research in the United States. On the other hand, why should researchers be held to such high standards when everyone else regularly and freely publishes similar information (or worse)?

CHAPTER SEVEN

International IP Law

A number of relatively obvious things can be said about the international intellectual property law scene. For example, observing that the contemporary world is a complex geo-political-economic environment is not an observation that requires a great deal of insight. Noting that intellectual property law issues present large sets of complicated matters has been stressed throughout this book. The past, present, and future find IP law regimes all over the world dealing with old media (as well as IP law that deals with other than media matters). Having to deal with the implications that reformatting media content from analog to digital had on all aspects of media production, distribution, and consumption is common across modern media types. Facing the reality that the reach, speed, and ubiquity of the Internet have all changed the stakes for content touched by intellectual property law in a global environment cannot be denied.

The commonplaces in the preceding paragraph serve as a useful yet daunting introduction to this chapter. In a single book chapter, one can barely scratch the surface of a topic with as many facets as one finds in international IP law. The material begs for its own volume (or set of books/series). And yet the very nature of the world in which we live demands attention to these features, as little, if any, intellectual property content is isolated from most of these factors. This book has so far been limited to US laws and circumstances; in fact, many of the most important questions about IP law now face the challenges brought on by numerous international implications. This chapter takes up those issues in summary without the pretense of exhaustive coverage.

The chapter begins with a broad overview of some of the cultural features that overlay the global IP law landscape. Included are questions of economics, business relations, and trade; government and political systems; international competition and cooperation; and "global cultural wars" in general. Second, the chapter describes and discusses some of the broad technical matters relating to the business of intellectual property management—including raising and resolving legal questions—in this environment. Finally, we present some case-based illustrations of the realities at hand.

Complexities of the International Scene

Global Economic Policies

Clearly, this volume is not the appropriate place for a wide-ranging discussion or debate over the relative success or failure of either the United States or capitalism in the global economy. A quick review of large factors especially as they relate to intellectual property will suffice.

By some measures, the position of the US economy in relation to the world is very solid. For example, many estimates indicate that exports will continue to be a strong factor supporting the US economy in and beyond 2008 (Schneider). While the United States continues as a leading importer in the world, the total volume of imports has leveled and slowed as other parts of the world, including Europe, Latin America, Asia, and the Middle East, continue to develop strong exporting economies (Quinlan). Active participation in the global economy presents both significant market potential for American intellectual property and represents significant risks for losses from piracy.

Intellectual property-producing industries play a significant role in that economic strength. The International Intellectual Property Alliance (IIPA) estimates that:

- The US "core" copyright industries accounted for an estimated $819.06 billion or 6.56% of the US gross domestic product (GDP) in 2005, up from 6.48% of the US GDP ($760.49 billion) in 2004.

- The US "total" copyright industries accounted for an estimated $1.38 trillion or 11.12% of GDP in 2005, up from 11.09% of the US GDP ($1.3 trillion) in 2004.
- The "core" copyright industries were responsible for 12.96% of the growth achieved in 2005. . . . This means that the growth contributed by these core industries (12.96%) was almost double their current dollar share of GDP (6.56%). (International Intellectual Property Alliance)

Notwithstanding the fact that the IIPA has a vested interest in highlighting (and perhaps overestimating) both the contributions of the sector and the costs to it (from what they label as piracy), there is no doubt that the IP content industries are full participants in US trade exports.

This high level of participation in the global economy puts the US intellectual property content industries in a vulnerable position with regard to violations of IP protections. Again, according to the IIPA:

> As a result of deficiencies in the copyright regimes of the 51 countries/territories highlighted . . . the US copyright-based industries suffered estimated trade losses due to piracy in these of over **$18.4** billion in 2007. On a global basis (that is, in all countries/territories including the US), IIPA conservatively estimates that total losses due to piracy were at least **$30–35 billion** in 2007, not counting significant losses due to Internet piracy, for which meaningful estimates are not yet available. (Smith 17)

As the most radical example, the United States decries the intellectual property policies used in China:

> Excessively high legal thresholds for launching criminal prosecutions offer a safe harbor for pirates and counterfeiters. Under China's Criminal Law, piracy of copyrighted works and counterfeiting of trademarked goods are subject to criminal procedures and penalties only when the authorities find the amount of piracy or counterfeiting to be "serious," "especially serious," "relatively large," or "huge". . . . Pirates and counterfeiters who structure their operations to fit below those thresholds face no possibility of criminal sanction. . . . The thresholds are so high that they appear to permit pirates and counterfeiters to operate on a commercial scale. (Office of the United States Trade Representative 1)

Generally speaking, these and similar estimates only consider hard media and do not take online piracy into account. The scope and impact of online losses are difficult both to calculate and to fathom but would certainly multiply the available figures exponentially. From the point of view of the US content industries, one not only perceives a major problem, but one might well wonder about the very survivability of industry segments in the face of such rampant, blatant, and illegal activities eating away at investments and profits.

However, the situation presents numerous contested features that complicate what "protectionists," such as the content industries represented by the IIPA, would have one believe and conclude about the risks, costs, causes of, and solutions to so-called "threats" to the US content industries by IP piracy. As noted by McLeod, Lessig, Vaidhyanathan, Ambrosi et al., and many others, global IP law questions have become linked with US trade policies. IP law questions cut across the international business efforts of a large number of industries, with the result that acceptance of the US intellectual property protection regime has become a litmus test for good relations with other countries despite a variety of contestable assumptions built into the US approach.

Obviously, it is not possible to note here all of the entities that control trade issues worldwide. A brief mention of the US scene will help illustrate the matter. Later, we will discuss the various entities involved in jurisdictional issues. The State Department and Commerce Department are principally tasked with controlling US export matters.

> The Commerce Department's Export Administration Regulations control the export of (1) goods, and (2) information and know-how, whether in tangible or intangible form, that can be used to manufacture, utilize, or reconstruct goods, including computer software and technical data. However the export of some forms of software and information, particularly those involving encryption, may also be controlled by the International Traffic in Arms Regulations (ITAR) issued by the State Department under the Arms Export Control Act. (Smedinghoff 397–98)

The State Department and Commerce Department are principally tasked with controlling US export matters. Much of that which is exported is subject to export licensing and Commerce Department controls under the Bureau of Export Administration commerce control list.

There are also a variety of efforts to control electronic communication of information over computer networks. Sometimes referred to as "transnational data flow laws," "these laws primarily regulate the communication about individuals—that is, personal data" (Smedinghoff 403). While the United States does not have a single data protection law that covers overseas transmission of both public and private sector records, numerous state and federal statutes apply. Some countries have developed omnibus privacy and data protection laws; a couple dozen countries feature a variety of laws and data administration commissions and/or agencies. The scope of these laws varies. One can generally say that all countries have an interest and stake in protecting their governments (and especially militaries) from spies and terrorism. One can also note that many countries outside the United States appear to take the protection of private data about their citizens more seriously than does the United States, for whom the development of markets and economic development appear to largely take priority.

As IP has become an important part of the US export scene, the US intellectual property protection scheme has become grafted onto trade laws such as the *US Trade Act of 1974*, as well as agreements signed via international forums such as the *1996 Copyright Treaty* and *1997 Performances and Phonograms Treaty* with the World Intellectual Property Organization (WIPO) as well as the World Trade Organization (WTO) agreements on *Trade-Related Aspects of Intellectual Property Rights* (*TRIPS*) (to name only a few of the major relevant agreements). As noted by Ambrosi et al.:

> TRIPS has proven a very effective tool for forcing developing countries to adopt a US-style "IP" system, regardless of whether this is in the best interest of their populations, because failure to comply means risking trade sanctions. . . . Globally, the anti-"piracy" maximalist copyright and patent campaign is quickly gaining ground, without widespread participation in debate and without public knowledge of what is at stake. The governments of Japan, the EU, Australia, and even some developing countries are increasingly adopting anti-"piracy" arguments initially developed by US incumbent industries.

The authors make a case that is representative of the arguments presented by others with their orientation: that the US approach is bad for the public distribution of knowledge, counter to aspects of IP law that foster innovation and creativity, unfair to native people in less-developed countries, overly restrictive of private use—perhaps to the point of trumping legal protections in favor of private use even within the United States (as well as globally)—and is generally overly protective of US content industries to the point of cultural hegemony. To wit:

> If allowed to continue unchecked, recent developments in copyright and patent law that expand the definition of and penalties for "piracy" will carry serious negative implications for fair use and the public domain, technologies and technological standards . . . education, and the knowledge commons. A growing, diverse movement views the current "intellectual property" regime as a threat to the democratization of education, civic participation, the promotion of creative expression, and protection of a shared human heritage of knowledge and creativity. . . . In the context of growing wealth inequality, stratification of access to knowledge via market mechanisms will further marginalize the poor. Developing countries, together with innumerable "civil society" groups, continue to argue that the "IP" package of brand names, patents and copyright,

delivered via TRIPS, WIPO or bilateral trade agreements, is really a means for already dominant firms to expand into regional and global monopolies. Moreover, despite a well developed discourse around the special need to combat audiovisual and other forms of "piracy" in the developing world, many point out that the real "pirates" in the South are the bio-pirates: Giant Northern pharmaceutical and agro-business firms that are busy taking out patents on medicinal plants and crop strains, among other "found" objects, developed over thousands of years by indigenous peoples. (Ambrosi et al.)

On this point, McLeod notes that:

Intellectual property laws . . . do nothing but exacerbate the unequal distribution of wealth between rich and poor nations by ensuring that those who already own property are able to use that power to increase their proprietary holdings. North American and European countries, particularly the United States, have led an unrelenting battle against developing countries to force them to adopt an intellectual property system that is advantageous to these already wealthy countries. (172)

As reflected in the figures provided by the IIPA (above), the entertainment and information segments of the US export and trade economy play a significant role in the global IP situation. However, IP involves a lot more than entertainment and information media. The scene includes medical (including genetic and pharmaceutical), agricultural, mechanical, and all forms of business methods developments. These and every kind of "idea fixations" are at play by way of the broad panoply of IP categories (copyright, trademark, trade secrets, patents, etc.) on a global scale across all range of geopolitical boundaries.

It is certainly the case that not all of these aspects involve new digital media. However, the global—and mostly digital—communication connectivity provided by the Internet, satellite, and cell phones (among other means) has, in many cases, thrust what might have previously been local, regional, and national commerce into the global arena. Once any commercial activity digitizes and transmits company data (or some other entity does that for them or with their data), the implications of global digital IP questions come into relevance. Your company might make tractors, bricks, boxes, or clothes; as such, the IP questions surrounding your business are of little interest to this text. However, once your product is "in" an online catalogue, you bring your sales and marketing team up to speed with the ins and outs of e-commerce, and make your ordering/purchasing/delivery chain available to customers (be they business-to-business or the public at large), your tractors, bricks, boxes, or clothes take on digital identities that raise interesting IP law questions in this globally connected world.

There are features in the international arena that push back against America's exportation of media-related materials. Principal among these are the European Union's restrictions referred to as the *Television without Frontiers Directive (TVWF Directive)*. This legislation "is the cornerstone of the European Union's audiovisual policy. It rests on two basic principles: the free movement of European television programmes within the internal market and the requirement for TV channels to reserve, whenever possible, more than half of their transmission time for European works ('broadcasting quotas')" (Europa). On the one hand, the *TVWF* helps "manage" media relationships among member nations. On the other, it is a powerful trade restriction tool, opposed by the US government, that enables EU member nations to fight against the co-option of their media industries by American exports.

Many of the US arguments concerning adoption of US-style IP laws "cut both ways" in developing countries. On the one hand, using the American system often puts the native innovators at a disadvantage due to the lack of IP infrastructure in their country and to the fact that group innovation cannot be protected. In effect, opting into the American system risks co-option. However, the Americans also make persuasive arguments in favor of the fact that the system can be used by developing countries and their citizens as a way to protect and benefit from innovation.

John Murphy, vice president for international affairs at the US Chamber of Commerce and executive vice president of the Association of American Chambers of Commerce in Latin America (AACCLA), made this "positive" argument in an address he delivered at the Americas Innovation Forum in Punta del Este, Uruguay, on March 31, 2008. Murphy argued that innovation and economic progress both require strong IP protection even more in developing than developed countries. Using as examples Singapore, Mexico, and other countries that have adopted US-style systems, Murphy illustrated why countries should cooperate with the US approach to IP law.

Global Culture Issues

One could spend a lot of time and effort over arguments concerning the degree to which the world is becoming "Americanized." Clearly, a thorough discussion of relationships among the developed and developing nations, international monetary and trade policies, trans-global wars, the nature of imperialism, and/ or the pros and cons of one or the other socio-political-economic model for just living, are all far beyond the scope of the present volume. Such issues and the roles that American-style culture plays in the development of life outside US borders have long been at risk prior to the development of digital new media.

As noted above, however, trade agreements leveraging "favored nation trade status" with the United States in order to spread the adoption of the US-style IP legal regime have been an important part of US international politics, especially in recent years as the digital/information revolution has come to the fore. Combined with the fact that the United States is the principal (though far from the only) producer of globally popular entertainment media as well as one of the primary players across all of the information economy activities, the moves to foster the adoption of the US-style IP legal regime (and its outcomes) are not insignificant.

For many native peoples, the US efforts smack of cultural hegemony and lack of good faith. The US approach insists on protecting the entertainment and information content that enriches US content holders. The global reach of media remarkably extends the influence of those industries. Yet others are struck by our lack of interest in the abilities of indigenous peoples to protect their IP from co-option, export, and capitalization by US firms. In other words, the US intellectual property regime appears in the global framework to work much better at enabling profit than in protecting innovation and the rights of innovators, and that profit seems directed back toward the United States in most cases.

McLeod names a number of countries that have begun to resist US-led influence, particularly with regard to patents, for a number of reasons. Some, like Brazil and Ecuador, are newly protective of their native knowledge in ways they previously had ignored. Since US-style patent law does not recognize indigenous, group-oriented knowledge development as patentable, traditional formulations (perhaps passed down through generations and centuries) have generally not been protected from exportation and synthesis by Western pharmaceutical companies. The result has been the loss of incalculable riches to the country of origin (175).

India has resisted co-option of its national sovereignty in these areas for years, to the point of incurring the political wrath of the Bush Administration and being labeled an "unfair trading partner." Zimbabwe, Bangladesh, and the Dutch have all taken action against the US-style regime. The European Union has been at the forefront of global legislation against genetically modified food, one of the new frontiers in the intellectual property portfolio of Western agrobusiness.

More specifically, with regard to products of the media industries, US interests face significant cultural opposition, as reflected, for example, by former French President Jacques Chirac's answer to the question, "Are you worried about American cultural imperialism?":

> No, not at all, because the Americans do fantastic things in many cultural domains. However, I do not want to see European culture sterilized or obliterated by American culture for economic reasons that have nothing to do with real culture. That is why I am for the cultural exception [i.e., leaving cultural productions out of international free-trade agreements], and especially for production and distribution quotas. (Redman and Sancton)

Comparing typical Hollywood film budgets with those of French filmmakers indicates the significant disadvantage at which overseas media industries operate. Yet it was reported that in 1995 "Hollywood releases play at one-fourth of France's 4,500 cinemas" (Rinaman). Therefore, one finds that many European leaders are heartily comfortable with the EU's "Television without Frontiers" protections referenced in the previous section on trade.

Then, of course, there are the broader cultural differences that separate East from West, developed nations from developing countries. For example, as noted earlier in this chapter, China's adherence to US-style IP protection has been virtually non-existent. It is equally difficult to imagine many countries firmly in the Muslim world to have much interest in protecting Western investments in idea-based property.

There have long been differences between the ways that the United States and other parts of the world interpret the bases and justifications for IP protection. The US articulation of idea-based innovation as "property" equivalent to real property is simply not universally agreed to. Watching Andreas Johnsen, Ralf Christensen, and Henrik Moltke's *Good Copy Bad Copy* <http://www.goodcopybadcopy.net> reminds one just how strongly many around the world either ignore US-style IP or find it dated or irrelevant.

In general, then, there are strong movements working against each other in the international IP law environment. US-style IP regimes are well established and growing as trade partners, and countries who want most-favored-nation trade status move in the protectionist direction dictated by the United States. On the other hand, there is a lot of push-back by countries who, for various reasons, are either unhappy with the US approach or who are culturally and/or politically alienated from the United States. China remains daunting, and

:ult to imagine that many of either the Muslim or African countries will show much interest in cooperating with US prerogatives for protecting US media and new media exports.

The Internet Changes Everything

Like other communication technologies, there is no universal agreement as to how the Internet should work. The medium includes both the technologies and the ways that people use them. As with television, for example, computational networks and content are put to a variety of uses across communities. State-owned and -operated entities are different from commercial enterprises, nonprofits, etc. The Internet is no different. To varying degrees, then, national communications infrastructures (including the Internet) face national control. To the degree that it is rigidly enforced, that control generally comes from within national borders as an effort by the country to regulate the information available to or about its people and government.

Though a distributed system without centralized and hierarchical control, the Internet is not totally chaotic; the entities that cooperate in its operation often do so via the implementation of standards that have been developed by a large number of mostly volunteer groups, sometimes sponsored by governmental agencies. In some ways and to varying degrees, these groups can be said to play a major role in "running the Internet." They include:

- Internet2 Project (UCAID)—For development of advanced network services for higher education and research and the VBNS high-speed backbone on which it will run. See also Abilene and Qbone and VBNS+; and the Canadian CA*net 3.
- Internet Society—Concerned with the evolution of the Internet and its social, political, and technical issues.
- Internet Engineering Task Force (IETF)—Develops technical standards for the Internet.
- Internet Architecture Board (IAB)—Oversees Internet protocols and procedures and the creation of Internet standards.
- Internet Assigned Numbers Authority (IANA)—Coordinates assignment of protocol numbers. See ICANN (below) for domain name assignments.
- Commercial Internet Exchange Association (CIX)—Nonprofit trade association for public data Internetworking service providers.
- CommerceNet—Nonprofit group that works to accelerate the application of electronic commerce on the Internet.

- W3C, World Wide Web Consortium—An industry consortium run by MIT that develops standards for the evolution of the Web.
- ICANN—Internet Corporation for Assigned Names and Numbers (supersedes some IANA functions) and list of Accredited Registrars.
- InterNIC at Network Solutions—Directory and Databases.
- Domain Name Buyers Guide.

And . . .

- Internet responsiveness or weather as maps from MIDS.
- Internet Domain Survey—run in January and July.
- IP Next Generation (IPNG). (Cerny)

There is also the Internet Governance Forum (IGF), which represents carriers, ISPs, governments, international organizations, academics, and others that meets once a year and deals with topics such as: openness (the free flow of ideas and information); security (protecting users and networks); e-criminals (child abusers, etc); cultural and linguistic diversity; and issues of access, particularly in the developing world. The IGF takes no votes and makes no decisions but advises bodies that run the Internet day-to-day, such as the Internet Corporation for Assigned Names and Numbers (ICANN). (Sarson)

And, of course, management of the Internet is another venue in which many folks around the world are unhappy with the significant amount of leverage the United States has over infrastructure and cultural affairs (Sarson). The IGF structure helps modify the negative feelings somewhat, but a group that meets once a year can only exert so much influence on the day-to-day operations of a vast set of global networks.

A central issue for intellectual property law is that there is no "ruling" international law in these matters. Although there are trade-related agreements and international standards oversight bodies, these functions only give the appearance of "global" control mechanisms. The questions then become: Whose laws apply?

What are the specific rules/laws for a given case?

The International Legal Environment for IP Law

In legal terms, the primary issues involved relate to "jurisdiction." Jurisdiction settles questions about which particular court or court system will be used as well as the power of a court to haul a party into court and render a decision that is binding on that party. Criminal jurisdiction requires that there has to be some connection between the agency/organization and the crime/criminal (territory, nationality, protection of national interests, protection of the people of a country). Civil jurisdiction requires some connection between the person or property and the territory. Jurisdiction applies to these important issues, among others: venue (location of a particular court), service of process (delivery of legal papers that initiates a lawsuit or legal proceeding), and the choice of law (the legal process of deciding which of the jurisdiction's laws applies).

Legal principles concerning jurisdiction on the Internet have emerged through case law. However, as Internet technologies have advanced, the development of legal principles has lagged. As noted above, courts must determine the degrees of connection among persons, property, acts, and geography to establish jurisdiction. A distinction between "active" and "passive" participation has been used to determine whether personal jurisdiction applies to someone operating a Web site (Wolf). In the archetypal cases, if someone operates a Web site on which they "interactively" do business, courts have sometimes found them to be within the jurisdiction of the court where their operation is based. If the material on the site is merely "passive" information (even if it is advertising), courts have found insufficient grounds for personal jurisdiction. However, this distinction is muddied by the evolving technologies of Web 2.0 in which few, if any, sites are either exclusively "interactive" or "passive," and by the fact that the law often has to deal with both Web site providers and users in cases in which users may be far away from the location of the provider. Further, the key determination for this so-called "standard" focuses exclusively on the conduct of commerce/businesses; there are many other ways to use Internet resources in addition to commerce, and those uses can and do produce circumstances requiring legal remedies invoking questions of jurisdiction.

The grounds for jurisdiction are usually based on geography, with the location of the court determining their range and latitude. However, in a global environment, matters at issue, the networks used, and the parties involved are most likely spread across vast distances and many national boundaries. Jurisdication will be shown to be even more complex when we take up virtual environments in Chapter 9. Further, as noted, once jurisdiction has been established, a given court determines/defines which legal principles to be used in each case. Local, regional, state, national, or international laws, rules, or treaties might be invoked, or the practices of national or international agencies or tribunals might be used.

A recent set of cases provides an excellent illustration of the legal com-plexities in global IP disagreements. *MPAA v. Jeboo* and *Jeboo v. MPAA* fea-ture suits filed by the Motion Picture Association of America in America and China and a suit filed by Jeboo in China. In *MPAA v. Jeboo*, five US movie studios and the MPAA sued Jeboo for providing copyright-pro-tected movies to Internet cafes. After winning court cases in the suit, the MPAA announced both the "win" and a "settlement" in which Jeboo was said to have "apologized." In response, Jeboo sued for defamation (libel), claiming that they only settled in order to "move on" and that they had ad-mitted to no wrongdoing. See Clint DeBoer for a report about the initial court win and announced settlement; see Mark Hefflinger for a report on the subsequent breakdown of the arrangement and the *Jeboo* countersuit.

Two kinds of agencies/organizations contribute to the global legal envi-ronment: public/governmental organizations referred to as intergovernmental organizations (IGOs) and private/nongovernmental organizations (NGOs). Some examples of IGOs with policies and practices that are relevant to global new media issues include the United Nations and its Commission on Interna-tional Trade Law, as well as its Conference on Trade and Development, and the United Nations Education, Scientific, and Cultural Organization (UNESCO); the EU and a number of its entities; the Council of Europe; the Organization for Economic Cooperation and Development; the World Trade Organization; the International Telecommunications Union; and the WIPO. Some examples of NGOs include the Alliance for Global Business; the Global Business Dia-log on Electronic Commerce; the International Chamber of Commerce; and the International Electrotechnical Commission (Smedinghoff).

When parties submit to an international agency/court, they may agree to the standards of that venue. When dragged into a national/state court, the court may pick either its own national/state law, the international law that country/state recognizes, or the guidelines provided by an IGO or NGO.

In determining the applicable laws, all of the categories we have studied throughout this text are clearly relevant. However, in the global arena, there are three primary aspects that get more attention than other features: copyright, patent, and international trade agreements.

In questions concerning copyright law, adjudication begins with the na-tional laws that apply. However, these can also confuse matters somewhat, as they take precedence within some nations, may not be accepted in "other" countries, and are not fully harmonized. International treaties are also considered. Important among these in the copyright area are: *The Berne Convention for the Protection of Literary and Artistic Works*, *WIPO*, the *Copyright Treaty*, the *Performances and Phonograms Treaty*, and the *Universal Copyright Convention*.

In the area of patents, the *Paris Convention for the Protection of Industrial Property*, the *Patent Cooperation Treaty*, and the *TRIPS* (*Trade-Related Aspects of Intellectual Property Agreement*) are important.

Among the treaties and trade agreements at risk, *GATT/TRIPS* and *NAFTA* carry the most weight.

New Media Cases Illustrating International IP Law

Pebble Beach Co. v. Caddy, No. 04–15577, 2006 WL 1897091 (9th Cir. July 12, 2006)

The corporation behind the famous US golf course Pebble Beach <www.pebblebeach.com> filed suit against a small British inn named Pebble Beach Bed & Breakfast <www.pebblebeach-uk.com> for trademark infringement and dilution. The accused, Michael Caddy, moved to dismiss the case for lack of personal jurisdiction and insufficiency of service of process. Although Caddy could have simply stayed in England and refused to appear (in which case the Court might have found against him for non-appearance), he came to the United States and fought the claims. The trial court granted Caddy's motion to dismiss, noting that Caddy's business did not conflict with that of the Pebble Beach golf course because he did not direct his business toward the United States or California. Pebble Beach appealed, and the Court of Appeals upheld the trial verdict, finding that Pebble Beach had not satisfied the three-factor "effects test" that would show that a defendant committed an intentional act expressly aimed at the state of jurisdiction that causes harm in the state of jurisdiction in order to be sued there. The Court further said that a non-interactive, "passive" Web site such as Caddy's was inadequate to establish jurisdiction. The appeals court also found that Caddy is not a cybersquatter because he had a legitimate business in England under the name he has used there.

Copiepresse v. Google, The Court of First Instance in Brussels, Nr. 06/10.928/C (Feb. 13, 2007)

Copiepresse (CP) is a Belgian collective rights management organization that represents Belgian newspapers. CP sued Google over the Google News service that copies headlines, the first sentence (or portion of sentence) of articles, and links without prior permission from Belgian newspapers or the reporters who write the stories. Google argued (in a Belgian court) that their practice constitutes fair use, based on two exceptions: (1) that their use is an account of the news, and (2) that criticism or review of the news is fair use. However, the practical operation of Google News impedes their defense. The "accounts of news" exception usually applies to a commentary on the news, and Google News reproduces news without any commentary. Further, the "criticism or review" function requires careful examination of a collection of elements, and in Google's case, no human performs this task. Given the voluminous nature of the materials used, it is not practical for Google to get consent from reporters and writers. The end result? Google loses in Belgium.

Under US law (e.g., *Kelly v. Arriba Soft*), Google News would likely win, because its use would be considered "transformative"(and thereby be protected). Under Belgian law, transformation of an underlying work is viewed negatively and as a violation of an author's moral rights. The Belgian court wrote that:

> - [We] Conclude that Google may not claim any exception as stipulated in copyright law and related rights;
> - Conclude that the activities of Google News (i.e. the reproduction and communication to the public of the titles of articles and the short extracts from articles) and the use of the Google "cache" (i.e. the registration accessible to the public of the so-called "cache" memory of articles and documents) breach copyright law;
> - Order Google to remove from all these sites (specifically from Google News as well as the visible cache links in relation to the search engine Google web) all articles, photographs and graphic representation of authors for whom the voluntary third parties intervening justify that they hold the rights.

The court also levied fines. Copiepresse and Google have been in ongoing negotiations in an effort to reach a settlement, action that the Court finding against Google rather "forced" them into.

Google Inc. v. Daniel Giersch. Office For Harmonization in the Internal Market (Trade Marks and Designs), Second Board of Appeal R 252/2007-2 (Feb. 26, 2008)

After losing court battles in Germany over the issue, Google filed cases in other European venues, including the Office for Harmonization in the Internal Market of Germany, against Daniel Giersch (of Monaco) for infringement of the "G-mail" trademark. Daniel Giersch started using the name "G-Mail" in 2000, which was four years prior to Google's use of it. Giersch's service scans messages, sends them via the Internet, then prints and hand delivers them at the receiving end. After Giersch became aware of Google's plan to offer "G-Mail" in Germany, negotiations between the parties resulted in an impasse and, subsequently, Giersch sued Google for infringement. Giersch won both in multiple court cases and before the Office of Harmonization in Germany; his trademarks are registered there, in Switzerland, Monaco, and Norway (Broache).

Summarizing International IP Law in New Media

The importance of the global environment to US intellectual property interests is self-evident. The scope of the stakes and risks and the amount of business already being done in intellectual content clearly mandate that significant attention must be paid to protecting intellectual property within a just and equitable system that is sensitive to the varied circumstances across diverse economic and geopolitical boundaries. There is, however, a wide gap between recognizing needs while acknowledging costs and benefits and producing systems that accomplish wildly varying goals. The international scene challenges governments, industries, businesses, and creative innovators alike. Intellectual property policies are among the most highly charged and contested matters in global economics.

The United States has taken the lead in developing practices with global reach; some international agencies, including those guiding Internet policies, have also contributed energies. However, the fact that the United States has leveraged its strong position in trade negotiations into agreements based on US approaches to IP neither guarantees success nor produces equity. As we've seen throughout this text, the US intellectual property regime is highly contested and is technologically challenged, even within the United States. Taking global implications into consideration increases the complexities and challenges exponentially. It is clear that the United States cannot afford inaction. The economic risks from ineffective protection of intellectual property are staggering. However, the United States is also responsible, in its own "legal" and "business as usual-like ways" for engendering global skepticism over the wisdom of adopting US style IP laws. Finding rapprochement among protectionism, cultural hegemony, creativity, and technological innovation is a key challenge in the global digital environment.

As also noted throughout this book, the IP law complexities faced by governments, industries, and businesses are now shared by everyday users of the Internet and are particularly acute for creative producers and distributors who do not have access to a stable of lawyers with expertise in the global environment. Each area of IP law, copyright, patent, trademark, trade secrets, and the Content torts, enters the everyday lives of Internet users via the products made through digital innovations. The entire system implicates intellectual property laws, as the content and mechanisms of exchange fully partake in the features that differentiate digital content from analog material: everything along the pipeline can be reproduced and re-distributed with accuracy, ease, and in prodigious amounts by users with modest technological means and know-how. Contemporary creatives must learn to navigate these troubled waters—in many cases without adequate guidance—in ways that stay within the bounds of current laws and treaties featuring high ambiguity over jurisdiction, statute instability, and contestation over socio-political and economic equity. [ELL]

Discussion Questions

1. Discuss the nature of the United States as "cultural imperialist." Should our efforts be pitched toward distributing our intellectual property as globally and profusely as possible? Should we use our IP regime as a way to leverage that spread of US-produced content?
2. Should international agencies "control" the United States's ability to mandate its IP regime for other nations?
3. Should the United States pay reparations to developing nations for the value of intellectual property that has been appropriated over the years?
4. You are building a Web presence for your company. Should you plan to accommodate the laws of all the nations from which your site can be accessed? Will you open field operations in each country? Offer alternative versions of the site? Or will you attempt to get by with a single, US-based site that assumes compliance with US laws and expectations only?
5. Discuss international piracy, fully considering the fact that available values of costs and losses only account for "hard" media. What kinds of steps should be taken to stem the tide of international digital piracy?

CHAPTER EIGHT

Digital Rights Management

Most of the new content we purchase and consume is, at some point in its life, digital. Book manuscripts are files on an editor's computer; music is many hundreds of sound files on an engineer's computer, and even the most traditionally produced Hollywood film is a digital file during DVD production. Increasingly, this content is also being distributed digitally. Publishers, producers, and creators see the exciting possibilities of a digital world but fear the implications of easy and virtually cost-free replication of digital data. One response to this has been the rise of Technological Protection Measures (TPM), so-called Digital Rights Management technologies. Digital Rights Management, or DRM, is a technology that enforces a restriction on the use of content. DRM might require a user to enter her unique password before viewing or printing a PDF file, or it might prevent her from copying an audio file to more than a certain number of computers. In some schemes, the DRM might be tied to monitoring software that periodically checks in with a network server to verify that the user or the device is still authorized by the rights holder. DRM is controversial for a number of reasons. Many content producers see it as their only effective weapon against widespread piracy, while privacy advocates worry about access to sensitive user information, and librarians and archivists fear DRM may interfere both with traditionally protected uses of content and with long-term archiving.

TPM and DRM suggest ways to protect intellectual property on the "control side" in cooperation with the "penalty side" aspects of the *Digital Millennium Copyright Act (DMCA)*. On the one hand, TPM and DRM may someday effectively lower the number of infringements. On the other hand, however, TPM and DRM are somewhat "above the law" in that they are solutions invoked by producers and distributors without legal review. In effect, control-side, code level restrictions treat all consumers as potential criminals and may obviate users' rights and protections by restricting the ways that digital materials can be used—again, without legal review. The use of TPM and DRM is therefore of great interest in a book about IP law and practices in new media. This chapter provides a brief introduction to the topics and notes a small number of instances that illustrate the problematic nature of these controls.

How DRM Works

There isn't a single, simple definition of DRM that describes all implementations. Even the term itself is controversial: Some feel the phrase "rights management" is euphemistic, suggesting that "digital restrictions management" or even "handcuffware" are more appropriate (Stallman). Whatever the preferred term, DRM is a framework with both technical and legal components. One could say that "technology constructs and the law enforces," or, as Lawrence Lessig describes the DRM-enforcing *DMCA*, "It is law protecting software code protecting copyright" (Lessig, "Jail Time in the Digital Age"). In some cases, the technology itself may not have been designed with copyright protection in mind. In fact, the *DMCA* provisions of the *United States Copyright Law* could be invoked to challenge unauthorized uses of works that are in the public domain or otherwise not subject to copyright protection.

In these relatively early days of DRM, there are a number of different models and implementations. On one end of the spectrum are so-called lightweight, or "speedbump" models, which inform the user of use limitations, but offer only minimal technical resistance to unauthorized uses (Felten). They are mildly inconvenient, designed to stop a casual infringe, but do not constitute an insurmountable obstacle. The FairPlay technology embedded in content in the Apple iTunes music library has been cited (Doctorow) as a speedbump example: A user is limited to a certain number of authorized computers on which a file can be played, but once an audio CD is created from the content, it is as portable, transferable, and DRM-free as an audio CD purchased in a record store. At the other end of the spectrum are chains of end-to-end enforcement. Had it withstood legal challenge in 2005, the Federal Communications Commission's attempted broadcast flag regulation would have required that all digital video recorders obey do-not-copy instructions embedded in digital television broadcasts (American Library Association). The broadcast flag would have been one link in an emerging chain of DRM for high-definition video and television content. High Definition Television (HDTV) offers a connection protocol, the High Definition Media Interface, or HDMI, that can recognize and enforce High Definition Content Protection (HDCP) instructions from a compliant device such as a DVD player or gaming console.

Other measures sometimes lumped into a DRM definition might more accurately be labeled as "rights identification systems." Visual watermarking, in which information about the copyright owner, terms of use, or other restrictions, are displayed on top of or alongside image data, is one example of rights identification. Rights languages such as Open Digital Rights Language (ODRL) and the Extensible Rights Markup Language (XrML) can also be used to identify and declare rights.

Acts vs. Tools

The various DRM and rights identification schemes come together in the federal copyright law. The 1998 *Digital Millennium Copyright Act* added Chapter 12 to the *United States Copyright Law*, "Copyright Protection and Management Systems." The chapter has five main sections: 1201 and 1202 prohibit circumvention of protection systems and define the protections for copyright management information; the last three sections deal with penalties. Section one (1201) actually includes three different prohibitions. 1201(a)(1) prohibits circumvention of a technological measure controlling access to a work. 1201(a)(2) prohibits trafficking in any technology designed to circumvent access control. Section 1201(b) prohibits trafficking in any technology designed to circumvent controls that protect against copying or other protected rights of the copyright holder. A crude shorthand of this confusing array of rules might be:

1201(a)(1) ACTS: no breaking access controls
1201(a)(2) TOOLS: no selling tools to break access controls
1201(b) TOOLS: no selling tools to break copy controls

Noticeably absent is a prohibition on the act of breaking copy controls.

Such a prohibition is not included, so that Chapter 12 does not contradict the existing limitations on the copyright holder's rights, and to keep from punishing users making non-infringing uses of content (Peters).

Interestingly, in drafting the *DMCA*, Congress at one point considered removing the access protection provisions—1201(a)—from Title 17 altogether: "The Committee on Commerce adopted an amendment that moves the anti-circumvention provisions out of Title 17 and establishes them as free-standing provisions of law. The Committee believes that this is the most appropriate way to implement the treaties, in large part because these regulatory provisions have little, if anything, to do with copyright law" (Commerce Committee). Eventually, however, the prohibitions were reinserted into Chapter 12 of Title 17, in effect creating a new type of protection for works that has little or nothing to do with the traditionally protected rights of the copyright holder (Nimmer 396–99). This creates a somewhat strange and paradoxical situation: one may be prohibited from defeating technical protection measures that protect access, but once access has lawfully been gained, whether or not further protection measures may be defeated is subject to evaluation of the traditional and technology-neutral existing exemptions within copyright law: "Nothing in this section shall affect rights, remedies, limitations, or defenses to copyright infringement, including fair use, under this title" (17 U.S.C. sec. 1201(c)(1)).

The prohibitions outlined in section one, generally lumped together as the anti-circumvention provisions, protect the gadgets, software, and other technical features that make up DRM. The section concludes with a lengthy list of exceptions and additional requirements that manufacturers of VHS and 8mm video recorders must comply with. Among the exceptions explicitly mentioned are for reverse engineering (17 U.S.C. sec. 1201(f)) and encryption research (17 U.S.C. sec.1201(g)). Recent history has shown, however, that application of the encryption research exemption, as well as analysis of the traditional exemptions in copyright law in light of the *DMCA*, can be problematic.

Strange but True: Tales of Digital Rights Management

Secure Digital Music Initiative (SDMI)

One of the most well-known examples of encryption research that ran afoul of the *DMCA*'s anti-circumvention provisions occurred when a team of computer scientists interacted, in 2001, with the Secure Digital Music Initiative (SDMI).

SDMI was a group of recording industry and technology companies seeking to design protection systems to detect and prevent unauthorized copying and distribution of audio recordings. By designing an unbreakable new protection technology and selling music wrapped in it and achieving market penetration with SDMI-compliant portable music devices, the recording industry hoped to have a real weapon against rampant music piracy. In September 2000, SDMI issued a public challenge to the digital community to try to defeat SDMI's technological protection measures (TPM). SDMI's primary protection strategies involved watermarks: an algorithm applied to a digital file that effectively creates a traceable but inaudible signature on top of the audio signal (Craver et al., "SDMI Challenge FAQ"). SDMI contended that it would not be possible to remove the watermark without causing significant damage to the audio file itself, making stealing watermarked files an unattractive choice for would-be music pirates. SDMI offered a prize of $10,000 to anyone who successfully defeated their watermarking technology, providing the challenger was willing to transfer intellectual property rights to their process to the SDMI.

A team led by Princeton University computer scientist Ed Felten claimed success in defeating the technique less than a month after the challenge was issued (Bray). Rather than claim the monetary prize and submit their code to SDMI, however, Felten's team chose instead to present their results at the Fourth International Information Hiding Workshop in Pittsburgh in April 2001. On April 9, 2001, the Recording Industry Association of America (RIAA) mailed Dr. Felten a letter warning him that "any disclosure of information gained from participating in the Public Challenge would be outside of the scope of the activities permitted by the Agreement and could subject you and your research team to actions under the *Digital Millennium Copyright Act* ('*DMCA*')" (Oppenheim). In the version of this letter preserved on the Princeton Department of Computer Science's Web site, the *DMCA* is invoked no less than five times in the page-long letter. The RIAA and, presumably, the SDMI, asserted that the researchers had agreed to certain conditions upon clicking an "I Agree" box on the "hacksdmi.org" Web site. Dr. Felten and his colleagues felt the letter presented enough of a threat of a lawsuit to keep them from presenting their results at the Hiding conference. Reading from a prepared statement, Dr. Felten said, "Litigation is costly, time-consuming, and uncertain, regardless of the merits of the other side's case. Ultimately we, the authors, reached a collective decision not to expose ourselves, our employers, and the conference organizers to litigation at this time."

The dispute between Felten's team and the SDMI centers on three questions. Were the researchers bound by any agreement or license to keep their results private? Is writing a paper describing results the same as sharing actual code? Most important, what exactly does the *DMCA* prohibit, and what encryption research activities does it exempt? (Samuelson 2028). There would be no conclusive answer to any of these questions in the Felten case. When several reports of the cancelled presentation appeared in the media, both the RIAA and SDMI were quick to claim no intention of suing the researchers. Felten and his colleagues then presented a request for declaratory judgment in US District Court. The suit requested the Court to find that the paper and presentation were not in violation of the *DMCA* but also to find the *DMCA* itself unconstitutional on the grounds that Congress exceeded its enumerated powers in enacting it. The Department of Justice, named as one of the defendants in the suit, moved to dismiss, and in November 2001 the Court agreed with the defense that there was no credible threat of litigation against the scientists. Finding the request for declaratory judgment therefore without grounds, the judge denied it. In the meantime, Prof. Felten et al. took the companies at their word and presented their SDMI results at a USENIX conference (Craver et al., "Reading between the Lines").

Many in the engineering and computer science communites expressed opposition to the anti-circumvention portions of the *DMCA*, both before and after the Felten case. In her "Viewpoint" column, Past President Barbara Simons of the Association of Computing Machinery expressed these concerns about the *DMCA*:

> The law does not address issues such as the robustness of a technological measure. The publication of an analysis of flaws in a weak and poorly designed technology that is supposed to control access to a copyrighted work could be considered a violation of the DMCA.
>
> A critical aspect of the anti-circumvention provisions of the DMCA is that intent to circumvent copyright is not a requirement for being found in violation of the law. In other words, someone who has made no illegal copies of a copyrighted work and who intends for his or her work to be used only to better understand some aspect of science could be charged under the DMCA. (Simons)

This comment brings us back to the origin of the *DMCA* and the tension that exists between traditional copyright protections and new supra-copyright access protections added with the *DMCA*. The Princeton and Rice University team would not be the last computer science researchers to be threatened with action under provisions of the *DMCA*.

Cases Illustrating DRM

United States of America v. Elcomsoft Co., Ltd. and Dmitry Sklyarov. USDC (N.D. Cal. 2002)

On July 16, 2001, a Russian programmer named Dimitry Sklyarov was arrested and charged with trafficking in circumvention software, making him the first person to be criminally prosecuted under the terms of the *DMCA*. Section 1204 defines criminal penalties for violation of sections 1201 and 1202, including no more than five years' imprisonment for the first offense and up to ten years for any subsequent offense (17 U.S.C. § 1204(a)). Sklyarov, a Ph.D. student employed by a Russian software company named ElcomSoft, wrote a piece of software he called the Advanced eBook Processor Program (AEBPR), that reformats eBooks to allow viewing with software other than the proprietary eBook software. Sklyarov came to Las Vegas to present at the "hacker" conference DEF CON but was arrested as he was leaving his hotel to return to the airport and home (Electronic Frontier Foundation, "EFF's *United States v. Elcomsoft & Sklyarov* FAQ").

The Adobe eBook Reader, distributed free of charge by Adobe, uses "eBooks" content as sold by a number of third-party sellers. Sellers of eBooks use an Adobe Content server to generate unique vouchers that travel with the eBook and reside on the user's computer. The voucher provides permission to the eBook software to allow the book to be viewed on the screen. Specific book permissions can be customized so that, for example, one book may be printed in its entirety, while another can only be printed a page at a time, or a page per day, depending on the choice of the eBook publisher. As his DEF CON presentation (Sklyarov) and the court documents both describe, Sklyarov's AEBPR unlocked the contents of eBooks using the voucher intended to protect the contents, creating a Portable Document Format (PDF) version of the book with no restrictions on use:

> Thus, the restrictions imposed by the publisher are stripped away, leaving the ebook in a "naked PDF" format that is readily copyable, printable, and easily distributed electronically. The conversion accomplished by the AEBPR program enables a purchaser of an ebook to engage in "fair use" of an ebook without infringing the copyright laws, for example, by allowing the lawful owner of an ebook to read it on another computer, to make a back-up copy, or to print the ebook in paper form. The same technology, however, also allows a user to engage in copyright infringement by making and distributing unlawful copies of the ebook. (*United States of America v. Elcomsoft Co., Ltd. and Dmitry Sklyarov*)

Some three weeks after his arrest, Sklyarov was released from jail, but the US Department of Justice continued with its prosecution of Sklyarov and ElcomSoft. The case went to a jury trial in December 2002, and both Sklyarov and ElcomSoft were acquitted. After the trial, at least one juror reported that the jury found that, while the product was clearly illegal according to the *DMCA*, the law itself was so confusing that they could well believe that the Russian company could have failed to understand that their product was breaking the law (Bowman).

DRM is big business. For example, password recovery is the primary business of Elcomsoft, the firm that was prosecuted in the latter case. Microsoft has a significant business in DRM, and Jupitermedia (and a wide range of other operations) publishes an enormous amount of news and information about DRM issues.[1] Bill Rosenblatt, editor of DRM Watch, runs GiantSteps Media Technology Strategies, a management consultancy focused on the content industries and writes about DRM in the new media industries, under the philosophy that "digital rights technologies enable much more than media piracy prevention: they should be fundamental building blocks in the dissemination and transfer of information through digital networks."

The Chamberlain Group, Inc., v. Skylink Technologies, Inc., 02 C 6376 (2004)

In late 2003, The Chamberlain Group, manufacturers of garage door openers, sued Skylink Technologies for violating the *DMCA* by selling a door-opening remote designed to interoperate with Chamberlain's door-opening system. Skylink, which manufactures aftermarket remotes, had reverse-engineered its device to defeat Chamberlain's rolling code system. With a "rolling code," the code needed to open the door increments by three after each use, purportedly to prevent someone with a "code grabber" from recording the code during use, then returning to the garage later and gaining unauthorized access with the stolen code. Skylink's universal remote sent three codes in quick succession. If the first code failed to open the door, the second and third would reset the door opener, taking advantage of a resynchronization failsafe that measured two sequential failed codes to look for the appropriate increment of three between them. This re-synchronizing feature was designed to allow an authorized user to re-establish a connection legitimately lost, for example, if the remote was pressed many times outside of the range of the receiver in the door opener. Chamberlain claimed that by allowing the user to effectively reprogram the door opener, Skylink was defeating the Technological Protection Measure built in to the opener's microchip, and was therefore in violation of the new 1201 provisions of the law.

Consumers Union (publishers of *Consumer Reports*) wrote in their *amicus* brief to the Court in support of Skylink: "This case presents the question of whether companies can use the anti-circumvention provisions of the Digital Millennium Copyright Act ("DMCA") to foreclose competition for aftermarket products (such as replacement parts) without an underlying claim of copyright infringement and in the absence of evidence that consumers were not authorized to use the products they had purchased" (Urban and Schultz). In other words, one of the key questions in the Skylink case was whether the language in the *DMCA* protecting TPMs truly applies when there is no underlying copyright question. Did Congress intend for the anti-trafficking provision to create a new economic right separate from copyright or only to offer additional protection to an underlying copyrighted work?

In fact, Chamberlain argues that the computer code itself, that is, the door-opening code protected by the rolling code, was copyrightable. In its request for summary judgment, Chamberlain reveals that it, too, offers for sale universally compatible remotes intended to work with openers sold by other companies, but that it draws the line at offering a remote capable of defeating the rolling code systems manufactured by its competitors, such as Genie. It is of interest that, in this same document, Chamberlain's discussion of the harm caused by Skylink centers around the damage caused to the market for Chamberlain's universal remotes, specifically recounting how Skylink undercut the exclusive aftermarket remote provider relationship Chamberlain had enjoyed with Lowe's home improvement stores.

In her ruling denying Chamberlain's request for summary judgment, District Court Judge Rebecca Pallmeyer found that there were significant noninfringing uses for the Skylink remotes beyond defeating the rolling code system, since Skylink remotes interoperate with a number of other garage door systems, not just Chamberlain's. She also found that there was real reason to doubt whether Chamberlain had clearly demonstrated that the computer code was copyrighted. Although Chamberlain had filed registration papers with the US Copyright Office, the version of its code actually in use at the time it went to court against Skylink was different from that listed in the filed application. Furthermore, she found that owners of garage door openers are implicitly authorized to circumvent any protection measures on a number of grounds: that this is the established practice in the marketplace; that Chamberlain itself had participated in this market; and that Chamberlain had failed to notify consumers on product packaging or elsewhere that only Chamberlain-approved opening remotes could be used with their openers. She found, therefore, that Chamberlain had failed to meet another standard of section 1201(a), that access was effectively prohibited.

Chamberlain appealed, but the Federal Circuit upheld the lower decision. The Federal Court took a slightly different view of the case, namely that Chamberlain's claim had no merit because they had failed to prove any connection between the device and actual copyright infringement:

> The anti-circumvention and anti-trafficking provisions of the DMCA create new grounds of liability. A copyright owner seeking to impose liability on an accused circumventor must demonstrate a reasonable relationship between the circumvention at issue and a use relating to a property right for which the Copyright Act permits the copyright owner to withhold authorization—as well as notice that authorization was withheld. A copyright owner seeking to impose liability on an accused trafficker must demonstrate that the trafficker's device enables either copyright infringement or a prohibited circumvention.

Even though on its face the case seems almost ridiculous, and it is hard to imagine that Congress would have intended copyright law to be used to protect garage door openers, the federal decision in the *Chamberlain v. Skylink* case very clearly instructs us that liability for the act of circumvention can only be considered if there is an actual copyright violation as well. The ruling therefore ties the acts in section 1201(a) much more closely to the traditionally protected rights of the copyright holder than they would seem to be linked in a straightforward reading of the law. According to the logic applied in the Skylink case: if no unauthorized access and no copyright infringement, then no trafficking liability. This is a very different conclusion from the one drawn in other cases, such as *321 Studios*, where a software company was found to be in violation of the anti-trafficking provisions, which were considered on their own and not in conjunction with any acts of unauthorized access or copyright infringement (*321 Studios*).

EFF v. Sony BMG, Cal. Sup. Ct. Los Angeles Cty. (2005)

Throughout the first five years of the new millennium, the recording industry's distress about explosive growth of online music downloading and concurrent, multi-year losses in traditional album sales drove it to continue a feverish search for technical solutions to the piracy problem. The Recording Industry

Association of America (RIAA) took a leading role in a number of legal battles with major peer-to-peer software providers and networks, and even took the step of bringing suits against individuals alleged to be major file traders. New media formats like the Super Audio CD (SACD) and Digital Audio Tape (DAT), which both had stronger copy protection than regular audio CDs, were effectively "dead on arrival," neither embraced nor adopted by consumers in sufficient numbers to create a real market. Initiatives like the Secure Digital Music Initiative (SDMI) failed to gather enough industry support to take off, possibly due to a lack of confidence in the DRM following its widely publicized defeat by Ed Felten and his team, although it is possible that licensing terms and standardization of devices would have been as daunting had the project matured.

In October 2005, programmer Mark Russinovich discovered a strange piece of software on his computer, and after some diligent research, he discovered it to be a "rootkit" that had been installed without his knowledge when he placed a Sony CD into his computer. The software cloaked certain files and directories on the computer to mask itself, and when Russinovich attempted to manually remove the offending code, it disabled his CD player (Russinovich). He posted a blow-by-blow account of his detective work, and the story quickly spread through mainstream media. Although it admitted being the source of the software, Sony was slow to release updates that effectively and easily reversed the effects of the rootkit, and at first released patches that actually put users at risk for further and more severe damage to their systems. In a widely quoted interview with National Public Radio, Sony executive Thomas Hesse perfectly epitomized the company's tepid response: "Most people, I think, don't even know what a rootkit is, so why should they care about it?" (Hesse). Within a few weeks of the discovery, malicious viruses exploiting the file-hiding features of the Sony software were discovered. "'This is no longer a theoretical vulnerability; it is a real vulnerability,' said Sam Curry, vice president of Computer Associates' eTrust Security Management division. 'This is no longer about digital rights management or content protection, this is about people having their PCs taken over'" (Borland).

The software Sony clumsily installed, called XCP and developed by a Sony partner, First4Internet, was originally intended to prevent users from burning unlimited CD copies of an original audio CD, and to require them to use a media player packaged with the CD rather than a player already present on the user's computer. Speaking to reporters about First4Internet's software in July 2005, prior to the detection of the rootkit problems, Thomas Hesse, president of global digital business for Sony BMG, said: "The casual piracy, the schoolyard piracy, is a huge issue for us. Two-thirds of all piracy comes from ripping and burning CDs, which is why making the CD a secure format is of the utmost importance" (Reuters, "Sony Test").

Within a few weeks of the initial news about XCP, news of another Sony DRM technology, MediaMax, surfaced. While not as difficult to get rid of or as potentially dangerous to users' computers as was XCP, MediaMax installed itself on the users' computers even if the user answered "no" to the user agreement. MediaMax was suspected of collecting and transmitting information about user activity back to Sony. In the news reports and the litigation that followed, Sony's vague and misleading End User License Agreements (EULA) received the bulk of the criticism. The Electronic Frontier Foundation (EFF) and the state attorneys general from Texas and California filed a class action suit against Sony, eventually settling for the cost of replacing CDs and for $622,000 in damages in the state cases. Speaking after the settlement, California Attorney General Bill Lockyer said, "Companies that want to load their CDs with software that limits the ability to copy music should fully inform consumers about it, not hide it, and make sure it doesn't inflict security vulnerabilities on computers" (Kelzer). Sony ceased the manufacture and distribution of audio CDs containing the XCP and the MediaMax technologies.

DRM's Effectiveness for Protecting Content

What lessons can be gathered from these DRM cases in technical, strategic, and legal terms? It is far from proven that it is possible to build an unbreakable DRM technology, and even less clear that it is possible for the various players in the content industries to agree on a standard path. Arguably the two DRM schemes consumers are most likely to have encountered—the Content Scrambling System used in DVDs and the FairPlay DRM built into Apple's iTunes—are also among the weakest. Software to rip a perfect copy of the video contents of a DVD is widely available for download, even though the DeCSS software and the only vendor known to have attempted to sell physical CDs of DVD-copying software were targets of fierce copyright lawsuits in the early 2000s. iTunes's DRM is laughably easy to defeat, requiring either a burn to an unprotected CD and a re-import, or yet another readily available software download. More elaborate schemes, like the SDMI and the eBook reader, have also been swiftly defeated by skilled programmers.

As Edward Felten commented in the case of the Secure Digital Music Initiative, "'In the application SDMI has in mind,' he says, 'no watermarking scheme is strong enough.' The problem for SDMI, he says, is that the potential adversary has the watermarked file that is allowed to be played, the version that cannot be played and the music playback device. Any potential pirate can take the SDMI-compliant player apart to see how it works" (Talacko).

This statement highlights the fundamental dilemma faced by almost all DRM proponents. DRM is designed to protect content, but the ultimate goal is to sell both locked content and players or viewers capable of unlocking it. With any DRM scheme, be it an encryption scheme like CSS or eBook, or a flagging scheme like SDMI's watermark or the (attempted) broadcast flag, a consumer will always end up with both the problem and the solution in hand. The lazy consumer, the tech-aware and law-abiding consumer, and/or the technically challenged consumer will either choose to live within the limitations imposed by the DRM scheme or will choose not to buy the content at all. Tech-savvy scofflaws and consumers who are not aware that it may be illegal but can build or find the tools readily available may find it all too easy to circumvent access controls to share music, remix their favorite movies into YouTube versions, and copy and paste chunks of their electronic books for class papers.

If the digital restrictions in DRM-protected files are consistently defeated, content providers who want protection are left only with the legal safeguards provided by the *DMCA*. But as we have seen, the *DMCA* has been interpreted in a variety of ways by the courts, contributing to the perception that it is at best confusing and at worst intentionally opaque and self-contradictory. Further, experience has shown that DRM is not only used to protect content but, in doing so, is used to limit the ability of citizens to use media, hardware, and software that they (often) have purchased legally. DRM is a form of control at the code level (Lessig, *Free Culture*) that can be used by commercial media content providers to limit consumer behavior in ways that exceed the spirit or letter of the law (or both).

Triennial Rulemaking: Exemptions to the *DMCA*

Complicating the legal picture somewhat is the safety valve Congress wrote into the law that requires the US Copyright Office to evaluate the effect of the *DMCA* every three years, to solicit requests for new exemptions from the public, and to grant those exceptions it feels will help restore a balance of rights that may have been upset by the *DMCA* (Title 17, section 1201(a)(1)(C)). The so-called "triennial rulemaking" has now been held three times since the law was passed, and each time the number of exemptions has increased slightly. The Register of Copyrights traditionally takes a relatively narrow approach to the rulemaking. Although the call for public comment yields requests for many different types of relief—from very specific exemptions to blanket statements asserting a right of fair use—the Register only focuses on the act of circumventing access controls: "Thus, the task of this rulemaking appears to be to determine whether the availability and use of access control measures has already diminished or is about to diminish the ability of the public to engage in the lawful uses of copyrighted works that the public had traditionally been able to make prior to the enactment of the *DMCA*" (Peters). The Electronic Frontier Foundation, long an opponent of DRM and critic of the *DMCA*, criticized this narrow approach when they announced their intention to abstain from the latest round of rulemaking requests, concluding that "the *DMCA* triennial rulemaking is fundamentally unable to protect the interests of today's digital media consumers" (von Lohman et al.).

In 2006, the Copyright Office announced that six classes of works were exempt from the anti-circumvention rules, so long as the uses were noninfringing. The six classes, along with the specific access conditions, are:

1. Audiovisual works in a college's film or media studies departmental library, when circumvention is used for the purpose of making clips to be used in teaching
2. Obsolete computer programs and video games, when circumvention is used by a library or archive to preserve or archivally reproduce a published digital work
3. Malfunctioning or obsolete dongles (hardware keys) protecting computer programs
4. Literary eBooks when all editions contain access controls preventing electronic reading aloud
5. Firmware preventing wireless telephones from connecting to a wireless network
6. Sound recordings and audiovisual works on discs with copy protection, if the circumvention is for the purpose of testing or investigating existence of security flaws or vulnerabilities

Clearly these exemptions are written with specific cases and problems in mind. The sixth is very obviously a response to the Sony rootkit problems. The first exemption only applies to colleges and universities, leaving out teachers at the K–12 level, and only teachers in a Film or Media Studies department, not Computer Science, English, History, or Biology (and how would departments of Speech, Speech Communication, Communication, or a Multimedia Program be treated?). If the exemptions only cover the acts of circumvention, however, and don't excuse those developing and distributing the tools, how likely is it that an average user will be able to exercise the exemption? And further, how can DRM developers have hope of developing a failsafe system for content when any acts of circumvention are permitted?

> While there are companies that are very supportive of DRM, many leading advocates are strongly opposed. Primary among the opponents, perhaps, is the Electronic Frontier Foundation (EFF). EFF notes that "from the Internet to the iPod, technologies are transforming our society and empowering us as speakers, citizens, creators, and consumers. When our freedoms in the networked world come under attack, the Electronic Frontier Foundation (EFF) is the first line of defense." The EFF is very clear as to where it stands on DRM. In part: "Major entertainment companies are using 'digital rights management,' or DRM (aka content or copy protection), to lock up your digital media. These DRM technologies do nothing to stop copyright pirates, but instead end up interfering with fans' lawful use of music, movies, and other copyrighted works" (EFF, "Digital Rights Management and Copy Protection Schemes").

A Turning Tide?

In February 2007, a letter entitled "Thoughts on Music," from Apple CEO Steve Jobs appeared on the Apple Web site and received global media attention. Jobs described three possible scenarios for the future of digital rights management and the FairPlay system in iTunes. Alternatives one and two were to continue on the current course or to license FairPlay to other companies so that music files sold on the iTunes store would be interoperable with other devices. Jobs argued that this second approach would compromise the security of the FairPlay system. "The third alternative is to abolish DRMs entirely. Imagine a world where every online store sells DRM-free music encoded in open licensable formats. In such a world, any player can play music purchased from any store, and any store can sell music that is playable on all players. This is clearly the best alternative for consumers, and Apple would embrace it in a heartbeat" (Jobs). The Jobs letter came out at a time when grumbling about Apple's price of $.99 per song and monopoly of online music sales was growing. Within four months of the Jobs letter, EMI, one of the four largest music companies, and Apple had announced that they would begin selling DRM-free music through iTunes, though at a slightly inflated price of $1.29 per track. By the end of the summer of 2007, Wal-Mart and Amazon both sold DRM-free music on their sites, and by October, the price for DRM-free tracks on iTunes had dropped back to $.99 each (*The Economist*). By January, 2009, a number of additional record companies made their content on iTunes DRM-free.

Why the shift? Do these moves mean that DRM is dead? Most likely not, since this all happened at a time when major content producers were rapidly expanding into the direct digital market. YouTube made it obvious to television and movie producers that people will watch streaming video online, even if the video is of poor quality. It may be that effective DRM in music appears a lost cause, but there are still digital television, mobile media, and electronic books to consider, and the commercial owners of media content want to protect their investments. "Rumours of DRM's death are exaggerated. The technology will survive, if only to monitor the usage of certain files and to protect other digital goods, such as computer games and films" (*The Economist*).

Summarizing Digital Rights Management

In many ways, the DRM movement is at the very core of the most important issues on the current intellectual property scene. Contestation over the control of using digital content cuts across nearly every key new media industry. As noted in previous chapters, US intellectual property law, though professional-ized and complex, legally applies to every American, regardless of whether the laws seem just, or of the consumer's lack of ability to understand the laws, or her/his unwillingness to comply.

One can think about DRM through analogy with the automobile. Con-sumers do not often understand (or, for that matter, much care about) the technological details "under the hood" as long as the car works when the key is turned or the ignition button is pushed. To an extent, many corporate hold-ers of digital content and rights believe that intellectual property represents a similar situation. They believe that they should control use of the materials in protection of their legal rights, and if they can do so out of the consumers' view, all the better. DRM schemes seem the perfect solution, as they can be made to operate "under the hood" (at the code level), hopefully controlling "illegal" uses while consumers make "legal" use of the materials entitled by their purchases.

However—and unfortunately—the situation is not as clear-cut as the analogy suggests. First, among other aspects, many large corporate rights hold-ers have a very different view of the uses to which digital materials can legally be put than do many consumers and consumer advocates. For example, some in the music industry would like to force consumers to pay additionally and separately when they use a digital music file across various types of players. Some in the industry would like to monitor and control usage with that effect using DRM. The idea that once one has paid for a song, say via purchase of a CD, that one has to pay again (or purchase a copy of a different sort) if one wants to play it on a computer, play it on an MP3 player, put portions of it onto a cell phone as a ring-tone, or use excerpts of certain songs in personal or family-related e-mail, home movies, or slide show presentations, is a notion that runs counter to consumers' wants and expectations. Consumers have been conditioned by the multiple uses allowed under the first-sale doctrine (as it was in place in the analog era). This is just one example in which large corporate content and rights holders see DRM differently than do many consumers.

From industry perspectives, the financial losses from piracy in the digital realm are so extraordinary that no solution short of a virtual content lockdown that is fully under their control seems adequate. From the perspective of many consumers, DRM schemes produce untenable limitations to personal use. To many legal analysts and consumer advocates, interactions between the *DMCA* anti-circumvention clauses and DRM schemes produce a situation in which there are serious compromises of consumer protections found within intellectual property laws other than the *DMCA*. Joined to hidden click-through agreements and terms of service instruments, the "control" landscape appears to be tilted in favor of large corporate content and rights holders and against common citizen consumers.

However, as noted, despite the fact that DRM schemes most often operate out of public view, somewhere on various code levels, no scheme for widely distributed materials has withstood circumvention. While most consumers do not know how to "tinker under the digital hood," enough specialists with consumer advocacy leanings do know how to disable or circumvent DRM to the degree that using such schemes (and spending much money developing them) appears to be a business endeavor that risks high costs for short-term and perhaps only frustrating outcomes. DRM schemes appear to offer controls that are somewhat effective over mass distributions and large populations but ineffective in controlling willing piracy. What that amounts to, then, is the realization that effective DRM schemes are "preaching to the choir," as they work to constrain everyman from infringements she/he probably wouldn't commit, while not adequately keeping purposive thieves from wanton piracy.

In short, one is tempted to say that DRM just does not work. However, it is clear that new media industries will continue efforts toward developing and deploying content rights management and constraint systems and that consumers will continue facing controls over their use of digital content that are not the direct result of action taken by, or under supervision of, elected representatives. In other words, while much of the intellectual property law system is based on legislation and judicial action—both of which operate within the realms of representative government and our traditional justice system—one neither votes on nor follows case precedent when DRM goes to work controlling usage. Further, as shown by the Sony rootkit incident, DRM systems may well constitute large-scale infringement of consumers' rights—a paradoxical outcome given the goals for rights protection that DRM schemes are supposed to represent. [CS]

Discussion Questions

1. Make a list of the various DRM schemes controlling the digital media you utilize. Discuss your experiences with and the implications of these features. Do the schemes and outcomes benefit you as a consumer? Or do the schemes appear to limit you in unjust ways?

2. Describe the kinds of notifications you would like to see when DRM schemes are used. Should labels on the exterior of products clearly indicate the DRM schemes used? Is inclusion in click-through agreements or terms of service notices effective and/or adequate?

3. College students are often said to be among the "worst" pirates in the United States, perhaps due to their rebelliousness or because college networks and equipment provide the means for piracy. (Of course, that claim may not be true, as some students have faster and more open network access at home than at school.) Without revealing names or confidences, discuss the prevalence of piracy among your college peers. Are you and your classmates "pirates"? Do DRM schemes adequately limit your activities? Are you adept at breaking such schemes?

4. Discuss the proposition that efforts toward effective DRM schemes are (a) worthy enterprises that are required under current circumstances, or (b) a waste of time because they will never work.

5. Describe your experiences with the most effective DRM schemes you've encountered. In what ways did they work so well? Can you be positively disposed toward their further use?

CHAPTER NINE

Toward Tomorrow, Today

IP Law in Virtual Worlds

Reflecting on IP issues in virtual worlds can be directed by two broad considerations. In some ways, virtual worlds present a very challenging "frontier" for intellectual property law in the new media environment. Both this volume and everyday life remind us that the law lags behind innovation. There is currently no legislation specific to virtual worlds, yet globally large numbers of people regularly "inhabit" or "visit" virtual worlds. All of the IP issues so far presented apply in virtual worlds, overlaid by all of the issues raised by the global/international/networked environments in which virtual worlds are arrayed. While one would not expect an entire body of new law dedicated exclusively to virtual worlds, the total lack of legislation in this area points to how very difficult new media environments can be for both courts and citizens.

From a second perspective, the multiplicity of activities in virtual worlds raises direct legal issues in the present. As we'll demonstrate, people (and lawyers) are currently involved in disagreements founded in virtual world activities. Courts hear cases on questions for which they have little preparedness, using laws that are fully designed for the "real world" (RL) rather than for "virtual worlds." Many RL citizens (including most elected officials and judges) give no thought to the ways that laws should apply in virtual worlds. To the uninitiated, activities in virtual worlds either seem so "game-like" that activities within them should not much matter to the legal system, or it seems clear that normal law simply applies to matters that take place while people sit in front of their computers. After all, we've made the law work (sort of) for the Internet. Why won't it also work for virtual worlds?

However, the denizens of virtual worlds often feel as though they are not "in the real world" when they inhabit virtual spaces; after all, isn't that at least part of the point of a virtual world? They often have the sense that perhaps RL laws simply shouldn't or don't apply to their behavior(s) within "a game." Further, the law is not clear even about basic aspects involving virtuality.

Additionally, to this point, most of the relevant virtual worlds are proprietary, such that the contract law represented in their terms of service (ToS) or click-through/shrink wrap agreements may well "trump" intellectual property law in many ways. Generally, these contractual terms appear to tilt everything about virtual worlds in favor of the software and network provider, either stripping players/users of usual legal protections or modifying those features almost beyond recognition. If and when virtual worlds "go open-source" and are less proprietary, moving away from private contract language may bring virtual worlds closer to IP law as opposed to contract law. However, giving up the control private companies maintain over their products (and the virtual worlds produced therein), combined with the numerical profusion and geographic diffusion of open-source virtual worlds, might cause one to wish for the "good old days" when private companies used contract law and their ToS to keep order "as the town's only sheriff."

In short, virtual worlds present a series of challenges to IP law. RL laws are in place and—best as we can tell—can be (and have been) applied to virtual world cases. Jurisdictional issues are as complex as IP law, globalism, and the Internet can make them. And IP law is hardly the tip of the iceberg in virtual worlds. Ownership of every aspect and behaviors of every kind, not just IP law issues, are at play and at risk. For example, in his book *Virtual Law*, Duranske lists questions about currency, rules of evidence, inworld governance practices, property (real estate and objects), civil procedures, criminal law, securities law, and tax law as some of the topics that can be added to all of the IP categories covered in the current volume. Lawyers are beginning to specialize in virtual IP law. For example, Duranske lists the following in an appendix noting legal activities in *Second Life*: sixty lawyers and legal firms; ten dispute-resolution services; eight legal-service firms; and twelve bar associations and professional groups.

If IP law "lags behind" new media developments in general, IP law trails virtual environments even further. In this regard, virtual worlds present a useful extension of considerations central to this text and thereby serve as a very fertile example with which to close our considerations. We will examine three important aspects of this topic (jurisdiction, "buffer copies," and the first-sale doctrine), look at IP issues in an archetypal virtual world (*Second Life*), and then delve into recent court actions that illustrate some of the important issues.

Jurisdiction and Virtual Worlds

Given the nature of the status quo, traditional jurisdiction analysis applies, at this point, in virtual worlds. In theory, geography combines with extant legal mechanisms to enable the "usual" pursuit of justice. But as noted in Chapter 7 ("International IP Law"), jurisdictional questions are difficult to answer in a global and netted environment. Layers upon layers of ownership and control issues problematize solutions to virtual disputes. All of the questions of geography and the global 'Net come into play. Issues raised by the proprietary nature of the hardware, software, and the networks used further complicate things. User agreements and terms of service add another dimension to the mix. And, of course, the previously mentioned lack of law specific to virtual worlds leaves the entire process unmoored.

We have already examined in some detail the jurisdictional complexities introduced by the global reach of the Internet. These certainly apply in the case of virtual worlds, since providers, participants, and network operations are often widely distributed across geographical and jurisdictional boundaries. The use of governmentally authorized courts is certainly the status quo. However, there is little indication that the courts are prepared to deal with existential questions such as: To what degree are virtual property and behaviors real? Or, to what degree are real people and behaviors acquiring and using property in virtual worlds subject to "real law"? Or, perhaps, What are the rights of the embodied virtual presence, the avatar, and who defends them especially in cases in which the laws of the real world are at odds with the actions and needs of virtual embodiments? Even if the wise folks of the judicial system are able to get their collective heads around such questions, one has to wonder about the ability of legislative bodies around the globe to do so in the making of laws with which the judiciary operates. Jurisdiction and "space/geography" have another interesting "twist" in virtual environments. From the RL perspective, people "in" virtual worlds are stationed at their computers, inhabiting the geography of their location. From that perspective, some jurisdictional issues are clear:

perhaps the laws of the land on which they are stationed bind folks. Further, the worlds are created, stored, and manifested within the providers' servers. To some extent, jurisdiction might be established at their locations (many virtual worlds' ToS specify their home region as the jurisdiction of record, although that specification may or may not carry the day in court). However, many virtual worlds use a distributed computing model that finds their servers spread around the globe. If the purported violation occurs between two inhabitants of, say, *World of Warcraft* via servers located, for one, in the United States and, for the other, in Germany, which country should serve as the venue of record? Additionally, from the perspective of the users of virtual worlds, those worlds produce "other places" in which the activities at issue take place. To them, the infraction took place in a particular "sim" within *Second Life*, regardless of the fact that Linden Lab does not currently use a distributed model and maintains a server farm near its San Francisco, California, home.

It is clear that at this point IP law would totally ignore the distinction that a user makes when insisting that the purported violation took place in a specific virtual space (rather than in the RL location of participants or servers), as court actions in cases dealing with the World Wide Web indicate. However, as virtual worlds become more commonplace, ubiquitous, and persistent, those spaces may take on their own senses of jurisdictional boundaries, thereby increasing complexities for courts and legislators alike.

The Internet Corporation for Assigned Names and Numbers (ICANN) and other such bodies have shown that some international disputes can be moderated by extra-legal entities. But who and what would get hundreds of virtual world owners to agree to outside control, and who convinces the courts and lawmakers to defer the work to those bodies? One could answer, "The same forces that encourage the use of those entities for the current Internet would/ could do so for virtual worlds," and one might move in the direction of an affirmative plan. However, recall that the use of such entities for the Internet has not obviated recourse to the "normal" court systems for very many disputes. And in many ways, at least at this point, the Internet is more "open-source" and less proprietary than are virtual worlds. The "international arbiter" model probably works better in situations in which clear ownership is not present (open-source) than it does when propriety controls are the norm, as is the case in virtual worlds at the present time.

As noted, the software used for virtual worlds is proprietary. Its use is controlled largely by contract law: click-through and shrink wrap agreements and terms of service (ToS) trump a lot of IP law. Additionally, virtual worlds have community agreements and sometimes even enforcement mechanisms. These are extra legal but suffice for many resident disputes, although not all. And they are outside the legal system so may not protect user rights properly. We will examine a case involving *Second Life* that addresses both of these aspects (ToS and internal arbitration mechanisms).[1] As private use arrangements between provider and client, however, participation in virtual worlds might be most easily adjudicated within the confines of each virtual environment.

However, there is a substantial difference between instances in which terms of service or shrink wrap/click-through agreements are brought into a RL court of law and used as evidence, and the situation in which the courts are obviated, or taken out of play, by service or shrink wrap/click-through agreements that mandate mediation/arbitration or other adjudication procedures either within the virtual world or between users and providers within providers' conflict resolution facilities and practices. There is little RL precedent for taking the courts and their authority totally out of play, based merely on contractual agreements. Witness, for example, how often the courts are involved with labor-management issues in circumstances in which contractual agreements, and the negotiation mechanisms that enact them, break down between the parties. One would not think that virtual worlds would present a situation so essentially different that the normal court systems would tend do anything but act in their "normal" ways. However, most software includes such efforts to obviate or constrain users' legal recourse in the event of disagreements either among users or between users and providers, and users have yet to free themselves from those traditions by using the courts rather than following the contract law and using the provider as arbiter.

Buffer/RAM "Copies" and Reproduction Rights

As we noted regarding *20th Century Fox v. Cablevision* (p. 255, Chapter 1 footnote 18), if buffer copies were taken to be "fixed," then they would fall within the reproduction rights of copyright holders and implicate every sort of distribution of material. This is especially crucial in many virtual environments where most of what one sees, uses, and "lives in" is held in cache on each user's machine. A re-interpretation of this legal principle (from "buffer doesn't count" to "everything in RAM is a copy") would take us back to the most draconian interpretation of the *Green* and *White Papers*, before the final drafting of the *DMCA*, and would put questions of ownership and terms of use in virtual worlds on a different footing than currently is the case.

Currently, ownership and use of elements within virtual worlds is determined by the terms of service of the particular system; users and providers of "the game" agree to the status of the ownership. The agreements cede ownership of materials or rights to one party or the other (users or providers) and specify the range of permitted uses by both. These agreements are based on the status quo in which RAM/buffer copies are NOT taken as fixed copies requiring permissions for use. If RAM/buffer copies were taken as protected under copyright law, usage agreements would be obviated, and all ownership aspects would revert to the original copyright holder or those to whom they've granted rights. This change would require a set of new agreements between creators and users in virtual worlds. While it is possible that such agreements could be included simply as "new" terms of service, such a massive change in the status quo would almost certainly lead to challenges and court cases. Further, there is a question as to whether the wide range of permissions needed in order to participate in a virtual world could be gathered efficiently, especially, for example, in a "user created" environment such as *Second Life*, in which the majority of the content is the intellectual property of a very wide range of creative "residents" but freely displayed on the computers of all participants. Virtual worlds, their producers and users, appear to have a very strong stake in legislative outcomes involving the status of RAM/buffer copies.

First-Sale Doctrine and Transmission

Principles in the first-sale doctrine have been deeply curtailed by digital technologies. After purchase, the law enables one to do many things with an analog media item, including selling it and lending it to others and making a copy for backup purposes (among other things). The law also constrains some uses of analog materials, "first sale" notwithstanding; for example, mass copying and distribution or public performance without the proper permissions are forbidden. Laws concerning digital material change these foundational principles, as they generally forbid all further copying or transmission as activities that are controlled by the *Copyright Act* and especially the *DMCA*. Given the digital nature of everything in virtual worlds, it appears that the status quo in those cyberspaces stands with the general suspension of first-sale doctrine principles. Just as in RL, where curtailment of the protections provided by the first-sale doctrine has stripped citizens of rights established within copyright law itself, establishing virtual worlds as "first-sale-doctrine-free" zones presents serious limitations to the potentially legal use of materials by those acquiring the item.

For example, the ToS used by Linden Lab in *Second Life* (like those used by many other virtual world providers for their worlds) specifies that Linden Lab owns *everything* "inworld." They cede back to the user some intellectual property rights (and narrow or deny other IP rights). But a key feature is that this arrangement curtails the first-sale doctrine, as everything within *Second Life* belongs to Linden Lab, no matter how much time, effort, creativity, and resources a user put into making the item or how many Linden dollars "User B" paid "User/Creator A" for purchase of the object. Since "User/Creator A" never really owned the item in the first place (Linden Lab owns it), he or she cannot transfer to "User B" any of the traditional first-sale rights. While the *Second Life* software allows "User/Creator A" to "set permissions" on the object such that "User B" attains rights that resemble those under the first-sale doctrine (to duplicate or modify or resell the item), "User/Creator A" can also set those permissions to forbid all such uses. And, of course, the ToS specify that the object does not actually belong to "User B"; therefore, "User B" cannot make any further use of the object that might violate Linden Lab's ownership rights.

Closer Examination of IP Issues in an Archetype Virtual World: *Second Life*

Second Life (*SL*) is treated as an archetype in this work because it has some relatively unique features among current virtual worlds. Most virtual environments are primarily the work of the software company that creates, markets, sells, and operates the "world." In some cases, users can make modest modifications of the "game" and its components, but the content is primarily provided by the company while users provide behavior. In contrast, *SL* consists primarily of user-created content. Linden Lab provides "the base" (the software and terms of service, the server space and network connectivity to their servers where the world is maintained, the basic configuration of land, sea, sun, air—though users can modify most of those features, the wire-frame "avatar"—though, again, every user modifies that "representation"; and a variety of support functions), while users create/provide most other features of and in the virtual world. Users terra form "land," build buildings and all infrastructure, and design clothing and every sort of accoutrement one can imagine in a global 3D environment of almost limitless variety and creativity. This "user created-ness" raises the stakes for intellectual property law in virtual worlds, as compared to virtual spaces in which nearly everything is provided (and owned by) the company at hand.

Another feature that makes *SL* interesting is that it is neither a "game with quest" nor is it level-based, and it does not contain much violence, so is less a game than an online social environment. As such, it probably more resembles virtual worlds of the future than do the more highly populated quest and adventure online virtual world games such as *World of Warcraft*. As a result, we learn a bit more about the way IP law will work in virtual worlds by examining *SL* than we would from some other spaces.

Additionally, *SL* is exceedingly proprietary. At this point, it does not use a distributed computing model, nor is it open-source on the server side (although Linden Lab has released the code for the client side, making it open-source, and is working with developers to enable interoperability with other virtual spaces). Given its strongly proprietary model, *SL* has numerous and detailed policies specifically oriented toward IP questions and issues. In addition to providing extensive information about their policies toward copyrights, patents, trademarks, and the personal torts, Linden Lab (via the *SL* Web site) provides detailed information about how residents may protect their copyrights to virtual materials created inworld, as well as providing full instructions about *DMCA* notification and takedown procedures (for cases in which Linden Lab is notified of potential infringements or if residents want to claim infringements by others).[2]

Two additional factors make *SL* an interesting model. *SL* maintains a virtual economy (the currency is the "Linden," which—at the time of this writing—trades at roughly 270 Lindens to the US dollar). Millions of "real" dollars are exchanged by residents each week as they buy, sell, and trade virtual property with Linden values. In this regard, again, *SL* gives the appearance of being more viable as a model for the ways that virtual worlds will eventually take shape than do other worlds in which there is either no negotiable currency or currencies that produce minimal "churn." Finally, and directly toward our interests in this book, there is a developing set of cases/incidents resulting from participation in *SL*. Case experience and precedent are both useful adjuncts to our understanding of how IP law treats virtual worlds now and how that law might develop in the future as virtual worlds "build out."

Ownership of Property in Virtual Worlds

As the result of incidents and court cases that illustrated the folly in its early policies of allowing residents to retain full ownership of "purchase" of virtual property, and notwithstanding its good feelings and helpful customer service standards, Linden Lab now makes it clear that it owns everything in and about *SL*. Via its ToS <http://secondlife.com/corporate/tos.php>, it notes that it owns it all–not only the goods, but the account, and all the data that "residents" enter into the system. Linden Lab then grants use of the materials back to qualified users:

> 3.3 Linden Lab retains ownership of the account and related data, regardless of intellectual property rights you may have in content you create or otherwise own. You agree that even though you may retain certain copyright or other intellectual property rights with respect to Content you create while using the Service, you do not own the account you use to access the Service, nor do you own any data Linden Lab stores on Linden Lab servers (including without limitation any data representing or embodying any or all of your Content). Your intellectual property rights do not confer any rights of access to the Service or any rights to data stored by or on behalf of Linden Lab.
>
> 3.4 Linden Lab licenses its textures and environmental content to you for your use in creating content in-world. During any period in which your Account is active and in good standing, Linden Lab gives you permission to create still and/or moving media, for use only within the virtual world environment of the Service ("in-world"), which use or include the "textures" and/or "environmental content" that are both (a) created or owned by Linden Lab and (b) displayed by Linden Lab in-world.

Note that via the ToS, Linden Lab grants some rights back to users; yet it limits other rights. Specifically, it grants back copyrights, with the exception of retaining rights for the company to use everything in any way it wants. Mostly, this relates to its need to use resident-created material for promotion; otherwise, it would have to ask for permission every time it showed user-created graphics in support of *SL*. Since almost everything "in-world" is user created, Linden Lab would be at the mercy of the people who "play the game" every time it wanted to advertise or promote it using images of its own product (but of residents' making). As a result, it retains full rights to use the content for its purposes. Further, there is a very ambiguous relationship between the copyright protection promised every resident and the ability of residents to "use" items created by others in *SL*. For example, once one has created something in *SL*, one can "set" the degree to which other people may copy, buy/sell/give away, and/or modify the item. There is also the ability to set various levels of restrictiveness as to who can access the virtual land that one owns/controls (you can only "put down" made objects on your land, so to keep things "present in-world" 24/7, one has to own/rent virtual property). However, generally speaking, residents build structures on land and then leave them there in such a way that others can come and go regardless of whether or not the owners/creators of the structures are online. While the items themselves might be set "no copy, no modify," so that they cannot be taken, there are a variety of ways in which the items can be (and often are) put to use that cannot be controlled.

The best examples may be seen by viewing any of the hundreds of blogs about *SL*. On such blogs, one will see numerous in-world photographs depicting objects and scenes in *SL*. While it is the case that much of the use of such photography may be taken as fair use (due to the journalistic functions enacted therein), it is not clear that one can assume that *every* such image is exempted, yet permission to use the visual image of copyright protected graphic images is very rarely, if ever, obtained.

> 3.2 You retain copyright and other intellectual property rights with respect to Content you create in Second Life, to the extent that you have such rights under applicable law. However, you must make certain representations and warranties, and provide certain license rights, forbearances and indemnification, to Linden Lab and to other users of Second Life.

In other words, you retain the copyright, but everyone can use (without royalty or permission) everything you don't explicitly lock down. Further, one can only lock down the inworld item; making and distributing screen shots isn't controlled. That is a somewhat different interpretation of copyright protection than one comes to expect in RL.

The situation is much more complex regarding patent protection. Through its ToS, Linden Lab specifically abrogates all patent rights and claims within *SL*.

> You also understand and agree that by submitting your Content to any area of the Service, you automatically grant (or you warrant that the owner of such Content has expressly granted) to Linden Lab and to all other users of the Service a non-exclusive, worldwide, fully paid-up, transferable, irrevocable, royalty-free and perpetual License, under any and all patent rights you may have or obtain with respect to your Content, to use your Content for all purposes within the Service. You further agree that you will not make any claims against Linden Lab or against other users of the Service based on any allegations that any activities by either of the foregoing within the Service infringe your (or anyone else's) patent rights.

Why a "closed" position on patent when the company so openly offers copyright protection to all residents? In general, Linden Lab's leaders are philosophically opposed to software patents; in their view, software patents stifle innovation. They prefer "patent peace," where everyone gets to use the innovations.[3] While they are welcome to hold this point of view and have the legal right to impose it on users of their systems, one has to wonder how the imposition of such constraints modifies the enthusiasm that business, education, and industry might otherwise have for taking their enterprises into virtual worlds and *SL*. Further, if *SL* stands as the primary example of the future of 3D virtual

social worlds, citizens will have to come to grips with the loss of a very important protection of and incentive for technological innovation: patents.

Linden Lab recently established a program of significant size concerning
its trademarks. In effect, far too many people were using its marks, in most
cases without permission. Linden Lab attempted to pull back its marks by
invoking its rights and introducing policies and programs for proper usage.[4]

Attempting to get control over its trademarks was certainly the right thing
to do on the part of Linden Lab. However, these circumstances also illustrate
how proprietary software, and the virtual worlds they create, are at the behest
of the owners/operators who can change or fine-tune the rules at any time. In
case a analysis to follow, we will see how that ability to change the rules on the
fly makes virtual worlds fundamentally different than RL regarding the development and application of IP law.

Some of the Issues Raised by How Linden Lab Treats IP

These practices and policies illustrate how companies managing proprietary
digital materials, including virtual worlds, can change the legal playing field
through ToS and contracts.[5] Citizens' rights often get trumped in the fine
print. Such arrangements present a central problematic in the new media/digi-
tal environment. In many ways, IP laws and courts haven't kept up with the
pace of innovation; likewise, the development of contract law has not fared
much better. RL presents a rather comical dichotomy in this regard in that one
can only wonder how many judges and/or lawyers read the ToS for every Web
site they visit. We could hazard a guess that, in general, judges and lawyers (not
to mention elected officials and law makers) probably "click right through"
ToS and shrink wrap/click-through agreements just about as fast as do average
citizens. Yet, these legal specialists know that "ignorance is no protection from
the law." When they are involved "at the office," so to speak, in cases that turn
on these contractual issues, plaintiffs and defendants alike are held responsible
to the letter of the contractual arrangement. One wonders if the realities of
their private lives might someday lead to progressive changes in the law? In
some ways the digital revolution may, in the long run, be even more bound up
by these contract issues than by trouble over IP law itself.

Aspects inherent in the technologies involved with virtual worlds also
present issues. For example, streaming technologies (the way that most online virtual worlds work) are not really very secure. To wit—CopyBot, brought
about by the "libsecondlife project":

A brief description of what CopyBot was originally about:

You see the libsecondlife project consists of a loose group of programmers that all have the common goal of making an open source interface library for Second Life—but each of us has particular specific goals that range from making tools to access SL using alternative clients (text only interfaces, PDA access, textureless low bandwidth clients, etc.), others want to build NPC/Bots for use as store attendants, customer service providers (FAQ bots), or for use with games. Others want to enable the ability to backup SL content off the grid, or build content off grid using alternative tools (3D programs such as Maya or 3DS-Max) and then be able to load that content into SL. Some are hoping that once libsl is mature enough, it will even allow the development of open source sims that can be hosted outside of Linden Labs, and allow the official SL client to seamlessly connect from the Main Grid to these alternative sims using a relatively simple proxy on the client machines.

In the pursuit of these varied goals, one of the things that libsl needs to be able to do is fully decode the packets from SL that describe prims, textures, inventories and all the assets. It also needs to be able to, as the official client does, enable the creation of all of those. One member was working on decoding and creating avatar appearances and prims—he thought, an easy way to work on the code for both, and allow easy testing of both those, would be to connect one to the other.

Basically he took the code he was using to decode avatar appearances, and the code to set your appearance and linked them together—whenever it saw appearance information about another avatar it would recreate it and set the appearance of a bot's avatar to match. This started simply with setting the avatar's skin and clothing textures to match. And eventually grew to include attachments.

There was no initial intent to use this for IP violation, to steal peoples' content. Yes—it did occur to some, as others in the project started contributing time, effort, code to it, that it could be used to violate people's rights, to circumvent the system's permissions. Some of us talked about it and even discussed how or if it could be prevented. While some of this discussion was on-going, a youtube video of it in use was made, a copy of the code that linked decoding and creating was submitted to our publicly accessible source code repository, and someone outside of the team grabbed it, packaged it, and started distributing ...

Then the protests began ... Some facts ...

* As many have already pointed out, there is no way to prevent this type of activity. If the official SL client is able to display data for a particular account, then a bot logged in as that account will be able to retrieve and use that data.

* Use of encryption or similar will not work, because the official SL client must have a means of decrypting it, and if the official client can decode it—then that method can be reverse engineered out of it.

* Although copybot itself cannot make perfect copies of prims & textures, that's more of a function of the fact that work on that particular areas of SL had not started before November 2006.

* It is within the realm of possibility, that *ALL* content that a particular account can access can be decoded, stored off-line, and recreated. Including scripts, full downloads of textures, prim data, appearances, the terrain/land/parcel data for a sim, *ANY-THING* that you can make or upload using the official client—if your account has permissions to get information on it, then a bot could be made to download and recreate it. This in fact is the goal of more then one member of the libsecondlife project.

    And for those that believe the libsecondlife project team is just a vicious horrible group of hackers that should be flogged, I'd like to point out something.
    Members and contributors of and to the libsecondlife project have discovered, reproduced, reported and assisted in fixing a great many exploits that we discovered during the development of our library. These exploits range from ways of circumventing upload fees, to the ability to crash sims with a single packet of data. We've found ways to give accounts an unlimited number of L\$, or crash other peoples' clients at will. But none of these, *NONE* have we ever willfully distributed outside of our group. Each that we find, we report to Linden Labs. We help isolate it, and determine exactly what causes the exploit, then assist where we can in the testing/fixing process.
    As I write this, I know there are two currently unfixed exploits—one that easily allows objects constructed in a certain way to instantly crash clients and another such object that can crash sims. Both have been reported to LL, both should be fixed in the next grid update. If the libsecondlife project members were really out to do harm, rather than good—well . . . I leave it to you, as educators, to determine the extent of the damage that could be caused if we were a malicious group.
    Michael Cortez AKA Static Sprocket (libsecondlife project team member, used with permission)

So while Linden Lab reserves some copyright protections for resident creators, a number of technological "facts of life" constrain the ability to fully protect any creation in a virtual world.

When users create accounts, they acknowledge (as part of the click-through agreement) that:

Linden Lab is a service provider that may allow people to interact online regarding topics and content chosen by users of the service, and that users can alter the service environment on a real-time basis. Linden Lab generally does not regulate the content of communications between users or users' interactions with the Service. As a result, Linden Lab has very limited control, if any, over the quality, safety, morality, legality, truthfulness or accuracy of various aspects of the Service.

In addition to the ToS, Linden Lab maintains a series of "community standards" (CS) for behavior, and it uses its internal mechanisms to enforce both the ToS and the CS. The Community Standards set out six behaviors—the "Big Six"—violations of which result in suspension or, with repeated violations, expulsion from the *Second Life* Community.

In short, Linden Lab and *SL* operate within the context of extensively articulated yet contested and ineffective policies toward intellectual property. The cases below further illustrate the kinds of disputes founded in virtual worlds.

Without sounding overly cynical about the degree to which lawyers show up, with interest, whenever potential billable hours enter the scene (especially given that one of the authors of this text is a lawyer), interest in intellectual property rights and laws in virtual worlds is building rapidly. In an article published in *The Metropolitan Corporate Counsel*, Diane Duhaime presents the case in favor of lawyers coming to grips with virtual environments, noting that "In sum, exposure to or at least some basic knowledge of virtual environments is desirable for corporate counsel. It might not be long before your marketing department is requesting a review of advertising materials to be presented in Second Life, or a customer or employee is reporting an abuse of the company's trademark or other intellectual property rights in a virtual environment."

Virtual World Judicial Developments

Bragg v. Linden Research, Inc. and Philip Rosedale, No. 06–4925, USDC (E.D. Pa., May 30, 2007)

Bragg v. Linden began when Linden Lab excluded Mr. Bragg from *SL* and confiscated his virtual holdings for an alleged violation of the ToS. Mr. Bragg was accused of leveraging land sale auctions in *SL* to his advantage. His virtual property was taken/revoked, at an estimated value of about $5,000 US.[6] Bragg used the ToS to claim that (a) the ToS specified/assured that the virtual property was his, and (b) Linden Lab's in-world adjudication procedures were inadequate such that (c) his virtual property was seized without due process.

Bragg filed the case in a Pennsylvania state court in October 2006, but the case was moved to federal court in November 2006 and was heard by Judge Eduardo Robreno. In May 2007, Robreno ruled in favor of Bragg, and in doing so, virtually invalidated the ToS as legally binding, as well as agreeing that the internal appeal and adjudication procedures that Linden Lab uses in *SL* are woefully inadequate (Reuters, Eric). He defined the ToS as an unenforceable "contract of adhesion," so allowed the case (Bragg's claim that the ToS gave him ownership of his virtual property) to go forward (Linden Lab had asked for dismissal). Judge Robreno repeated his ruling on a second action (a Linden Lab motion to compel arbitration) by denying arbitration.

At least three things resulted (or may result) from this case: (1) Linden Lab settled with Bragg (undisclosed terms) for what was thought to be a return of his virtual property; (2) Linden Lab immediately changed its ToS to redefine ownership, making clear that Linden Lab owns everything in and about *SL*. This illustrates the slippery slope within proprietary virtual environments. While the Court's action did have a short-term and limited effect (the value of Bragg's holdings was returned to him), the company merely went into its rules and changed them, in effect obviating the long-term outcome of the Court's ruling; (3) in another way, this ruling could have a long-term effect if other courts use it as precedent for invalidating similar shrink wrap/click-through contracts and ToS Courts have often upheld software shrink wrap/click-through contracts and ToS as binding. However, "everyone knows" that virtually no one reads software fine print. With packaged goods, these agreements are contained within software packaging such that consumers can't read them before they've "agreed" by opening the package; online, the agreements often appear via pop-up windows through which users seldom read before clicking the "I agree" button so they can get on with their current/wanted activities. In almost all cases, the agreements consist of numerous lengthy paragraphs of overly legalistic technical terminology. There is a legal principle in contact law that holds that inaccessible contract terms may be less than legally binding. The rulings in *Bragg v. Linden* may provide fodder for judicial reinterpretations of the status of software and/or online shrink wrap/click-through contracts and ToS.

Eros, LLC, et al. v. Simon, et al., 1:07-cv-04447-SLT-JMA. USDC (E.D.N.Y. Oct. 24, 2007)

Six *SL* content creators filed a lawsuit in the New York Federal District Court, claiming copyright and trademark infringement against Thomas Simon (and unnamed others). Simon (known as Rase Kenzo in *SL*) allegedly exploited a flaw in the *SL* software to duplicate thousands of copies of Eros's products. Simon settled the case for about $600.00 after initially turning down an offered settlement that would have cost him ten times that much (Dannenberg).

Eros, LLC v. Robert Leatherwood and John 1–10 Does, 8:2007cv01158. (M.D. Fla. July 3, 2007)

Eros LLC pursued another suit, this time against an *SL* resident known as Catteneo. Eros LLC accused Catteneo of illicitly copying and selling an animated "virtual sex" bed for as little as L$4,000, a price that sharply under-cut Eros's price. On September 6, 2007, a motion to subpoena AT&T and Charter Communications for the RL identity of Catteneo was granted. Eros made similar requests of LL and PayPal. Eventually (via the subpoenas and detective work), Eros "established" that Catteneo was Robert Leatherwood of Texas; however, the nineteen-year-old denied being Catteneo for a time. A default judgment was entered against Leatherwood by the District Court for the Middle District of Florida, as through his denials of being Catteneo he did not attend the hearings.

By March 2008, Leatherwood admitted owning the account and settled with Eros. The terms were not announced but were thought to be a mere agreement to cease and desist from further commerce using the materials that Eros had created.

Summarizing IP Law in Virtual Worlds

We've proposed that this brief introduction to IP law in virtual worlds is a fitting end to the book, in that virtual worlds may provide a glimpse of future challenges to and complexities in IP law in new media. These environments are operating in their formative stages at this writing. Globally, tens of millions of people regularly participate in some form of virtual world. While console-based and hand-held gaming are the principal platforms in the multi-billion dollar computer gaming industry, 3D virtual, multiplayer, online games see burgeoning levels of activity and promise incremental gains in the future. Socially based virtual worlds are not yet as ubiquitous as quest-based gaming; however, the rapid increase in worlds such as *Second Life, There.com, Active Worlds, Kaneva, vSide,* and the *Sims Online* are sometimes thought to be more indicative of how online communicative interaction will work in the future than are games and/or the present 2D Web or electronic mail. Virtual worlds hold great promise as a growth industry.

The suite of intellectual property laws introduced in this volume presents enormous challenges to citizens, industry, and governments alike. Even prior to the age of computerized, digital communication and media, the breadth of IP law and its technical nature found each of its areas of interest standing as esoteric legal specialties. Overlaying the rapid and wide-ranging technological developments of the digital age as well as the global nature of contemporary economies onto an already complex IP law landscape produces an almost dizzying environment. Technical experts with interests in these areas—lawyers, judges, legislators, industry leaders, and teachers—face no easy task keeping up with the pace of change. As noted throughout this volume, legislation and the courts have lagged badly behind the pace of technological change.

Experts aside, everyman enters the scene equipped with computer, cell phone, MP3 player, digital camera and camcorder, DVR, digital television, an eBook reader, GPS location device, electronic mail, a personal Web site and blogs, corporate Web sites and blogs, membership in and active participation on FaceBook, MySpace, and LinkedIn, as well as "resident" status in *Second Life* and expert-player standing in *World of Warcraft*. The digital citizen steps forward as a full participant in new media both as a consumer and as a content creator. Armed and able with the means of production and instantaneous global distribution, today's new media users are up to their collective ears in content and processes with direct connections to, and investments in the ramifications of, IP law.

Yet the systems that develop and implement IP laws do not have everyday citizens in mind. For the most part, IP law has been, and continues to be, written by and for large, corporate, content- and rights-holding industries. User law is scant; most legislators are both uninterested in the plight of common citizens and generally supportive of the stronger controls advocated by corporate and industrial interests. In the arenas of IP law into which they now find themselves thrown, everyman stands alone.

One wonders if virtual worlds promise opportunities to modify the status quo. In some ways, applying RL intellectual property law to virtual worlds is so fraught with difficulties that the provision of a totally new regime to accommodate virtual worlds seems not beyond speculation. That system would almost certainly have to take the everyday user into more consideration than does the current IP legal system, as intellectual property activities in virtual worlds are more conducted by average citizens than by corporate entities. At this point, IP law written exclusively for and used in virtual worlds would be much closer to "user law" than is the current IP regime.

Even if an exhaustive change does not occur, perhaps the unique challenges presented by virtual worlds may bring about incremental, yet fundamental, changes in the current system. As noted in the discussion of the judge's rulings in *Bragg v. Linden Research, Inc. and Philip Rosedale*, a previously foundational feature of new media practice and law was brought into question. The very nature of previously accepted contract laws having to do with ToS, click-through/shrink wrap agreements, and the mediation procedures offered by software companies, were all compromised in the ruling, spurred by the judge's careful examination of the order of the day in the virtual world *SL*. Virtual worlds are so ubiquitous and are developing so quickly that additional cases will certainly be brought. Some of those cases will present opportunities to re-examine and redefine the very nature of relationships among products of the mind (intellectual property), the legal system, globalization, content creators, and digitally empowered users.

Nothing has changed; everything has changed.

Discussion Questions

1. Discuss your expectations for the use of "legal controls" during your participation in online, 3D virtual environments. What should primarily "rule"? The rules as set by the provider of the world? RL law?

2. What determines whether RL law applies to "inworld" activities? Duranske suggests the following as the test: "Real-world laws apply to virtual worlds to exactly the degree that virtual worlds attempt to offer real-world possibilities" (26). In other words, if the providers (and most users) present everything as a "game inside the magic circle," then the application of RL laws should be very limited. If, on the other hand, there are RL commerce and/or activities (education, "real" entertainment, business meetings, etc.), then RL laws should apply. Discuss this proposal.

3. To what degree should users' IP rights be protected within virtual worlds? Should they fully retain copyrights and patents for their creations therein? Why/why not? Discuss these questions both from the perspectives of users and providers.

4. At what point should an entire set of "laws for virtual worlds" supersede RL law? Who might be empowered to develop such principles?

5. Using *SL* as an example, participants "come into" *SL* from all over the world and interact in a visual space that gives the impression of geography, although the Linden Lab servers are all near its headquarters in San Francisco, California. Discuss the degree to which designating courts in and around San Francisco to be the appropriate jurisdictional venue seems just, wise, and/or practical, given the global participation in *SL*.

Notes

Introduction

1. Waxer and Baum 13.
2. Lessig, *Free Culture* 199–207.
3. The Copyright Office completed a study in 2006 making recommendations for orphaned works. Their report is available at <http://www.copyright.gov/orphan/>. The report suggested that legislation modify the *Copyright Act* with regard to orphaned works. Two of the legislators who encouraged the office to undertake the report, Sen. Patrick Leahy (VT) and Rep. Howard Berman (CA), have sponsored legislation for changes (see Oswald). However, as with most copyright-related legislation, there is significant contestation surrounding these proposals.
4. The historical normalcy of extensions was a key feature in *Eldred v. Ashcroft*, discussed in Chapter 1. A chart summarizing when works enter the public domain may be found in various places on the Internet, including: <http://www.uca.edu/divisions/general/gencounsel/copyright/expiration.asp> and <http://www.unc.edu/~unclng/public-d.htm>.
5. Litman, *Digital Copyright* 35–69.
6. Association of Research Libraries.
7. After three years of study, the Library of Congress's Section 108 Study Group has issued its report and recommendations concerning many of the issues surrounding digital preservation and archives. The report is available at <http://www.loc.gov/today/pr/2008/08-063.

html>.

8. Anderson 170–77.

9. The *Copyright Act* is found at 17 U.S.C. § 101 et seq. The *Patent Act* is found at 35 U.S.C. § 1 et seq. The *Trademark Act* is found at 15 U.S.C. § 1051 et seq.

10. *Uniform Trade Secrets Act* <http://www.law.upenn.edu/bll/ulc/fnact99/1980s/utsa85.htm>.

11. 18 U.S.C. § 1831 et seq.

12. Garner 293.

13. Garner 1443.

14. H.R. 683.

15. Statistics available at <http://www.uscourts.gov>.

16. Plitch 1.

17. 15 U.S.C. § 1125(d)(1)(A)(i).

18. <http://arbiter.wipo.int/domains/>.

19. <http://www.arbforum.com/domains/>.

20. <http://www.cpradr.org/ICANN_Menu.asp?M=1.6.6>.

21. <http://www.adndrc.org/adndrc/index.html>.

22. <http://uscode.house.gov/search/criteria.shtml>. Another user-friendly Web site containing the *United States Code* is sponsored by Cornell University and is located at <http://www.law.cornell.edu/uscode/>.

Chapter One

1. "'There are serious concerns that the court has, and serious questions raised, about the effectiveness of any order that this court might issue given the current state of affairs,' Judge White said, lamenting the fact that constitutional law might not be able to keep up with technological change." See Glater.

2. *Wikipedia* notes:

"In 1978, Apple Corps, The Beatles-founded record label, filed suit against Apple Computer for trademark infringement. The suit settled in 1981 with an amount of $80,000 being paid to Apple Corps. As a condition of the settlement, Apple Computer agreed to stay out of the music business. The case arose in 1989 again when Apple Corps sued, claiming violation of the 1981 settlement agreement. In 1991 another settlement of around $26.5 million was reached. . . . In September 2003 Apple Computer was sued by Apple Corps again, this time for introducing iTunes and the iPod which Apple Corps believed was a violation of the previous agreement by Apple not to distribute music. . . . The date for this trial has been set for March 27, 2006 in the UK." ("Apple Inc.") <http://en.wikipedia.org/wiki/Apple_Computer#Notable_litigation>.

These circumstances are also referred to in the "Legal Proceedings" sections of Apple's yearly filings with the US Securities and Exchange Commission; for example, the filing for the period ending March 26, 2005, may be found at <http://www.sec.gov/Archives/edgar/data/320193/000110465905020421/a05–7551_110q.htm>. The case culminated in May 2006 with a verdict in favor of Apple Computer. By the time of the last trial, the case hinged on trademark rather than copyright issues, as Apple Corps claimed that Apple Computer's use of an apple in its logo for the iTunes stores infringed on Apple Corp's trademarks. The Court found otherwise: "Apple Outsings Beatles in Trademark Court Battle," 8 May 2006, cnn.com <http://money.cnn.com/2006/05/08/technology/apple_beatles. reut/index.htm?cnn=yes>.

3. See McLeod; also Lessig, *Free Culture*, on the dangers inherent in making the citizenry at large into criminals.
4. Patterson 42–142, on the history before the *Statute of Anne*.
5. Patterson 181
6. Merges et al. 347.
7. Patterson 183.
8. Patterson 197.
9. The law would be validated by a variety of court cases, beginning with *Wheaton v. Peters* (1832). See the discussion of judicial action later in this chapter.
10. Waxer and Baum list the various changes, 12–13; Patterson 213; Goldstein 44.
11. Litman, "Copyright Legislation and Technological Change" 284–86.
12. Merges et al. 348–49.
13. "The Computer Software Rental Amendments Act of 1990: The Nonprofit Library Lending Exemption to the 'Rental Right: Executive Summary'" <http://www.copyright.gov/reports/software_ren.html>.
14. Litman, *Digital Copyright* 58.
15. International intellectual property history and issues will be discussed in Chapter 7. A large number of treaties, agreements, and negotiations have impacted the development of US copyright law since 1950, including *Patent Cooperation Treaty, WIPO, Copyright Treaty, Performances and Phonograms Treaty, Universal Copyright Convention, GATT/TRIPS*, and *NAFTA*.
16. For example, see the Section 108 Study Group, report and recommendations: <http://www.loc.gov/today/pr/2008/08–063.html>.
17. This treatment of the development of the *DMCA* draws heavily on Litman, *Digital Copyright*.
18. *Twentieth Century Fox Film Corp. v. Cablevision Systems* leads to concern that the courts may be returning to a narrow (draconian) interpretation of RAM/cache memory as "copying," an interpretation found in the *Green* and the *White Papers*.
19. 17 U.S.C. § 106.
20. H.R. Rep. No. 2222, 60th Cong., 2d Sess 6 (1909).
21. H.R. Rep. No. 2222, 60th Cong., 2d Sess 6 (1909).
22. 17 U.S.C. § 115(d).
23. To further complicate matters, the *Digital Performance Right in Sound Recording Act* attempts to exclude from compulsory licensing streaming music services. The definition of "digital phonorecord delivery" expressly excludes "a real-time, non-interactive subscription transmission of a sound recording where no reproduction of the sound recording or the musical work embodied there is made from the inception of the transmission through to its receipt by the transmission recipient in order to make the sound recording audible." 17 U.S.C. § 115(d).
24. 17 U.S.C. § 115 § 118 § 111I § 114(d)(2) § 114(d)(1) § 115 § 115(a)(1) § 115(a)(2) § 115(b) § 115(c) § 106(4) § 115(c)(3)(1995).
25. 17 U.S.C. § 115 (a)(2); see also Lessig, *Free Culture* 57.
26. *Palladium Music, Inc. v. EatSleepMusic, Inc.*, 398 F.3d 1193, 1200 (10th Cir. 2005).
27. Nimmer § 8.04[A].

28. *Staggers v. Real Authentic Sound,* 77 F. Supp. 2d 57, 64 (D.D.C. 1999).
29. Electronic Frontier Foundation. "A Better Way Forward: Voluntary Collective Licensing of Music File Sharing. 'Let the Music Play Whitepaper.'" April 2008. <http://www.eff.org/wp/better-way-forward-voluntary-collective-licensing-music-file-sharing>.
30. Ibid.
31. H.R. 24, *PRO-USE* (*"Preservation and Restoration of Orphan Works for Use in Scholarship and Education Act"*) <http://thomas.loc.gov/cgibin/query/z?c109:H.R.24:>.
32. H.R. 1201, *Digital Media Consumers Rights Act* <http://thomas.loc.gov/cgi-bin/query/z?c109:H.R.1201:>.
33. H.R. 2408, *Public Domain Enhancement Act* <http://thomas.loc.gov/cgi-bin/query/z?c109:H.R.2408:>.
34. H.R. 4536, *Benefit Authors without Limiting Advancement or Net Consumer Expectations (BALANCE) Act* <http://thomas.loc.gov/cgi-bin/query/z?c109:H.R.4536:>.
35. H.R. 4569, *Digital Transition Content Security Act* <http://thomas.loc.gov/cgi-bin/query/z?c109:H.R.4569:>.
36. H.R. 4861, *Audio Broadcast Flag Licensing Act* <http://thomas.loc.gov/cgi-bin/query/z?c109:H.R.4861:>.
37. McCullagh.
38. See Oswald.
39. See Vaidhyanathan.

Chapter Two

1. For example, see Bunker, and also Kudon.
2. The *No Electronic Theft (NET) Act,* 1997, enables criminal prosecution for copyright violations that do not result in monetary profit and/or for use in non-commercial works, thereby raising the stakes/risks for those who would seek fair-use protection.
3. See findings in *Star Trek* and *Seinfeld* cases.
4. See Crews.

Chapter Three

1. Jaffe and Lerner 11.
2. Jaffe and Lerner 68.
3. For details on this practice, see Rivette and Kline.
4. General Information Concerning Patents (Revised January 2005) "What Is a Patent?" <http://www.uspto.gov/web/offices/pac/doc/general/#ptsc>.
5. Note that the system works—and is unforgiving. While investigating Amazon.com's site, one of the authors clicked the 1-click® button, and an unwanted book was on its way.
6. An example of such a standard -setting organization is the Universal Serial Bus (USB) Implementers Forum, an industry-standards body incorporating leading companies from the computer and electronics industries. Notable members have included Apple Computer, Hewlett-Packard, NEC, Microsoft, Intel, and Agere. USB is a serial bus standard

to interface devices. It was designed for computers such as PCs and the Apple Macintosh; now, because of its popularity, it is used in numerous electronic devices such as video game consoles, PDAs, and cell phones.

7. McCarthy.

Chapter Five

1. Reprinted by US Department of Labor, "Definition of Trade Secret." <http://www.osha. gov/pls/oshaweb/owadisp.show_document?p_table=STANDARDS&p_id=10103>.

Chapter Six

1. Due to the tri-partite nature of the subject at hand, each of the three areas of interest will be taken in turn. Yet since there are three sets of materials, each will receive a more brief treatment than the single topics in previous chapters. The early development of rights of publicity, privacy, and defamation in the United States derive from the same sources and forces, so the treatment of their earliest history applies to all three. This text will not cover privacy laws dealing with the lending or banking industries and/or bank records; however, many electronic privacy issues circulate around private information contained in databases related to financial transactions.

2. This is one of the factors that limits the treatment in this text. One simply cannot review all of the state statutes/approaches within the framework of a book of this nature.

3. On appeal, however, although the Court of Appeals for the 9th Circuit affirmed the finding that the defendant was entitled to summary judgment, the Court did so after it held that the defendant was not an "information content provider" as contemplated under the CDA, and thus was immune from liability. See *Carafano v. Metrosplash.com, Inc.*, 339 F.3d 1119 (9th Cir. 2003).

Chapter Eight

1. <http://www.elcomsoft.com/>; <http://www.microsoft.com/windows/windowsmedia/for-pros/drm/default.mspx>; <http://www.drmwatch.com/standards/>.

Chapter Nine

1. For background on legal developments in virtual environments, see Anne Wells Branscomb, ed., "Emerging Law on the Electronic Frontier," part 1 of a special issue of *Journal of Computer-Mediated Communication* 2.1 (June 1996), especially these articles in Part One <http://jcmc.indiana.edu/vol2/issue1/index.html>: David R. Johnson, "Due Process and Cyberjurisdiction"; Tamir Maltz, "Customary Law & Power in Internet Communities"; Juliet M. Oberding, "A Separate Jurisdiction for Cyberspace?" and in Part Two <http://jcmc.indiana.edu/vol2/issue2/index.html>: Niva Elkin-Koren, "Public/Private and Copy-

258 INTELLECTUAL PROPERTY LAW AND INTERACTIVE MEDIA

right Reform in Cyberspace." See also Post and Johnson.

2. <http://blog.secondlife.com/2008/04/11/protecting-your-copyrighted-content/>; <http://secondlife.com/corporate/dmca.php>.

3. Navigate to <https://support.secondlife.com/ics/support/default.asp?deptID=4417>, then click "legal questions/More info" about Section 3.2 of the ToS and patents.

4. <http://secondlife.com/corporate/brand/trademark/index.php>.

5. Community Standards: <http://secondlife.com/corporate/cs.php>; Terms of Service: <http://secondlife.com/corporate/ToS.php>, including: "Welcome to Second Life! The following agreement (this "Agreement" or the "Terms of Service") describes the terms on which Linden Research, Inc. ("Linden Lab") offers you access to its services. This offer is conditioned on your agreement to all of the terms and conditions contained in the Terms of Service, including your compliance with the policies and terms linked to (by way of the provided URLs) from this Agreement. By using Second Life, you agree to these Terms of Service. If you do not so agree, you should decline this agreement, in which case you are prohibited from accessing or using Second Life."

6. That gamers look for exploits in games that improve users' performance and outcomes is almost gospel in the gaming community. In some ways, it's remarkable that Linden Lab found Bragg's behavior to be problematic. However, in this case, the outcome—Lindens—are a form of gaming credit that can be negotiated for real currency, so "rigging" the bidding process in land auctions was thought to be a serious violation and threat to the common order.

Glossary

Affirm: When an appellate court affirms the lower court's ruling, it agrees with the ruling and upholds it.

Amicus Curiae: A Latin phrase meaning "friend of the court." It has come to signify non-parties who ask to have a voice in cases pending before appellate courts. Upon permission from the appellate court, the non-parties may file *amicus* briefs to help frame the legal issues before the court. The general rule, however, is that only parties to the dispute may submit briefs and arguments to the court.

Answer: After the plaintiff files and serves a complaint, the defendant is granted a limited amount of time to answer each of the allegations in the complaint.

Anti-circumvention: Legal constraints against "going around" (or hacking) the access, usage, and copy restrictions embedded within digital media content.

Appellant: The party who files an appeal from the decision in the trial court.

Appellee: The party who responds to an appeal from the decision in the trial court.

Briefs: The legal memoranda prepared by the parties and submitted to the court. Briefs contain the factual basis and legal theories of the parties' positions.

Cache: Temporary storage area in a computer's memory system where frequently accessed data can be kept for rapid access. Various cache locations contain copies of information, limiting the need to retrieve new originals.

Causes of Action: The legal theories of recovery asserted by the plaintiff. For example, trademark infringement is a cause of action.

Commons: The "space" in which materials in "the Public Domain" reside. Citizens share ownership and control of the materials in "the Commons."

Complaint: The opening document filed by a plaintiff in a civil lawsuit. The complaint sets forth the basic facts and causes of action upon which the plaintiff seeks relief.

Compulsory License: Governmental requirement that holders of certain kinds of intellectual property rights must grant use to others, generally in exchange for a royalty.

Concurring Opinion: Individual judges on appellate panels will, from time to time, issue their own concurring opinions when they feel a need to expound on a point of law or make a distinction of law that is not otherwise noted in the majority opinion. A concurrence does not have the force of law of a majority opinion, but it may help a particular judge establish a principle that may, in future cases, be built into a majority opinion.

Cybersquatting: Acquiring and holding a URL for the purpose of extracting payments for its use from parties with a more legitimate claim to the URL than the cybersquatter.

Default Judgment: Judgment in favor of the plaintiff when the defendant fails to appear before a court (or answer a summons).

Defendant: In a civil legal matter, the party who responds or defends against the plaintiff's claims.

Dicta: That portion of a judicial opinion that is not central to the holding but allows the court to elaborate on factual and legal issues in an effort to clarify its holding.

Digital Rights Management (DRM): Technology that enforces a restriction on the use of digital content.

Dissenting Opinion: One or more judges in the minority may choose to write a dissenting opinion that elaborates on the reasons why the minority believes the majority opinion is incorrect. While some dissenting opinions read a bit like "sour grapes," not infrequently, as the law evolves, what started as a minority opinion may in later times shift to become the majority opinion of an appellate court.

Doctrine of Equivalents: In patent law, an infringement need not be an "exact" or "word-for-word" copy in order to be "equivalent" and infringe.

First-Sale Doctrine: The buyer of merchandise may transfer it (sell it, trade it, give it away) without permission once it has been purchased/obtained.

Guidance Gap: The time between the development and implementation/deployment of new technologies and the development of laws that effectively adjudicate conflicts that involve aspects of the technologies.

Hacker/Hacking: Discovering vulnerabilities and/or exploiting them within computing systems and networks via technological skill and creativity.

Holding: That portion of a judicial opinion where the court issues its ultimate finding of law. In appellate decision, it is the holding that serves as precedent for future litigants.

"Magic Circle" Test: Deciding whether a virtual world is so much a "game" that it is, or should be, protected from intrusion by "out-of-game" elements (such as laws).

Majority: In appellate courts, which generally contain panels of judges (three to nine), when there is not unanimity in decision-making, the majority of justices who agree issue a majority opinion, which becomes the binding law.

Markman Hearings: Preliminary patent hearing at which the court interprets and adjudicates the terms for subsequent proceedings. In essence, the Markman Hearing clarifies the terms at issue and sets the parameters for cases that result in the action.

Massively Multiplayer Online Role-Playing Game (MMORPG): Computer-based role playing games in which a large number of players interact in an online virtual space.

Media Commodification: The notion that commercial media turn members of the audience into "the product" via the process of setting a value on their media consumption and then "selling" them to advertisers based on the size or features of the potential or actual audience for a given media item.

Minority: As noted above, the minority is the portion of an appellate panel that has fewer votes for its position and, ultimately, does not prevail in setting new law.

Motions: Any litigant who desires the court to take action on the litigant's case may file a motion (i.e., a legal paper asking the court for relief).

Natural Rights: The concept of a universal right inherent in the nature of living beings. An idea developed by Thomas Hobbes and others, natural rights are taken as not contingent upon beliefs or laws.

Orphaned Works: Materials, once copyright-protected, for which the location of the rights owner is difficult or impossible.

Peer-to-Peer Networks (P2P): Distributed computer networks (usually between "lay" participants rather than governmental or formal businesses) using diverse connectivity and cumulative bandwidth rather than centralized servers and network facilities. Uses peer nodes rather than "clients" and "servers."

Personal Jurisdiction: The inherent power of a court to hail a litigant before it. The rules concerning personal jurisdiction are complex and, at times, inconsistent, but they center around whether a party (usually a defendant) has had sufficient contact with the forum where the court is located to allow the court to compel the defendant to appear.

Plaintiff: In a civil legal matter, the party who brings the claim or claims.

Prosecution History Estoppel: Patent applicants who make amendments to their applications (to avoid infringing previous patents) cannot make infringement claims based on the pre-amendment patent terms (that were later amended).

Public Domain: Materials that are not owned or controlled by anyone and that may be freely used by all. Sometimes referred to as "the commons," as the material is held "in common" by the people of a given area, government, or jurisdiction.

RAM: Random access memory is the writable and, generally, volatile memory in computers and storage devices.

Remand: When an appellate court issues a decision, it may remand or return the case to the lower court for further proceedings, if the effect of the appellate court's ruling necessitates further proceedings.

Reverse: When an appellate court rules that the lower court made an error, the appellate court often reverses the ruling, undoing the legal effect of the lower court's ruling.

Safe Harbor: Exemptions found in the *DMCA* that protect Internet service providers (ISPs) from legal responsibility for the content of materials crossing their networks or stored in their facilities.

Stare Decisis: The decision of a judge (in US law, usually at the appeals court level) becomes precedent for future decisions.

Subject Matter Jurisdiction: In addition to having power to compel parties to appear, courts must also have jurisdiction to hear the subject matter of the dispute. In certain types of intellectual property disputes, patents and copyrights for example, the federal courts (as opposed to state courts) have exclusive subject matter jurisdiction to hear these types of cases.

Summary Judgment: A trial judge may grant summary judgment in favor of a party if the party demonstrates that there are no genuine issues of material fact that would necessitate a trial, and the judge can rule on the case as a matter of law. Parties frequently attempt to pursue summary judgment because if they prevail, they can dramatically shorten the time and expense of litigation.

Trial Court—Lower Court: As noted above, the entry-level court where litigants initially bring their dispute.

Writ of Certiorari: An appeal for review of cases by a higher court to determine whether any irregularities or errors justify review of the case. The Supreme Court uses its discretion in selecting cases proposed via such writs.

Works Cited

Ambrosi, Alain, Valérie Peugeot, and Daniel Pimienta. *Word Matters: Multicultural Perspectives on Information Societies*. Caen, France: C & F Éditions, 2005.

American Law Institute. "Overview, Institute Projects." <http://www.ali.org/index.cfm?fuse action=about.instituteprojects>.

———. *Restatement of the Law of Torts*: As Adopted and Promulgated by the American Law Institute. Washington, D.C., 1939.

American Library Association. "Appeals Court Shoots Holes in FCC's Broadcast Flag Rule." *American Libraries* 36.6 (2005): 17.

Anderson, Chris. "The Long Tail." *Wired* Oct. 2004: 170–77.

"Apple Inc." *Wikipedia*. <http://en.wikipedia.org/wiki/Apple_Computer#Notable_litigation>.

Association of Research Libraries. *Monograph & Serial Expenditures in ARL Libraries, 1986–2004*. Washington, D.C., 2004.

Bangeman, Eric. "RIAA Trial Verdict Is in: Jury Finds Thomas Liable for Infringement." *Ars technica* 4 Oct. 2007. <http://arstechnica.com/news.ars/post/20071004-verdict-is-in.html>.

Barker, Colin. "Patent Office to Re-Examine 1-Click." *CNET News.com* 19 May 2006. <http://news.com.com/2100–1014_3 6074259.html?part=rss&tag=6074259&subj=news>.

biojudiciary.org. "History and Introduction to the U.S. Patent System." Accessed 23 June 2006. <http://www.biojudiciary.org/subpage1.asp?tid=100>.

Black, Sharon. *Telecommunications Law in the Internet Age*. San Francisco, CA: Morgan Kaufmann Publishers/Academic Press, 2002.

Bollier, David. "Reclaiming the Commons." <http://www.bollier.org/reclaim.htm>.

Borland, John. "'Bots' for Sony CD Software Spotted Online." *CNet News.com* 10 Nov. 2005. <http://www.news.com/Bots-for-Sony-CD-software-spotted-oline/2100–1029_3–5944643.html>.

Bowman, Lisa M. "Elcomsoft Verdict: Not Guilty." *CNet News.com* 17 Dec. 2002. <http://news.cnet.com/2100–1023–978176.html>.

Boyette, Randi. "Words That Hurt—And Kill." <http://www.adl.org/ADL_Opinions/Education/20071213-op-ed.htm>.

Bray, Hiawatha. "Hackers Go One Up." *The Boston Globe* 26 Oct. 2000. 3rd ed., sec. Business.

Bridis, Ted. "XM Faces Lawsuit about Handheld 'Inno.'" *USA Today* 16 May 2006. <http://www.usatoday.com/tech/news/2006–05–16-xm-satellite-lawsuit_x.htm>.

Broache, Anne. "Behind Google's German Courtroom Battle." *CNET News.com* 14 Sept. 2006. <http://news.cnet.com/Behind-Googles-German-courtroom-battle/2100–1032_3–6115056.html>.

Bunker, Matthew D. "Eroding Fair Use: The 'Transformative' Use Doctrine after Campbell." *Communication Law and Policy* 7 (2002): 1–24.

Center for the Study of the Public Domain, Duke University Law School. "Orphan Works Analysis and Proposal." Duke Law School, 2005. <http://www.law.duke.edu/cspd/pdf/cspdproposal.pdf>.

Cerny, Jim. "Who Runs the Internet?" <http://www.unh.edu/Internet/web/whoruns.html>.

Cohen, Adam. "One Friend Facebook Hasn't Made Yet: Privacy Rights." *The New York Times* 18 Feb. 2008. <http://www.nytimes.com/2008/02/18/opinion/18mon4.html?_r=1&scp=28&sq=right+of+privacy&st=nyt&oref=slogin>.

Commerce Committee. *Committee Report 2 of 3—House Report 105–551—Digital Millennial Copyright Act of 1998.*

"Copyright Casebook: 2Live Crew and the Case of the Pretty Woman." *Copyright Website* 23 Nov. 2007. <http://www.benedict.com/Audio/Crew/Crew.aspx#>. *Copyright Law of the United States.* 1976.

Cortez, Michael (aka Static Sprocket). "A Bit about Libsecondlife." E-mail to the SL Educators' Listserve, SLED. 17 Nov. 2006.

Craver, Scott, Patrick McGregor, Min Wu, Bede Liu, Adam Stubblefield, Ben Swartzlander, Dan S. Wallach, and Edward W. Felten. "SDMI Challenge FAQ." 2000. <http://www.cs.princeton.edu/sip/sdmi/faq.html>.

———. "Reading between the Lines: Lessons from the SDMI Challenge." 10th USENIX Security Symposium. Washington, D.C.: USENIX, 2001.

Creative Commons. "Creative Commons." 24 May 2008. <http://creativecommons.org/>.

———. "Creative Commons Attribution 3.0 United States." 24 May 2008. <http://creativecommons.org/licenses/by/3.0/us/>.

Crews, Kenneth D. "The Law of Fair Use and the Illusion of Fair-Use Guidelines." *Ohio State Law Journal* 62 (2001): 599–702.

Dannenberg, Ross. "Case: *Eros v. Simon* (Settled 2007)—Second Life." *Patent Arcade.* <http://www.patentarcade.com/2008/04/case-eros-v-simon-settled-2007-second.html>.

Davidson, J. Scott, and Lewis C. Lee. *Intellectual Property for the Internet.* New York: John Wiley & Sons, 1997.

DeBoer, Clint. "MPA Wins China DVD Lawsuit." *Audioholics.com* 6 Mar. 2008. <http://www.

audioholics.com/news/industry-news/mpa-wins-china-dvd-lawsuit>.

Devaiah, Vishwas. "A History of Patent Law." Alternative Law Forum. Accessed 21 June 2006. <http://www.altlawforum.org/PUBLICATIONS/document.2004–12–18.0853561257>.

Doctorow, Cory. "VLC will play iTunes Music Store Tracks." *BoingBoing.net* 26 Mar. 2004. <http://www.boingboing.net/2004/03/26/vlc-will-play-itunes.html>.

Duhaime, Diane. "Why Should Corporate Counsel Become Familiar with Virtual Environments? Aren't They Just Fun and Games?" *The Metropolitan Corporate Counsel* Feb. 2008: 14. <http://www.metrocorpcounsel.com/pdf/2008/February/14.pdf>.

Duranske, Benjamin Tyson. *Virtual Law*. Chicago: American Bar Association, 2008. *The Economist*. "The Slow Death of Digital Rights." 13 Oct. 2007.

Eldred, Eric. "Battle of the Books: The eBook v. the Antibook." Accessed 30 June 2006. <http://www.eldritchpress.org/battle.html>. 1998.

Electronic Frontier Foundation. "About EFF." <http://www.eff.org/about>.

———. *Apple v. Does*. <http://www.eff.org/cases/apple-v-does>.

———. *A Better Way Forward: Voluntary Collective Licensing of Music File Sharing*. Aug. 2004. <http://www.eff.org/wp/better-way-forward-voluntary-collective-licensing-music-file-sharing>.

———. "Digital Rights Management and Copy Protection Schemes." <http://www.eff.org/issues/drm>.

———. "EFF's *US v. Elcomsoft & Sklyarov* FAQ." <http://w2.eff.org/IP/DMCA/US_v_Elcomsoft/us_v_elcomsoft_faq.html>.

Elkin-Koren, Niva. "Public/Private and Copyright Reform in Cyberspace." *Journal of Computer-Mediated Communication* 2.1, Part 2 (June 1996). <http://jcmc.indiana.edu/vol2/issue2/index.html>.

Europa. Activities of the European Union, Summaries of Legislation: Audiovisual and Media. Television Broadcasting Activities; "Television without Frontiers" (TVWF) Directive. <http://europa.eu/scadplus/leg/en/lvb/l24101.htm>.

Felten, Ed. "What Is a Speedbump?" *Freedom-to-Tinker.com* 2004. <http://www.freedom-to-tinker.com/index.php?p=586>.

Ferrera, Gerald R., Stephen D. Lichenstein, Margo E.K. Rader, Ray August, and William T. Schiano. *CyberLaw: Text and Cases*. Cincinnati, OH: South-Western College Publishing/Thompson Learning, 2001.

FindLaw. *California Civil Code—Section 3344–3344.1 [Astaire Celebrity Image Protection Act]*. <http://caselaw.lp.findlaw.com/cacodes/civ/3344–3346.html>.

Fink, Steven. *Sticky Fingers: Managing the Global Risk of Economic Espionage*. Chicago: Dearborn Trade, 2002.

Frey, Jason. "A Web Page of One's Own." *The Wall Street Journal* 14 July 2008. <http://online.wsj.com/article/SB121562102257039585.html?mod=djem_jiewr_IT>.

Garner, Bryan A., ed. *Black's Law Dictionary*. 8th ed. St. Paul, MN: Thompson-West Group, 2004.

Glater, Jonathan D. "Judge Says Wikileaks Site Can Have Its Web Address Back." *The New York Times* 29 Feb. 2008. <http://bits.blogs.nytimes.com/2008/02/29/judge-says-wikileaks-can-have-its-web-address-back/index.html?th&emc=th>.

Goldberg, Morton David. *Computer Software 1989: Protection and Marketing, Volume II*. New York: Practising Law Institute, 1989.

Goldman, Eric. "11th Circuit Freaks Out About Metatags—*North American Medical v. Ax-*

iom." *Technology & Marketing Law Blog* 8 Apr. 2008. <http://blog.ericgoldman.org/archives/2008/04/11th_circuit_fr.htm>.

Goldstein, Paul. *Copyright's Highway: From Gutenberg to the Celestial Jukebox.* Stanford, CA: Stanford UP, 2003.

Gordon, Wendy J. "Fair Use as Market Failure: A Structural and Economic Analysis of the Betamax Case and Its Predecessors." *Columbia Law Review* 82.8 (1982): 1600–57.

Hanneman, Henri W. *The Patentability of Computer Software.* Deventer, The Netherlands: Kluwer Law and Taxation Publishers, 1985.

Hassett, Rob. "Rights of Privacy and Publicity in Interactive Media." <http://www.internetlegal.com/articles/rightsof.htm>.

Hefflinger, Mark. "Chinese Movie Download Service Jeboo Sues MPA." *Digitalmediawire.com* 22 May 2008. <http://www.dmwmedia.com/news/2008/05/22/studios-win-%244.1m-judgments-against-movie-linking-sites>.

Hesse, Thomas. Interview. "Sony Music CD's under Fire from Privacy Advocates." *Morning Edition*, National Public Radio. Broadcast 4 Nov. 2005.

Hirtle, Peter. "Copyright Term and the Public Domain in the United States." 1 Jan. 2008; 24 May 2008. <http://www.copyright.cornell.edu/public_domain/>.

———. "Research, Libraries and Fair Use: The Gentlemen's Agreement of 1935." *Journal of the Copyright Society of the U.S.A.* (2006).

Holson, Laura M. "A Settlement by Vonage over Patents." *The New York Times* 9 Oct. 2007. <http://www.nytimes.com/2007/10/09/business/09vonage.html?th&emc=th>.

Hovey, Craig. *The Patent Process: A Guide to Intellectual Property for the Information Age.* New York: John Wiley & Sons, 2002.

H.R. Rep. No. 94–1476, 94th Cong., 2d Sess. 65, 1976.

ICANN, "Domain Name Dispute Resolution Policy." <http://www.icann.org/udrp/udrp-policy-24oct99.htm>.

———. "Timeline for the Formulation and Implementation of the Uniform Domain-Name Dispute Resolution Policy." <http://www.icann.org/udrp/udrp-schedule.htm>.

International Intellectual Property Alliance. "IIPA's New Economic Study Reveals the Copyright Industries Remain a Driving Force in the U.S. Economy." Press Release. 30 Jan. 2007: 1. <http://www.iipa.com/pdf/IIPA2006CopyrightIndustriesReportPressReleaseFINAL01292007.pdf>.

Jaffe, Adam B., and Josh Lerner. *Innovation and Its Discontents: How Our Broken Patent System Is Endangering Innovation and Progress, and What to Do about It.* Princeton, NJ: Princeton UP, 2004.

Jaszi, Peter. "Copyright Term Extension Act of 1995." Washington, DC, 1995. 24 May 2008. <http://web.lexis-nexis.com.turing.library.northwestern.edu/congcomp/document?_m=1b451f2b246713874c9db02b19f77dab&_docnum=12&wchp=dGLbVzW-zSkSA&_md5=410c25a53b837dbcdf603835fa6aa7aa>.

———. *Eric Eldred et al. v. John D. Ashcroft*, Petition for Writ of Certiorari, Brief of Amici Curiae by American Law Library Association et al.

Jobs, Steve. "Thoughts on Music." 6 Feb. 2007. <http://www.apple.com/hotnews/thoughtsonmusic/>.

Johnsen, Andreas, Ralf Christensen, and Henrik Moltke. *Good Copy Bad Copy.* <http://www.goodcopybadcopy.net>.

Johnson, David R. "Due Process and Cyberjurisdiction." *Journal of Computer-Mediated Commu-*

nication 2.1, Part 1 (June 1996). <http://jcmc.indiana.edu/vol2/issue1/index.html>.

Kaplan, Benjamin. *An Unhurried View of Copyright*. New York: Columbia University Press, 1967.

Kelzer, Gregg. "Sony Settles Rootkit CD Suit with Texas, California." *Information Week* 20 Dec. 2006.

Kudon, Jeremy. "Form over Function: Expanding the Transformative Use Test for Fair Use." *Boston University Law Review* 80 (2000): 579–612.

Ladas & Parry, LLP. "A Brief History of the Patent Law of the United States." Accessed 1 June 2006. <http://www.ladas.com/Patents/USPatentHistory.html>.

Legal Information Institute, Cornell University Law School. *CRS Annotated Constitution: Fourth Amendment*. <http://www.law.cornell.edu/anncon/search/display.html?terms=Privacy&url=/anncon/html/amdt4frag1_user.html?>.

Lessig, Lawrence. *Free Culture: How Big Media Uses Technology and the Law to Lock Down Culture and Control Creativity*. New York: Penguin Press, 2004.

———. *The Future of Ideas: The Fate of the Commons in a Connected World*. New York: Random House, 2002.

———. "Jail Time in the Digital Age." *The New York Times* 30 July 2001. <http://www.nytimes.com/2001/07/30/opinion/30LESS.html>.

———. "Little Orphan Artworks." *The New York Times* 20 May 2008. <http://www.nytimes.com/2008/05/20/opinion/20lessig.html>.

Leval, Pierre N. "Toward a Fair Use Standard." *Harvard Law Review* 103 (1990): 1105–36.

Linek, Ernie. "A Brief History of Trade Secret Law, Part 1." *BioProcess International*. Oct. 2004: 1–4. <www.bannerwitcoff.com/%5Carticles/briefhistory1.pdf>.

———. "A Brief History of Trade Secret Law, Part 2." *BioProcess International* Nov. 2004: 20–26. <www.bannerwitcoff.com/%5Carticles/briefhistory2.pdf>.

Litman, Jessica. "Copyright Legislation and Technological Change." *Oregon Law Review* 68 (1989): 275–361.

———. *Digital Copyright*. Amherst, NY: Prometheus Books, 2001.

———. *Law 760: Trademarks & Unfair Competition*. <http://www-personal.umich.edu/~jdlitman/classes/tm.htm>.

———. "Lawful Personal Use." *Texas Law Review* 85 (2007): 1871–920.

Long, Tony. "RIAA Hits a Sour Note with Its File-Sharing Witch Hunt." *Wired News* 11 Oct. 2007. <http://www.wired.com/culture/lifestyle/commentary/theluddite/2007/10/ludite_1011>.

Loren, Lydia Pallas. "Redefining the Market Failure Approach to Fair Use in an Era of Copyright Permission Systems." *Journal of Intellectual Property Law Association* 5 (Fall 1997): 1–58.

Madison, Michael J. "Rewriting Fair Use and the Future of Copyright Reform." *Cardozo Arts and Entertainment Law Journal* 23 (2005): 391–418.

Maltz, Tamir. "Customary Law & Power in Internet Communities." *Journal of Computer-Mediated Communication* 2.1, Part 1 (June 1996). http://jcmc.indiana.edu/vol2/issue1/index.html>.

McCarthy, Caroline. "Amazon, IBM Settle Patent Lawsuit," *CNet News.com* 8 May 2007. <http://www.news.com/Amazon,-IBM-settle-patent-lawsuit/2100-1014_36182178.html>.

McCullagh, Declan. "Congress Readies Broad New Digital Copyright Bill." *CNET News.com* 23 Apr. 2006. <http://news.com.com/2100-1028_3-6064016.html>.

McGonagle, John J., and Carolyn M. Vella. *The Manager's Guide to Competitive Intelligence*. Westport, CT: Praeger, 2003.

Mclaughlin, Kathy. "Mother Fights Record Companies' Lawsuit on Her Own." *USA Today.com* 25 Dec. 2005. <http://www.usatoday.com/news/nation/2005-12-25-download-suit_x. htm>.

McLeod, Kembrew. *Owning Culture: Authorship, Ownership, & Intellectual Property Law*. New York: Peter Lang, 2001.

Merges, Robert P., Peter S. Menell, and Mark A. Lemley. *Intellectual Property in the New Technological Age*. 2nd ed. Gaithersburg, VA: Aspen Law & Business, 2000.

Murphy, John. "Intellectual Property & Development." *Latin Business Chronicle* 28 (Apr. 2008). <http://www.latinbusinesschronicle.com/app/article.aspx?id=2328>.

Mylott, Thomas R., III. *Computer Law for Computer Professionals*. Englewood Cliffs, NJ: Prentice-Hall, 1984.

Nichol, Kenneth. *Inventing Software: The Rise of "Computer-Related" Patents*. Westport, CT: Quorum Books, 1998.

Nimmer, David. *Copyright: Sacred Text, Technology, and the DMCA*. The Hague, The Netherlands: Kluwer Law International, 2003.

Nimmer, Melville B., and David Nimmer. *Nimmer on Copyrights: A Treatise on the Law of Literary, Musical and Artistic Property, and the Protection of Ideas*. New York: Matthew Bender, 2005.

Oberding, Juliet M. "A Separate Jurisdiction for Cyberspace?" *Journal of Computer-Mediated Communication* 2.1, Part 1 (June 1996). *http://jcmc.indiana.edu/vol2/issue1/index.html*.

Office of the US Trade Representative. "Trade Delivers: WTO Case Challenging Weaknesses in China's Legal Regime for Protection and Enforcement of Copyrights and Trademarks." Apr. 2007. <http://www.ustr.gov/assets/Document_Library/Fact_Sheets/2007/asset_upload_file908_11061.pdf>.

Oppenheim, Matthew J. Letter to Professor Felten from Recording Industry Association of America. 2001. <http://www.cs.princeton.edu/sip/sdmi/riaaletter.html>.

Orphan Works Act of 2008. 24 May 2008. <http://www.thomas.gov/cgi-bin/query/z?c110: H.R.5889:>.

Oswald, Ed. "Orphaned Works Legislation Faces Pushback from Artists, " *BetaNews* 13 May 2008. <http://www.betanews.com/article/Orphaned_Works_legislation_faces_pushback_from_artists/1210704196>.

Paradise, Paul R. *Trademarks Counterfeiting, Product Piracy, and the Billion Dollar Threat to the U.S. Economy*. Westport, CT: Quorum Books, 1999.

Patrick, Robert, and David Hunn. "Lori Drew Indicted in Megan Meier MySpace Suicide Case." *St. Louis Post-Dispatch* 15 May 2008. <http://www.stltoday.com/stltoday/news/stories.nsf/stcharles/story/8CBA59D32CDFA0B88625744A0050D3F6?OpenDocument>.

Patterson, L. Ray (Lyman Ray). *Copyright in Historical Perspective*. Nashville, TN: Vanderbilt University Press, 1968.

Peters, Marybeth. *Recommendation of the Register of Copyrights in Rm 2005–11; Rulemaking on Exemptions from Prohibition on Circumvention of Copyright Protection Systems for Access Control Technologies*. 2006.

Plitch, Phyllis Bounty Hunter. "New Law Put Squeeze on Net Domain-Name Cybersquatters." *The Wall Street Journal* 20 Dec. 1999: 1. <http://online.wsj.com/article/SB945645226160009853.html>.

Ponte, Lucille. "The Emperor Has No Clothes: How Digital Sampling Infringement Cases Are Exposing Weaknesses in Traditional Copyright Law and the Need for Statutory Reform." *American Business Law Journal* 43 (2006): 515–60.

Post, David G., and David R. Johnson. "The Great Debate—Law in Virtual World." *First Monday* 11.2 (2006). <http://www.firstmonday.org/issues/issue11_2/post/index.html>.

Quinlan, Joseph. "Global Asset Allocation: 2008 Outlook. Jan. 2008. <http://www.kiplinger.com/businessresource/summary/archive/2008/emerging-quinlan-08.html>.

Redman, Christopher, and Thomas Sancton. "We Are Not an Average Nation: An Exclusive Talk with Jacques Chirac." *Time* 11 Dec. 1995: 59. <http://www.time.com/time/magazine/article/0,9171,983832-2,00.html>.

Reuters. "Sony Tests Technology to Limit CD Burning." 1 June 2005. *CNET.co.uk.* <http://news.cnet.co.uk/digitalmusic/0,39029666,39189658,00.htm>.

Reuters, Eric. "Judge Rules against 'One-Sided' TOS in Bragg Lawsuit." *secondlife.reuters.com* 31 May 2007. <http://secondlife.reuters.com/stories/2007/05/31/judge-rules-against-one-sided-ToS-in-bragg-lawsuit/>.

Rinaman, Karen. "French Film Quotas and Cultural Protectionism." Aug. 1996. <http://www.american.edu/ted/frenchtv.htm>.

Rivette, Kevin G., and David Kline. *Rembrandts in the Attic: Unlocking the Hidden Value of Patents.* Boston: Harvard Business School Press, 2000.

Rosenblatt, Bill. "About DRMwatch.com—From the Managing Editor." <http://www.drm-watch.com/article.php/3097951>.

Roseneor, Jonathan. *CyberLaw: The Law of the Internet.* New York: Springer, 1997.

Russinovich, Mark. "Sony, Rootkits and Digital Rights Management Gone Too Far." 31 Oct. 2005. Mark's Blog. <http://blogs.technet.com/markrussinovich/archive/2005/10/31/sony-rootkits-and-digital-rights-management-gone-too-far.aspx>.

Samuelson, Pamela. "Anti-circumvention Rules: Threat to Science." *Science* 293.5537 (2001): 2028.

Sarson, Richard. "ICANN Makes a Very British Compromise over Net Policing." *The Guardian* 29 May 2008. <http://www.guardian.co.uk/technology/2008/may/29/internet.politics>.

Satterlee, Stephens, Burke, & Burke, LLP. "Rights of Publicity on the Net." <http://ssbb.com/rights.html>.

Schneider, Andrew C. "Exports Will Lift GDP Growth Again in 2008." *The Kiplinger Letter* 26 Nov. 2007. <http://www.kiplinger.com/businessresource/forecast/archive/exports_to_lift_gdp_growth_071126.html>.

Seidel, Arthur H. *What the General Practitioner Should Know about Trademarks and Copyrights.* Philadelphia, PA: American Law Institute, 1976.

Shawn Bentley Orphan Works Act of 2008. 24 May 2008. <http://www.thomas.gov/cgi-bin/query/D?c110:1:./temp/~c1103r174C::>.

Simons, Barbara. "The ACM Declaration in *Felten v. RIAA.*" *Communications of the ACM* 44.10 (2001): 23.

Sklyarov, Dimitry. "ElcomSoft—Ebooks Security—Theory and Practice." DEF CON Nine. Las Vegas, NV, 2001. <http://www.cs.cmu.edu/~dst/Adobe/Gallery/ds-defcon2/ds-defcon.html>.

Smedinghoff, Thomas J., ed. *Online Law: The SPA's Legal Guide to Doing Business on the Internet.* Reading, MA: Addison-Wesley Developers Press, 1996.

Smith, Eric H. Letter to Stan McCoy. 11 Feb. 2008. <http://www.iipa.com/pdf/2008SPEC

301COVERLETTER.pdf>.

Solove, Daniel J. . *The Digital Person: Technology and Privacy in the Information Age*. New York: New York UP, 2004.

Stallman, Richard M. "Words to Avoid." *Free Society: Selected Essays of Richard M. Stallman*. Boston: GNU Press, 2002: 191–96.

Stim, Richard. *Patent, Copyright & Trademark: An Intellectual Property Desk Reference*. 8th ed. Consolidated Printers Inc., Jan. 2006.

"Summaries of Fair Use Cases." <http://fairuse.stanford.edu/Copyright_and_Fair_Use_Overview/chapter9/9-c.html>.

Talacko, Paul. "Towards a Piracy High Watermark: Copyright Protection: Paul Talacko Looks at the Initiative to Create Secure Music Standards and the Digital Watermarking Technology." *Financial Times* 29 Dec. 2000, sec. Inside Track.

Tehranian, John. "Infringement Nation: Copyright Reform and the Law/Norm Gap." *Utah Law Review* 3 (2007): 537–50.

Uniform Trade Secrets Act. Drafted by the National Conference of Commissioners on Uniform State Laws, 1985. <http://www.law.upenn.edu/bll/archives/ulc/fnact99/1980s/utsa85.htm>.

Urban, Jennifer M., and Jason Schultz, for Consumers Union. "Brief of Amicus Curiae Consumers Union in Support of Appellee." *The Chamberlain Group, Inc., v. Skylink Technologies, Inc.* (02 C 6376), 2004.

US Copyright Office. *Copyright Office Basics*. 23 Mar. 2008. <http://www.copyright.gov/circs/circ1.html>.

———. *Duration of Copyright*. Washington, DC, 2004.

———. *Highlights of Copyright Amendments Contained in the URAA*. Washington, DC, 2006.

———. *How to Investigate the Copyright Status of a Work*. Washington, DC, 2006.

———. Report on Orphan Works: A Report of the Register of Copyrights. Washington, DC, 2006. <http://www.copyright.gov/orphan/orphan-report-full.pdf>.

US Department of Labor. "Definition of Trade Secret." <http://www.osha.gov/pls/oshaweb/owadisp.show_document?p_table=STANDARDS&p_id=10103>.

Vaidhyanathan, Siva. *Copyrights and Copywrongs: The Rise of Intellectual Property and How It Threatens Creativity*. New York: New York UP, 2001.

Vijayan, Jaikumar. "What's in a Name? Cybersquatting Case Has an Answer." *Computerworld* 13 Feb. 2008. <http://www.computerworld.com/action/article.do?command=viewArticleBasic&articleId=9062559&source=NLT_AM&nlid=1>.

von Lohman, Fred Hinze, and Gwen Hinze. *DMCA Triennial Rulemaking: Failing the Digital Consumer*. San Francisco, CA: Electronic Frontier Foundation, 2005.

Warren, Samuel D., and Louis D. Brandeis. "The Right to Privacy." *Harvard Law Review* 4 (1890–91): 193–220. <http://www.lawrence.edu/fast/boardmaw/Privacy_brand_warr2.html>.

Watson, Jason. "A History of the United States Patent Office." 17 Apr. 2001. April 2005. <http://www.m-cam.com/~watsonj/usptohistory.html>.

Waxer, Barbara, and Marsha L. Baum. *Internet Surf and Turn Revealed: The Essential Guide to Copyright, Fair Use, and Finding Media*. Boston: Thompson Course Technology, 2006.

Wex Legal Information Institute, Cornell Law School. "Publicity." <http://www.law.cornell.edu/wex/index.php/Publicity>.

Wikinews. "Woman Found Guilty of Plotting to Sell Coke Documents to Pepsi." 2 Feb. 2007.

<http://en.wikinews.org/wiki/Woman_found_guilty_of_plotting_to_sell_Coke_documents_to_Pepsi>.

Wolf, Christopher. "Standards for Internet Jurisdiction." FindLaw. <http://library.findlaw.com/1999/Jan/1/241482.html>.

Womble Carlyle. "Trade Secrets Battle in Detroit—MSC Software Corp. vs. Altair Engineering Inc. and Seven Former MSC Employees." *Trade Secrets Blog* 20 Nov. 2007. <http://wombletradesecrets.blogspot.com/2007/11/trade-secrets-battle-in-detroit-msc.html>.

World Intellectual Property Organization. *Berne Convention for the Protection of Literary and Artistic Works.* 24 May 2008. <http://www.wipo.int/treaties/en/ip/berne/trtdocs_wo001.html>.

Cases

A&M Records, Inc. v. Napster, Inc., 239 F. 3d 1004 (9th Cir. 2001).

Abdul-Jabbar v. Gen. Motors, 85 F.3d 407, 415–16 (9th Cir. 1996).

Acuff-Rose Music Inc. v. Campbell, 972 F.2d 1429 (6th Cir. 1992).

Ahn v. Midway Mfg. Co., 965 F. Supp. 1134 (N.D. Ill. 1997).

Alexander G. Lunney v. Prodigy Services Company, &c., Respondent, et al., 99 N.Y. Int. 0165, no. 164 (Dec. 2, 1999).

Almeida v. Amazon.com, Inc., 456 F.3d 1316 (11th Cir. 2006).

Amazon.com v. Barnesandnoble.com, 239 F.3d 1343 (Fed. Cir. 2001).

Baker v. Selden, 101 U.S. 99 (1879).

Bally Total Fitness Holding Corp. v. Faber, 29 F. Supp. 2d 1161 (C.D. Cal. 1998).

Berger v. New York, 388 U.S. 41 (1967).

Big O Tire Dealers, Inc. v. Goodyear Tire & Rubber Co., 561 F.2d 1365 (10th Cir. 1977).

Blumenthal v. Drudge, 992 F. Supp. 44 (D.D.C. 1998).

Bosley v. Wildwett.com, 310 F. Supp. 2d 914 (N.D. Ohio 2004).

Bragg v. Linden Research, Inc. and Philip Rosedale, No. 06–4925, USDC (E.D. Pa., May 30, 2007).

Bridgeport Music v. Dimension Films, 410 F.3d 792 (6th Cir. 2005).

Brown v. ACMI Pop, N.E.2d (Ill. App. Ct., Aug. 2, 2007).

Campbell v. Acuff-Rose Music, Inc., 510 U.S. 569, 579 (1994).

Carafano v. Metrosplash.com Inc., 207 F. Supp. 2d 1055 (C.D. Cal. 2002).

Carafano v. Metrosplash.com, Inc., 339 F.3d 1119 (9th Cir. 2003).

Cardtoons, L.C. v. Major League Baseball Players' Ass'n, 95 F.3d 959 (10th Cir. 1996).

Carson v. Here's Johnny Portable Toilets, Inc., 698 F.2d 831, 835 (6th Cir. 1983).

Castle Rock Entertainment v. Carol Publ'g Group, 150 F.3d 132 (1998).

CBC Distribution and Marketing, Inc. v. Major League Baseball Adv. Media, L.P., F.3d (8th Cir. 2007).

CompuServe v. Cyber Promotions, Inc., 962 F. Supp. 1015 (S.D. Ohio, C2–96–1070, 1997).

Copiepresse v. Google, The Court of First Instance in Brussels, Nr. 06/10.928/C (Feb. 13, 2007).

Cubby v. CompuServe Inc., No. 90 Civ. 6571. USDC (S.D.N.Y. Oct. 29, 1991).

Cyber Promotions, Inc. v. America Online, Inc., 948 F. Supp. 436 (E.D. Pa. 1996).

Dendrite International, Inc. v. John Doe No. 3, 342 N.J. Super. 134 Appellate Division (2001).

DVD Copy Control Assn., Inc. v. Bunner, 31 Cal. 4th 864, 889 (2003).

DVD-CCA v. Bunner, Court of Appeals of the State of California, 6th Appellate District, HO21153 Santa Clara County Super. CT. No. CV786804, (Feb. 27, 2004).

eBay, Inc. v. MercExchange, 126 S. Ct. 1837 (2006).

EF Cultural Travel BV v. Explorica, Inc., 274 F.3d 577 (1st Cir. 2001).

EFF v. Sony BMG. Cal. Sup. Ct., Los Angeles Cty. (2005).

Eldred v. Ashcroft (01–618) 537 U.S. 186 (2003).

Eldred v. Reno, 74 F. Supp. 2d 1 (1999).

Eldred v. Reno, 239 F.3d 372 (2001).

Elena Cisneros v. Robert Sanchez. 1:05-cv-00259 USDC (S.D. Tex. Dec. 7, 2005).

Eolas Techs. v. Microsoft Corp., 399 F.3d 1325 (Fed. Cir. 2005).

Eros, LLC, et al. v. Simon, et al., 1:07-cv-04447-SLT-JMA. USDC (E.D.N.Y. Oct. 24, 2007).

Eros, LLC v. Robert Leatherwood and John 1–10 Does, 8:2007cv01158. (M.D. Fla. July 3, 2007).

Feist Publications, Inc. v. Rural Telephone Service Co., 499 U.S. 340 (1991).

Festo Corp. v. Shoketsu Kinzoku Kogyo Kabushiki Co., 535 U.S. 722 (2002).

Flanagan v. Epson America, Inc., No. BC007036, Cal. Sup. Ct., Los Angeles Cty. (1991).

Folsom v. Marsh, 9 F.Cas. 342, 6 Hunt Mer. Mag. 175, 2 Story 100, No. 4901 (1841).

Fox v. Encounters Intern., 318 F. Supp. 2d 279 (D. Md. 2002).

Goldman v. United States, 316 U.S. 129 (1942).

Google Inc. v. Daniel Giersch. Office for Harmonization in the Internal Market (Trade Marks and Designs), Second Board of Appeal R 252/2007-2 (Feb. 26, 2008).

Graham v. John Deere, 383 U.S. 1 (1966).

Graver Tank & Mfg. Co. v. Linde Air Products, Co., 339 U.S. 605 (1950).

Griswold v. Connecticut (No. 496) 151 Conn. 544, 200 A.2d 479, reversed (1965).

Haelan Laboratories, Inc. v. Topps Chewing Gum. Inc., 202 F.2d 866 (2nd Cir. 1953).

Harper & Row v. Nation Enterprises Case Media, 471 U.S. 539 (1985).

Henley v. Dillard Department Stores, 46 F. Supp. 2d 587 (N.D. Tex. 1999).

Hustler Magazine, Inc. v. Falwell, 485 U.S. 46 (1988).

Hustler Magazine, Inc., v. Moral Majority, Inc., Old Time Gospel Hour, Jerry Falwell, 606 F. Supp. 1526 (C.D. Cal. Apr. 23, 1985).

IBM Corp. v. Amazon.com, Inc. No. 06–452 (E.D. Tex. filed Oct. 23, 2006).

IDX Systems Corp. v. Epic Systems, Corp., 285 F.3d 581 (7th Cir. 2002).

Jane Doe v. Friendfinder Network, Inc. and Various, Inc. Civil No. 07-cv-286 Opinion No. 2008 DNH 058 (2008). <http://www.citmedialaw.org/sites/citmedialaw.org/files/2008–02–7-Friendfinder%20Order.pdf>.

Kalem Co. v. Harper Bros., 222 U.S. 55 (1911).

Katz v. United States, 389 U.S. 347 (1967).

Kelly, et al. v. Arriba Soft Corp., et al., USDC (C.D. Cal.), Southern Division Case No. SA CV 99–560 GLT[JW] (1999).

Kelly, et al. v. Arriba Soft Corp., et al. Appeal from USDC (C.D. Cal. Feb. 6, 2002).

Kelly, et al. v. Arriba Soft Corp., et al. (9th Cir. 10; July 7, 2003).

Kewanee Oil Co. v. Bicron Corp., 416 U.S. 470; 94 S. Ct. 1879 (1974).

KNB Enters. v. Matthews, 78 Cal. App. 4th 362 (Cal. Ct. App. 2000).

KSR Int'l Co. v. Teleflex Inc., 127 S. Ct. 1727 (April 30, 2007).

Loufrani v. Wal-Mart, Opposition Nos. 91/150,278, 91/154,632 and 91/152,145.

March Madness Athletic Ass'n v. Netfire, Inc., 2005 U.S. App. LEXIS 1475 (5th Cir. Jan. 24, 2005).

Marcus v. Rowley and San Diego Unified School District, 695 F.2d 1171 (9th Cir. 1983).

Markman v. Westview Instruments Inc., 517 U.S. 370 (1996).

Mazer v. Stein, 347 U.S. 201 (1954).

McIntyre v. Ohio Elections Commission (1995).

McRoberts Software Inc. v. Media 100 Inc., 329 F.3d 557 (7th Cir. 2003).

Metro-Goldwyn-Mayer Studios Inc. v. Grokster, Ltd. (04–480) 545 U.S. 913 (2005).

Michaels v. Internet Entm't Group, Inc., 5 F. Supp. 2d 823 (C.D. Cal. 1998).

Moseley v. Victoria's Secret Catalogue, Inc. (01–1015) 537 U.S. 418 (2003).

National Association for the Advancement of Colored People v. Alabama, 357 U.S. 449 (1958).

Newcombe v. Adolph Coors Co., 157 F.3d 686 (9th Cir. 1998).

New York Times v. Sullivan, 39, 376 U.S. 254 (1964).

Nixon v. Administrator of General Services, 433 U.S. 425 (1977).

North American Medical Corp. v. Axiom Worldwide, Inc., 2008 WL 918411 (11th Cir. Apr. 7, 2008).

NTP, Inc. v. Research in Motion, Ltd., 418 F.3d 1282 (Fed. Cir. 2005).

O'Grady v. Superior Court, 139 Cal. App. 4th 1423 (Ct. App. 2006).

Olmstead v. United States, 277 U.S. 438 (1928).

Palladium Music, Inc. v. EatSleepMusic, Inc., 398 F.3d 1193, 1200 (10th Cir. 2005).

Panavision Int'l, L.P. v. Toeppen, 141 F.3d 1316 (9th Cir. 1998).

Paramount Pictures Corporation v. Carol Publishing Group, et al., USDC (S.D.N.Y. 1998).

Pebble Beach Co. v. Caddy, No. 04–15577, 2006 WL 1897091 (9th Cir. July 12, 2006).

PepsiCo Inc. v. Remond, 54 F.3d 1262 (7th Cir. 1995).

Perfect 10, Inc. v. CCBill LLC, 481 F.3d 751 (9th Cir. 2007).

Pesina v. Midway Mfg. Co., 948 F. Supp. 40 (N.D. Ill. 1996).

Phillips v. AWH, 415 F.3d 1303 (Fed. Cir. 2005) (en banc).

Playboy Enters., Inc. v. Welles, 279 F.3d 796 (9th Cir. 2002).

Polaroid Corp. v. Polarad Electronics Corp., 287 F.2d 492 (2nd Cir. 1961).

Procter & Gamble Mfg. Co. v. Hagler, 880 S.W.2d 123, 128–29 (Tex. App. 1994).

Qualitex Co. v. Jacobson Products Co., 514 U.S. 159 (1995).

Rambus Inc. v. Infineon Techs. AG, 318 F.3d 1081 (Fed. Cir. 2003).

Recording Industry Association of America, Inc., v. Verizon, Inc., 359 U.S. App. D.C. 85 (2004).

Robert Thomas v. Bill Page et al., No. 04 LK 013, Circuit Court for the Sixteenth Judicial Circuit, Kane County, Ill. (2007).

Salinger v. Random House, Inc. 811 F.2d 90 (2nd Cir. 1987).

Shoars v. Epson America, Inc., No. SCWI 12749, Cal. Sup. Ct., Los Angeles Cty. (1989).

Smyth v. Pillsbury Corp., 914 F. Supp. 97 (E.D. Pa. 1996).

Sony Corp. of Amer. v. Universal City Studios, Inc., 464 U.S. 417 (1984).

Staggers v. Real Authentic Sound, 77 F. Supp. 2d 57, 64 (D.D.C. 1999).

State ex rel. Macy v. One Pioneer CD-ROM Changer (1993) and *Davis v. Gracey*, 111 F.3d 1472 (10th Cir. 1997).

State Street Bank & Trust Co. v. Signature Financial Group, 149 F.3d 1368 (Fed. Cir. 1998).

Stern v. Delphi Internet Servs. Corp., 626 N.Y.S. 2d 694 (1995).

Steve Jackson Games v. U.S. Secret Service (1993).

Stratton Oakmont, Inc. v. Prodigy Services Co., 1995 WL 323710 (N.Y. Sup. Ct. 1995).

Sue Scheff, Parents Universal Resource Experts vs. Carey Bock and Ginger Warbis, Case Number: 03-022937 (18). Circuit Court, Broward County, Fla. (Sept. 2006).

321 Studios v. MGM Studios, No. C 02–1955 SI. USDC (N.D. Cal. 2004).

The Chamberlain Group, Inc., v. Skylink Technologies, Inc., 02 C 6376 (2004).

Times Mirror Company v. Superior Court (CA), 53 Cal.3d (1991).

TiVo v. EchoStar, 516 F.3d 1290 (Fed. Cir. 2008).

Toney v. L'Oreal USA, 406 F.3d 905 (7th Cir. 2005).

TrafFix Devices, Inc. v. Marketing Displays, Inc. 532 U.S. 23 (2001).

Twentieth Century Fox Film Corp. v. Cablevision Systems Corp., 478 F. Supp. 2d 607 (S.D.N.Y. 2007).

Two Pesos, Inc. v. Taco Cabana, Inc., 505 U.S. 763 (1992).

U-Haul Int'l, Inc. v. WhenU.com, Inc., 279 F. Supp. 2d 723 (E.D. Va. 2003).

United States v. M.J. Trujillo-Cohen, CR-H-97–251 (S.D. Tex. 1997).

United States v. Smith, No. 91–5077 (5th Cir. 1992).

United States of America v. Elcomsoft Co., Ltd. and Dmitry Sklyarov, USDC (N.D. Cal. 2002).

Universal City Studios, Inc. v. Reimerdes, No. 00 Civ. 0277 (LAK), USDC (S.D.N.Y. Aug. 17, 2000, amended Sept. 6, 2000). [Defendants' Reply Brief in].

Wal-Mart Stores, Inc. v. Samara Brothers, Inc., 529 U.S. 205 (2000).

Warner-Jenkinson Co. v. Hilton Davis Chem. Co., 520 U.S. 17 (1997).

Whalen v. Roe, 429 U.S. 589 (1977).

Wheaton v. Peters, 33 U.S. 591 (1834).

Williams & Wilkins Co. v. United States, 420 U.S. 376 (1975).

Zacchini v. Scripps-Howard Broadcasting Co., 433 U.S. 562 (1977).

Zazu Designs v. L'Oreal, 979 F.2d 499 (7th Cir. 1992).

Zeran v. America Online Inc. No. 97–1523, (4th Cir. 1997).

Index

G

J

Q

R

About the Authors

Edward Lee Lamoureux received a BA (speech) from California State University, Long Beach (1975), an MA (Speech Communication) from Washington State University (1980), and a PhD (Rhetoric and Communication), from the University of Oregon (1985). An associate professor, Ed has been at Bradley University since 1985, where he has served as director, Basic Speech; acting director, Office for Teaching Excellence and Faculty Development; acting associate dean, College of Communication and Fine Arts; co-founder, acting director, and director, Multimedia Program; and co-director, Bradley University New Media Center. Lamoureux teaches Introduction to New Media Theory; Issues in New Media Theory; Intellectual Property Law; Field Research Methods (ethnography) in Virtual Worlds (in the Multimedia Program); and Theory and Literature of Rhetoric (in the Department of Communication).

Prof. Lamoureux's research interests include ethnography, rhetoric, religious communication, conversation, and teaching and learning in virtual worlds; his creative production has included audio production and Web work as well as communication training via digital embellishments. He served as editor of the *Journal of Communication and Religion* (sponsored by the Religious

Communication Association) for two consecutive three-year terms beginning in 1998. He taught the first online course at Bradley (by more than two years) and the first Bradley course(s) in virtual worlds. Lamoureux has published and presented numerous academic papers and frequently provides consulting resources to education and industry. He was an invited expert witness at the Library of Congress-sponsored Section 108 Copyright Hearings.

Ed is Professor Beliveau in *Second Life®*, where he also performs (guitar and voice) as "the Professor."

Steven L. Baron is a partner at the Chicago law firm of Mandell Menkes. He has significant experience in complex commercial litigation and dispute resolution, with particular emphasis on matters involving intellectual property, media law, and First Amendment law. Mr. Baron has successfully counseled clients, engaged in litigation, and resolved a broad range of disputes involving media and entertainment companies, advertising agencies, information technology businesses, internet service providers, and other clients with significant commercial, intellectual property, and media interests. Mr. Baron has appeared before state and federal courts, arbitrators, and mediators in Illinois and around the country on matters involving copyrights, trademarks, and trade secrets.

Mr. Baron received a JD degree from the University of Minnesota and the BA from the University of Wisconsin-Madison. He is a frequent author and lecturer on topics involving media and intellectual property and is an adjunct professor at Bradley University where he has taught a course on intellectual property law at the Slane College of Communications and Fine Arts.

Claire Stewart is the head of digital collections at the Northwestern University Library in Evanston, Illinois. She holds a BA in English Literature from Saint Mary's College and an MLIS from Dominican University. She has served in various positions at the Northwestern University Library since 1994. Claire is a campus expert on copyright, digitization, and multimedia collections.

General Editor: **Steve Jones**

Digital Formations is an essential source for critical, high-quality books on digital technologies and modern life. Volumes in the series break new ground by emphasizing multiple methodological and theoretical approaches to deeply probe the formation and reformation of lived experience as it is refracted through digital interaction. **Digital Formations** pushes forward our understanding of the intersections—and corresponding implications—between the digital technologies and everyday life. The series emphasizes critical studies in the context of emergent and existing digital technologies.

Other recent titles include:

Leslie Shade
   Gender and Community in the Social
   Construction of the Internet

John T. Waisanen
   Thinking Geometrically

Mia Consalvo & Susanna Paasonen
   Women and Everyday Uses of the Internet

Dennis Waskul
   Self-Games and Body-Play

David Myers
   The Nature of Computer Games

Robert Hassan
   The Chronoscopic Society

M. Johns, S. Chen, & G. Hall
   Online Social Research

C. Kaha Waite
   Mediation and the Communication
   Matrix

Jenny Sunden
   Material Virtualities

Helen Nissenbaum & Monroe Price
   Academy and the Internet

To order other books in this series please contact our Customer Service Department:
   (800) 770-LANG (within the US)
   (212) 647-7706 (outside the US)
   (212) 647-7707 FAX
To find out more about the series or browse a full list of titles, please visit our website:
   WWW.PETERLANG.COM